Walter George Muelder

Toward a Discipline of Social Ethics:

Essays in Honor of Walter George Muelder

Toward a Discipline of Social Ethics

PAUL DEATS, JR. Editor

:says in Honor of Walter George Muelder

ston University Press   Boston, Massachusetts 1972

Contents

Contributors

PAUL DEATS, JR. is Professor of Social Ethics and chairman of the Division of Theological and Religious Studies, School of Theology and Graduate School, Boston University.

C. ERIC LINCOLN is Professor of Sociology and Religion, Union Theological Seminary, New York City, and editor of the C. Eric Lincoln Series in Black Religion, published by Doubleday.

JAMES M. GUSTAFSON is Professor of Religious Studies, Yale University and former Professor of Christian Ethics, Yale Divinity School.

ALAN F. GEYER is Dag Hammarskjöld Professor of Peace Studies, Colgate University and former Editor of *The Christian Century*.

RALPH B. POTTER, JR. is Professor of Social Ethics, Harvard Divinity School and a member of the Center for Population Studies at Harvard University.

TEX S. SAMPLE is Associate Professor of Church and Society, St. Paul School of Theology, Kansas City, and former Director of Social Relations, Massachusetts Council of Churches.

JOSEPH D. STAMEY is chairman of the Department of Philosophy and also teaches in the Department of Religion, McMurry College, Abilene, Texas.

J. PHILIP WOGAMAN is Professor of Christian Social Ethics, Wesley Theological Seminary and former Professor of Social Ethics, University of the Pacific.

FATHER FRANÇOIS HOUTART is Secretary-General of the International Federation of Institutes of Social and Socio-Religious Research (FERES), University of Louvain, Belgium.

GEORGE MCGOVERN is Democratic Senator from South Dakota, former Professor of History and Government at Dakota Wesleyan University, and served as chairman of the World Council of Churches Consultation on Racism in London, May 1969.

PRESTON N. WILLIAMS is Houghton Professor of Theology and Contemporary Change, Harvard Divinity School and former Martin Luther King, Jr. Professor of Social Ethics, Boston University School of Theology.

JAMES K. MATHEWS is resident bishop of the Boston area of the United Methodist Church and a member of the Central Committee of the World Council of Churches.

L. HAROLD DEWOLF is Dean and Professor of Systematic Theology, Wesley Theological Seminary and former Professor of Systematic Theology, Boston University School of Theology.

Deats, Lincoln, Geyer, Sample, Stamey, and Wogaman received their doctorates from Boston University as students of Dean Muelder.

Acknowledgements

THIS *Festschrift* would not have been possible without the initial approval by then President Arland F. Christ-Janer and the financial support by Boston University.

Many alumni of Boston University contributed suggestions for the volume, but the responsibility was exercised by an Editorial Committee composed of Earl Kent Brown, Paul Deats, Jr. (Chairman), Alan F. Geyer, C. Eric Lincoln, J. Robert Nelson, F. Thomas Trotter, and J. Philip Wogaman.

Editorial criticism of manuscripts was shared by members of this committee and, in addition, by Robert Hamill, John Lavely, Malcolm McVeigh, Donald E. Messer, James Nash, Leroy S. Rouner, Tex Sample, and Joseph Stamey.

Miss Dorothy Lord provided the basic bibliography of Walter Muelder's writings. She and Miss Helen Bowman rendered invaluable assistance and counsel throughout the project. Mrs. Jean Morceau, Mrs. Frances Poe, and Miss Judy Schechtman shared in typing when deadlines were imminent. Mrs. MaryAnn Lash and Mrs. Roberta Clark of Boston University Press were cordial and helpful guides. Mrs. Linda Schell translated the initial draft of Father Houtart's essay.

My wife, Ruth, inevitably shared in the headaches, perplexities, and excitement of editing, never quite sure why everything always takes longer than it should.

To all of the above, to the contributing authors, and to Walter Muelder for providing the occasion and motivation, my warm appreciation.

Paul Deats, Jr.

Toward a Discipline of Social Ethics:

Essays in Honor of Walter George Muelder

Walter G. Muelder: An Appreciation of His Life, Thought, and Ministry

C. Eric Lincoln and Paul Deats, Jr.

T HERE is always an element of mystery about a human being, a dimension impossible to capture in language, spoken or written. Persons are truly known only in face-to-face experience and can never be adequately reproduced as objects of reporting. What is true for everyone is intensified when one attempts an intellectual portrait of the rare individual who has woven many strands of involvement and responsibility into an intricate and unified life-style. To write with meaning and validity about the life and ministry of Walter Muelder is an opportunity to share personal experiences; but it also presents the writers with the exacting problem of translating a person onto paper.

There is an almost formidable consistency in the way the experience of knowing Muelder is recalled by students and colleagues. Phrases such as "patience and determination," "intellectual rigor and honesty," and "pastoral concern for persons" always seem to surface. Certainly these are some of the hallmarks of his personality, clues to an interweaving of ideas and concepts and commitments about love and truth and justice and human worth which, for many generations of students and professional associates, have characterized their experience of the Dean.

In 1964, at the 125th anniversary celebration of the Boston University School of Theology, Walter Muelder told how his mother, then in her eighties, had recently read his *Methodism and Society in the Twentieth Century*. Her response, according to his report, was an exclamation: "Why, Walter, that's the story of our family!" She had found in his history streams of German Methodism and historical scholarship, Boston University and personalistic philosophy, Social Gospel and ecumenical concern — all bound up with the life and experience of the Muelder family.

The family was a kind of seedbed which could produce sons of Walter's stripe. He was born into the family of Epke Hermann Muelder on the first day of March in the year 1907, in Boody, Illinois. His father was a Methodist minister who, when Walter was about a year-and-a-half old, decided to give up his small parish in rural Illinois to study at the Boston University School of Theology. Walter wrote of his father:

He had been an immigrant youth, educated in a German speaking Methodist College in Missouri, and had studied the great names of German 19th century theology under professors bent on refuting them. The result was confusion. He learned that way off in Boston was a university where the new scholarship was taken seriously and related constructively to the Christian life. So off to Boston with wife and three small sons he went to study under Bowne, Knudson, Sheldon, Buell, Warren, Black — and to sit under great Boston preachers and to attend the path-breaking Ford Hall Forum. Here he wrestled until he received the blessing of God — a gospel he could preach without fear or favor and with compassion to his generation.[1]

The family returned to Illinois, and son Walter received the B.S. from Knox College in 1927. Retracing his father's footsteps to Boston (and later back to Germany), he was awarded the S.T.B. from the School of Theology in 1930, spent a year at the University of Frankfurt, and returned to complete his Ph.D. in philosophy at Boston

University in 1933. He wrote his dissertation on Troeltsch under Professor E. S. Brightman. In 1930 Muelder was appointed Frank D. Howard Fellow for his study in Germany and was subsequently Borden Parker Bowne Fellow in the Department of Philosophy at Boston University. Upon graduation, the young Dr. Muelder was one of the last to be ordained in a German-speaking Methodist conference. He entered the Methodist ministry in 1933 and was appointed to serve in rural Wisconsin. The next year he married Martha Grotewohl, who in due time presented him with three daughters: Sonya, Helga, and Linda.

By the time Walter Muelder returned to Boston University as dean and professor in 1945, he was already known as a socialist, a pacifist, and a persistent critic of the capitalist system and racial discrimination. He was an active member of the Methodist Federation for Social Action. There were, of course, complaints to the University about his appointment and about his public statements to Boston audiences. After one particularly strident flurry of criticism, Muelder submitted his resignation to President Marsh. The president refused to consider accepting it, but Muelder kept a copy of the letter in his pocket as a reminder that job tenure should not compromise integrity. He always counseled his students not to get fired for wrong reasons, but for issues of substance; the Dean took the moral commitments of his students no less seriously than he took his own.

While giving of himself unstintingly to professional and public causes, in his efforts to reserve some reasonable place in his life for his family, Muelder has eschewed the dubious distinction of being a "joiner." For the most part his memberships are limited to organizations he thinks critical to his work or professional interests. He is a fellow of the American Academy of Arts and Sciences, a member of Phi Beta Kappa, a post-doctoral fellow of the Society for Religion in Higher Education, and a former officer in the Fellowship of Reconciliation and the American Civil Liberties Union. In the late 1940s he was a participant in the New York Conference on Science, Philosophy and Religion. He has kept alive interests in both the American Philosophical Society and the American Theological Society. Some colleagues sensed a more theological language and a conservative mood when Muelder returned from World Council of Churches Faith and Order meetings. But the rigor of his philosophical method was never long hidden.

His guiding precepts are philosophical and personal. His advice to his students is always "Keep your categories clean" and "Final truth must be coherent with all of experience." These are the principles he himself has chosen to live by, the lights by which his life has been illuminated.

THOUGHT

The greatest influence on the developing thought of Walter Muelder was that of the Personalists at Boston University, particularly Edgar S. Brightman. It is not surprising then that one of the stanchions in his system is the notion that "truth is of, by, and for persons." Muelder always trusted his own teachers, never doubting that they knew what they were teaching. One can be sure that he never took anything simply on authority; but to know him is to understand his assertion that he had no unresolved authority problems.

Certain thinkers and their works exercised more lasting influence on Muelder than others, often by focusing attention on problems which enticed him to serious study. Ernst Troeltsch, for example, provided the problem for Muelder's dissertation, the enduring problematic for his thought, and the categories with which he subsequently approached many questions. One of his early articles, based on doctoral studies of sectarian groups in California, was "From Sect to Church" and was widely used in texts on sociology of religion. Similarly, it was Edgar S. Brightman, his greatest teacher, who instilled devotion to coherence as the test of truth in both philosophy and life.

For his first Matriculation Day address at the School of Theology in 1945, Muelder relied heavily on Arthur Koestler's *The Yogi and the Commissar* for illustrative categories. In the 1950s his teaching was greatly indebted to the idea of the small community developed by Arthur Morgan and Baker Brownell and to the work of Gunnar Myrdal, especially *An American Dilemma*. Paul Sigmund in *Ideologies of the Developing Nations* furnished seminal material in the

4

1960s. Nevertheless, in trying to understand Muelder, it is difficult to single out one strand of influence; thus one's understanding is forced to come to terms with Muelder's own professed reliance upon plural and cumulative causation (following R. M. MacIver and Gunnar Myrdal). Convergent emphases, sustained attention to concepts offering illumination and insight lead to evaluation and reintegration at a higher level. One does not find great gaps or leaps or sudden changes of direction or orientation. Muelder disdains fads. One does find growth, development, and emergent coherence of patterns of thought and style of life.

His students, bringing to him their confusion about the great issues of the times, have been surprised at how few questions of deep import the Dean has not already considered and thought through. There are few events he cannot, with seeming ease, place in proper historical, philosophical, and social context. His productivity, remarkable for a teaching administrator, has not been due solely to his brilliance of mind, his breadth of education, or focus of energy, although these have all been important. Most critical has been the fact that Muelder has never had to take time each day or each week to rethink his position on fundamental questions. He knows his mind and does not have to begin fresh each morning with an uncoordinated hodgepodge of ideas and notions. He has probably always been confident that truth and wisdom are more likely to result from disciplined reflection by an informed and oriented mind than from unfocused group discussion or a vague consensus. Some colleagues, in their own struggle with indecision, have found Dean Muelder's characteristic ease of knowing his way something to envy; others have resented what they perceived at the time to be rigidity or a puzzling conformity to tradition. Almost all learned in time to respect the integrity of his judgments and to understand that they are formed under the most rigorous criticism rather than easy commitment to consensus or unthinking conformity. Muelder has never changed his mind easily; he yields only to persuasive logic or firm evidence. He has learned from many sources, but he is not simply eclectic. Each new concept must fit into a coherent framework, which is itself capable of revision but is unlikely to warrant discard because of fundamental error.

Muelder's intellectual perspective means that he takes very seriously the historical dimensions of philosophy as well as the metaphysical questions traditionally dealt with. Metaphysics is for him, as for his teacher, Brightman, a matter of practice as well as theory; it is primarily a matter of orientation. Brightman introduced his *Person and Reality* with this statement about guiding principles:

We shall go ahead, then, in a search for constructive and coherent orientation; that is, for a truth somehow involved in the whole of human experience. . . . Wonder is the beginning of metaphysics. No one without curiosity can enter. Metaphysical wonder is a wonder about how everything hangs together. The metaphysician is a synoptic man. . . . Abstraction is omission. Temporary omissions enable thought to start; permanent omissions compel thought to falsify. The goal of metaphysics is complete concreteness. The true is the whole. Neither analysis nor synopsis is the whole truth. . . . Reason is more than formal logic, even than symbolic logic. The practical reason has the primacy over the theoretical; but nothing has the primacy over reason.[2]

These are guiding principles for Muelder, too. Yet Muelder came to see earlier and more clearly than Brightman the necessity for the philosophical whole to be open to empirical insights from the social sciences. In 1951 he wrote "Norms and Valuations in the Social Sciences." Fifteen years later he contributed a chapter to the papers for the Conference on Church and Society entitled "Theology and Social Science" which dealt more explicitly with theological issues and was more critical of both disciplines. His study of Hegel and his commitment to dialectical method have also helped him deal effectively with interdisciplinary material. Here, too, he was guided by the criterion of coherence; and both life and thought were disciplined by the "concrete unity of theory and practice." Along with L. Harold DeWolf, Muelder was to reformulate Brightman's Moral Laws, adding communitarian dimensions not present in Brightman.

Muelder never left philosophy as he turned to theology, nor did he surrender either as he explored economics and other social sciences. He has led the discipline in defining social ethics as an interdisciplinary enterprise.[3] A practicing academic and former student of

Muelder's writes of this interdisciplinary concern: "In the end, Muelder may well be correct on how important this is. And if my perception of parochial disciplinary professions is at all accurate, we need to hear more about the interdisciplinary nature of truth. It is so obvious, but to most professors, so obscure and threatening." [4] All the more reason for a man with Muelder's self-confidence to stake out and man a lonely outpost, as he has manned so many others in his time. This former student sums up his impressions of the Dean in terms of "his thoroughness and seriousness as a scholar; his eagerness to examine before acting; a desire to investigate whether individuals, the church or other institutions live out the verbiage they profess and to remind them of their words; an effort to take positions that have retaining power, i.e., to view faddism in a proper perspective; his ability to be, in many respects, a man before his time." [5]

A fair assessment of Walter Muelder's contributions to philosophy and social ethics does indeed at times suggest a certain precociousness scarcely understood by some of his critics. A case in point is the "institutionalist" label given Muelder by Edward Leroy Long in his *A Survey of Christian Ethics,* despite Muelder's well-known criticism of much institutional practice both as a Socialist and as a pacifist.[6] Professor Long divides motifs in "The Formulation of the Ethical Norm" from those in "The Implementation of Ethical Decisions," placing Muelder in the latter (possibly because Long refers only to *Foundations of the Responsible Society* and not to its intended companion, *Moral Law in Christian Social Ethics,* which treats the formulation of the norm). Under the second rubric, Long classifies Muelder as an institutional type and in his analytic treatment describes the institutional motif as "probably the most traditional and widespread form of Christian social teachings. . . . It often emphasizes," says Long, "the restrictive and negative functions of the state and thus breeds a social conservatism." [7] Anyone who is acquainted with the continuing work of Muelder will be puzzled as to whether the difficulty is with this critic's understanding of Muelder or with the typology itself. Long makes the institutional type hinge on a Niebuhrian conception of power expressed in structures of justice and order:

Any thinker may rightly be interpreted in terms of the institutional motif if: (a) the importance he attaches to the organizational control of power is greater than the importance he attaches to power as the means by which organization is maintained; (b) he counsels obedience to existing authority because the authority commands intrinsic respect, not merely because it can coerce subservience; (c) he believes that holding an "office" or "role" calls for actions which are different from what the individual would perform acting by himself in bondage to the Gospel ethic of love; or (d) he considers given existing orders, such as the state, to be created by God for the expression of Christian concern even though ambiguity and sin are involved in the use of such orders in order to attain particular objectives.[8]

Finally, Muelder is placed in a third kind of institutionalism category designated "Institutionalism Antithetical to Power."

Of course, Muelder is properly an institutionalist in the sense that he knows that institutional*ization* is an inevitable process in group life, while institutional*ism* is a perpetual danger, and that understanding and critical participation are required if institutions are to function to further rather than thwart the goals of human community. He is also an institutionalist in that he has never allowed himself the luxury of purely individual expression or ad hoc improvisation. But for Muelder the exercise of responsibility in and through institutions is always directed toward *changing* institutions and using them as further instruments of change. This is clearly reflected in his work: *Methodism and Society in the Twentieth Century,* published in 1961.

Still other reservations must be noted in respect to Long's categorization. First, Muelder has a positive appreciation of power. He has been critical of Niebuhr's conception of power, but he has also criticized the group-dynamics orientation for typically failing to come to grips with the problem of power. Secondly, Muelder takes a positive, although never uncritical, view of the state. He has consistently opposed a Leninist view of the the state and has seen the necessity for political power to be used to control economic power. But there has been no easy "obedience to existing authority" in this scholar who has written carefully about dissent and revolution. Finally, it is inaccurate to classify Muelder as a social conservative, except perhaps in a given instance at a point in time on one issue. Long notes that Muelder deals with five institutions—family, education, politics, economics, and religion. Each institution requires *critical* participation. Muelder's most sustained criticism has been of economic and political institutions *in their present forms.*

In 1964 Muelder suggested that "many institutions on which people have relied in the past and are still trying to do with today have become obsolescent."[9] But here he referred to war, segregation, colonialism, denominationalism, the sovereign nation-state—specific institutional forms which required reordering. Muelder confesses difficulty in understanding self-professed radical students and the New Left of the late 1960s, who think all institutions are unnecessary, who lack depth of historical perspective, and who do not appreciate the ethical interpenetration of ends and means. In dealing with institutions, he has appropriated H. Richard Niebuhr's contention that "no great change in political or economic life has ever taken place without a recollection of the past. . . . The search in common memory for the great principles which lie back of accustomed ways and of which these are perversions as well as illustrations can be a very radical and pregnant thing."[10]

The Dean's carefully developed answers to questions put by his students is a legendary aspect of his teaching. Professor Pat McConnell used to counsel classes the two taught jointly: "Don't let him get started lecturing; ask him a question before he begins." It was good advice. As the answer unfolded, it became apparent that there were unrealized dimensions to the innocent question. The answer would typically begin further back in history, take account of a wider social and cultural context, and have theological depths of which the questioner was unaware until the Dean had touched all the bases. The answer might be overwhelming, but it was never dogmatic. The students felt instructed rather than defeated, for the spirit was open and receptive to critical responses and disagreement. Still the teacher was demanding in his expectations—of persons and of institutions. He had most difficulty with "soft" men—those who could not summon the courage to speak and who thus nourished some inner disagreement until it became all wrapped up with resentment and exploded.

MINISTRY

When Walter Muelder accepted an appointment to his first pastorate in 1933, he began a ministry which was to transcend traditional categories in a parish that was eventually to encompass "mankind as the unit of cooperation." For the clairvoyant, there may have been some intimation of his future interests in the fact that five years earlier, in 1928, he had been a student delegate to an important conference of the Federal Council of Churches; or that in 1926 while a student at Knox College he joined what today's students would call a conspiracy for the elimination of the ROTC unit from his campus. Were these the beginnings of his lifelong commitment to ecumenism and to pacifism? Perhaps. One thing we do know: for Muelder, the call to minister meant there should be "in every place a voice" [11] to speak for those who could not speak for themselves and to air issues so that nothing in the public interest should be decided by default.

From his pastorate in rural Wisconsin, Muelder went to Berea College in Kentucky to chair the Department of Philosophy and Bible. It was there in the southern Appalachians that the young scholar got a firsthand education in the meanness and nastiness of poverty. It was there too that he became active in the Fellowship of Reconciliation and began to sharpen his political awareness as secretary of the local unit of the Socialist Party.

He became Professor of Christian Theology and Christian Ethics at the University of Southern California in 1940, but his ministry was not limited to teaching. Having earlier become identified with the labor movement in a boilermaking job and in railroad towns in the Midwest, he was now active in community leadership when black people moved into Los Angeles as part of the wartime migration from southern farms to northern and western cities. A German name linked with radical ideas had managed to get the young Muelder in trouble in more than one community, but such trouble was a part of his developing sense of mission and ministry.

From 1945 to 1972 Muelder was Dean of the School of Theology and Professor of Social Ethics at Boston University. This means that, including his years of study, half of his life has been spent at this institution. What has been his ministry at Boston University? First of all, he is a great teacher and pastor. There are few students who have sat under him or who have been counseled by him who have not been impressed by this fact.

An administrator at Ohio Wesleyan remembers:

When I think of Dr. Muelder and the contribution he has made to my role in life, I think of a variety of moments and subjects: the excitement of watching him create as he responded to the questions that we used to compose ahead of time in order to stimulate the class; the ability to emphasize the significance of compromise without destroying principle; the awareness one had that he knew what you were doing, that he was deeply concerned about your intellectual growth, and yet the impression he gave of insisting that this was to be and not to be talked about; the little statements that somehow still seem to hold — "You are only crucified once, make it for something worthwhile;" "There is a point of no return in compromise;" the amazing awareness he had of personal problems that you faced and how he could call you in for that well-timed conversation.[12]

Muelder was always a teaching dean. He typically offered two courses a semester (a lecture and a seminar) in addition to handling his administrative duties and scholarly writing. He used to comment that moving into the classroom was not an extra duty but welcome relief from administration. His courses had a focus on history, especially in "History of Western Ethics and Social Philosophy," "History of the Social Teachings of the Churches" (Troeltsch), "Development of Social Christianity in America," and "History of Theories of Social Reform" (with serious attention to Marxism). He also kept up with Roman Catholic social philosophy, the labor movement, and race relations. He taught a comprehensive course in "Christian Ethics and Social Reconstruction." Over the years he shared courses with Pat McConnell, Harold DeWolf, Paul Deats, and Preston Williams. He was always willing for a younger colleague to take over a course without showing any defensiveness about property rights.

His demands as a teacher were always balanced by his grace as a pastor. He spent unnumbered hours listening to students and colleagues, and still other hours, often with Martha, visiting sick members, the bereaved, or new parents in the School of Theology community. There was a reserve some students never seemed to get past, for the Dean did not make light conversation easily. He could really relax in a game of horseshoes, but typically he felt most comfortable when the talk turned serious.

One doctoral graduate recalls his early exposure to a directed study, alone in the Dean's office with Muelder, Plato, and the ghost of Socrates, with the trusted Dorothy Lord guarding the exit. The student nervously brought in his stack of books (to convince the tutor of his scholarly efforts) and his list of questions (to forestall questioning by the tutor). Sooner or later the student's questions ran out and the Dean's questions began; then pedagogy and logic overcame grace and affection. When the stumbling reply came, "I know it but I can't say it," the cool response was, "If you can't say it, you don't know it." But it was clear to the student that the aim was not a victory in logic or the triumph of ideas, but the growth of the learner; what was expected was sharp and clear understanding, not agreement. Even so the student found it difficult to disagree with his teacher — not just because of fear of being told he was wrong but because he found the teacher's argument so convincing. When he was finally able to articulate a real debate, he went home to celebrate his "maturity." Later he could not recall the issue debated, but the *fact* of the debate has remained for him a turning point of his own intellectual growth.

Long before it was fashionable to do so, Dean Muelder recognized the responsibility of America's educational institutions to be involved in helping minorities help themselves. Unlike others who claimed to be concerned, the Dean characteristically moved to translate concern into action. He brought promising black students to the School of Theology, and somewhere he found the financial means to keep them there. The record is revealing: A 1968 study by the Rockefeller Doctoral Programs in Religion compared the number of doctorates in religion awarded blacks between 1953–1968. The twenty-eight institutions awarding such doctorates granted a total of thirty-eight for this period. Eighteen of them were granted by the Boston University School of Theology. To complete the picture during Muelder's tenure, we must add thirteen doctorates awarded to blacks by the school during the period 1945–1952 and two more for 1969 and 1970. Thus the total is thirty-three, nine of these in Muelder's own field of social ethics.

The truth is that while he was certainly conscious of the peculiar inequities and disabilities suffered by some of his students because of various forms of social discrimination, Muelder himself tended to see the individual first. Race or nationality were accidents of birth attached to a particular person. One was not first black, white, or Chinese, but a person in a community of persons, having peculiar needs of his own. A former student from a "different background" has written:

Dean Muelder's commitment to the values of person and community transcended the boundaries of nationality and color. As one of the many foreign students who has had the privilege of studying under the Dean, I would like to say how much responsible concern he had for them, especially with their often intangible but difficult problems of special psychological adjustments to the different environs, without himself falling into the pitfalls of sentimentality and paternalism. Also his deep understanding of and sympathy to the problems of theology and Christianity in the context of cross-cultural and international involvements will be gratefully remembered by many who knew his thought and life.[13]

1972 marks the twenty-seventh year of Walter G. Muelder's ministry at Boston University School of Theology, and in a real sense, despite his broader spectrum of commitments, Boston University has stamped him and has been indelibly stamped by him. Twenty-seven years can make a deep imprint on a man or on an institution, and Dean Muelder's twenty-seven years here are no exception.

One of his first tasks as dean was to raise funds for and to plan the Theology building at 745 Commonwealth Avenue, which was ready in 1949. He never wanted to be a fund-raiser, and he kept his focus on education and the church. When he came to Boston University in 1945, he found a faculty of twelve, most of them Methodists and practically all of them alumni of the University. By 1972 there were thirty full-time faculty members, reflecting a diverse background of religious, educational, and international experience. All were brought to the School of Theology under Muelder's leadership, a leadership always fully shared with the Committee of Full Professors even though authority for nomination was his alone. During his tenure, the faculty went through four major curriculum reforms, the one with the largest "core" lasting from 1956 to 1966. Over fifteen hundred students have received their first professional theological degree (S.T.B. or Th.M.) during Muelder's time as dean. The size of the advanced degree program has grown to the point where now the Division of Theological and Religious Studies grants the third largest number of doctorates in the University's Graduate School. Muelder himself has been first or second reader for over seventy Ph.D. or Th.D. dissertations (about three a year over twenty-seven years), a significant number of these being interdisciplinary and having as second readers professors from the departments of sociology, psychology, political science, or philosophy.

Muelder exercised strong initiative in making the faculty and curriculum more international and ecumenical. The strong offerings in ecumenics, missions, and world religions were combined into a single department in 1961. He sponsored a continuing summer Ecumenical Institute especially designed for conciliar leaders, encouraged students to study at the Ecumenical Institute at Bossey, Switzerland, as well as at London, and supervised numerous dissertations dealing with ecumenical issues. Professors Eddy Asirvatham and Amiya Chakravarty of India, and Daud Rahbar of Pakistan were, successively, teachers of world religions. Muelder suffered some criticism because Chakravarty was not *formally* a Christian. Nils Ehrenstrom, for twenty-five years director of studies at the World Council of Churches, became the first Professor of Ecumenics. Other faculty represented experience in Africa, Asia, Europe, and the Middle East. The Dean encouraged still others to spend sabbatical time overseas.

Further ventures were undertaken in pastoral care and counselling — particularly with the establishment of the Danielsen Counselling Center — and in religion and the arts, collaborating with the School of Fine and Applied Arts. Ethics and the biological and medical sciences were considered in a special conference in late 1969 in conjunction with the Boston meeting of the American Association for the Advancement of Science.

Few administrators are more aware of the obligations of office than Muelder; he is careful to separate expression of opinion as a person from that as institutional representative. Yet he has spoken out and signed petitions critical of public policy, whether that of the government or of a corporation or of the University. He has served Boston University under four presidents and always been solicitous of a broad degree of academic freedom such as was nurtured especially during the long tenures of Daniel L. Marsh and Harold C. Case. Needless to say, the Dean has continued his interest in preserving and extending that freedom for his faculty and students.

Because of his long experience and his deep identification with the purposes of the University, as well as because of his intellect and character, Muelder has been a strong dean in all-University affairs. The university administration has made repeated demands upon his wisdom and upon his time — to chair the selection committee for the sixth president, to write the statement of university goals, to counsel his colleagues on school and university policies.

The Department of Philosophy has always listed him as a member of its faculty and many of its graduate students register for his courses on the history of ethics. In 1954 he was recognized as the ninth University Lecturer. His topic, "The Idea of a Responsible Society," was taken from World Council of Churches materials and later expanded into a book — *Foundations of the Responsible Society*. Similarly, the Lowell Institute Lectures of 1951 became another book, *Religion and Economic Responsibility*.

Walter Muelder is, of course, a committed churchman — Methodist and ecumenical. He has exercised a continuing prophetic role in the institutional church, whether serving on official general church boards, or working with unofficial responses within the church, or joining in a sponsored study of social thought and action in Methodism.[14] Over the years he has been a delegate to Methodist General Conferences, leader in the Massachusetts Council of Churches, member of the Department of the Church and Economic Life and the

Division of Christian Life and Work of the National Council of Churches. From 1952 there has been a growing involvement at every level of ecumenicity. In that year Dr. Muelder was a delegate to the World Council of Churches Conference on Faith and Order at Lund, Sweden. In 1953–1954 he was visiting professor at the Ecumenical Institute at Bossey, and he later served as chairman of the Institute Board. He was consultant at the World Council's Evanston Assembly in 1954, delegate to New Delhi in 1961, to Geneva (Church and Society) in 1966, and to Uppsala in 1968. In 1964, he was a World Methodist Council observer at Vatican Council II. Some of his most distinguished ecumenical service came as co-chairman (with Madeline Barot) of the World Council of Churches Commission on Cooperation of Men and Women in the Church, and as chairman of the Commission on Institutionalism.

There is an abiding ecumenical thrust in theological education as Muelder conceived and practiced it. This was expressed not only in the School of Theology but also in the Association of United Methodist Theological Schools and the American Association of Theological Schools. It was in large part due to the ideas and energy of Muelder that in 1968 three Catholic and four Protestant seminaries in Boston formed the Boston Theological Institute, of which he was founding president and chairman of the board. He has been a vigorous participant in the Consultation on Church Unity.

His contributions have been recognized by honorary degrees from his alma mater (Knox College) and from other educational institutions of both Protestant and Catholic affiliation.

Walter G. Muelder has played — and enjoyed — many roles: pastor, professor, dean, churchman, social activist. Throughout his life he has been committed to disciplined social action on the part of the church and other institutions. Pacifist, civil libertarian, philosopher, great teacher, lover of truth and justice, husband and father, his life reveals a rare quality of integration. The unity of thought, word, and deed has been guided by moral laws, so that his left hand has considered and, on the whole, approved what the right hand was doing.

NOTES

1. Walter G. Muelder, "Christian Social Ethics Looks Forward," *Nexus* 21 (May 1964): 3–4.

2. Edgar S. Brightman, *Person and Reality,* Peter A. Bertocci, Jannette E. Newhall, and Robert S. Brightman, eds. (New York: The Ronald Press Co., 1958), p. 15.

3. See especially Muelder's "Theology and Social Science," in *Christian Social Ethics in a Changing World,* J. C. Bennett, ed. (New York: Association Press, 1966).

4. Letter from Glenn R. Bucher, College of Wooster, 15 April 1971.

5. Ibid.

6. E. L. Long, Jr., *A Survey of Christian Ethics* (New York: Oxford University Press, 1967), pp. 213–15.

7. Ibid., p. 301.

8. Ibid., p. 168.

9. Muelder, "Christian Social Ethics," p. 7.

10. H. R. Niebuhr, *The Meaning of Revelation* (New York: Macmillan Paperback, 1941/ 1962), pp. 5–6.

11. Title of a book by Muelder; see Bibliography.

12. Letter from Robert Lisensky, Vice-President for Academic Affairs, Ohio Wesleyan University, 23 April 1971.

13. Letter from Chai Sik Chung, Chairman, Department of Sociology, Heidelberg College, 21 April 1971.

14. Muelder's temperate and objective treatment of the Methodist Federation for Social Action (*Methodism and Society in the Twentieth Century,* esp. pp. 212–228) occasioned sharp debate in the committee of sponsors. This was the second of four Methodist Social Thought and Action volumes published by Abingdon Press for the General Board of Christian Social Concerns. It was largely Muelder's prestige which brought this project to a faculty committee at Boston University School of Theology.

PART I

The Tasks and Methods of Social Ethics

1 The Quest for a Social Ethic

Paul Deats, Jr.

T H E R E is, at present, no coherent discipline of social ethics. However, through the labors of Walter G. Muelder and others of his generation, there is an emerging comprehension of the varieties of ingredients which form the matrix of inquiry, of the complex of considerations which impinge on the mind of one trying to "do ethics." No one has yet fully and cogently arranged these ingredients and considerations in a systematic way so that the discipline can become truly cumulative.

INTRODUCTION

A social ethic is not an easy achievement. There can be no simple elaboration from a given kerygma or eternal form. There are, to be sure, lessons from history; as Austin Warren suggests: "The 'highest' conscience — the most ethically rarefied intelligence — has not come into being without a history; it starts with, stands on, corrects, refines upon the ethical experience of a nation, a culture, a race."[1] History provides guidance for decision; it offers a variety of models of doing ethics and instructive illustrations of their use; but the present choice must still be made. It is good, perhaps essential, to have a charter, a constitution, as a principle of limitation upon present urgency; but the use or interpretation of that historic norm also requires critical judgment.[2] In addition, most, if not all, of the ethical models of the past are philosophical or theological ones designed for individual guidance rather than for shaping social policy, except in a "Christian civilization." Except for utilitarianism and pragmatism, the categories refer to intent, duty, conscience, and the good. The struggle for political consciousness has been difficult.

Further, as Eric Sevareid noted in 1970: "The best-phrased philosophical concepts have a way of coming apart at the semi-colons under the impact of events."[3] Thus it is not only the remembered history of ethical reflection and decision but also the experienced recent history of problems with ethical dimensions which sets the agenda for social ethics. These events need some order, some conceptual lenses, some framework of interpretation. The consequent borrowing of concepts and theories from the behavioral sciences leads some to wonder whether social ethics is — or can become — an autonomous discipline or should be content to be synthetic, a derived discipline of practice, using theory developed elsewhere (e.g., in the behavioral sciences and theology).

The Problem of a Social Ethic. The nature of social ethics is not adequately given in history, or in theology, in the facts themselves, nor even in watching practitioners operate. One cannot conclude that social ethics is what those who call themselves social ethicists do, or say they do, when they ply their craft. It takes only minimal acquaintance with the literature or marginal eavesdropping at meetings of the American Society of Christian Ethics to suggest that diversity of practice makes generalization difficult. For at least many of the professionals have been preoccupied with what James Gustafson calls a misplaced debate, pitting contextual or situation ethics against principles or laws.[4] Social ethics has often been practiced as a part of practical theology, related to action programs of churches and oriented to issues. Further, many individual practitioners have been highly individualistic, each following his own special interest.

It should not be surprising that the professionals are in disagreement then about the status of the discipline. In 1966 Max L. Stackhouse ventured that "social ethics is becoming a distinct discipline." He argued from the growth of a professional society and the coming of age of ethics as no longer "merely an implication of theology."[5] Three years later Beverly Harrison wrote: "It is no secret that, methodologically, the 'discipline' of Christian ethics is in disarray." She went on to describe the situation: "Disagreements among the theological giants of the previous era as to how the language of theological reflection is related to the language of moral reflection, always very much present but obscured then by the euphoria of new life in theology, have surfaced with a vengeance. In such a situation there is a serious danger that the very 'content' of the discipline comes to be understood as that discussion of appropriate methodology which goes on among the practitioners."[6] Gibson Winter shares the general conclusion, but with a different explanation: "Perhaps because everybody works a bit at social ethics, no one really works at it; at least, no such discipline has ever developed in a systematic way."[7]

How do we decide the issue? The answer rests on a normative understanding of what social ethics *ought to be*. I propose to approach the question historically and inductively, seeking in the conflicts of theories guidelines for a normative definition. I will look briefly and selectively at what has happened in society and in social ethics, especially in the four decades from 1931 to 1971. Then I will ponder the requirements of a discipline, finally suggesting possibilities for the emergence of a discipline.

The Historical Setting. Social ethics is at once very ancient and very new. In a sense there has always been a social ethic, at least since the time of the Old Testament prophets. The social dimensions are less clearly articulated in the New Testament. Yet Ernst Troeltsch traces over the centuries two major ways in which the Church solved the "great problem of Christian supernaturalism—that of uniting and adapting itself to the practical life of Society . . . on a great scale and in a popularly effective way . . . In Catholicism, by means of a universal Church, which regulates, supervises, and finally itself effects the ascent of Nature to Grace; in ascetic Protestantism, by a highly individualistic congregational system . . . and through the ascetic self-control of individuals." Troeltsch ends his study with this statement of the remaining problem:

Protestant ecclesiasticism, which began as the reform of Catholicism, and which built up a new uniform and compulsory Christian civilization, was led to an ever greater extent to sever its social doctrines from these early universal ecclesiastical developments. The first great structure which arose out of this process of separation was Ascetic Protestantism. It has founded and evolved the main body of Protestant civilization. But its power is weakening, and Protestantism is thus faced by new tasks, both in its own sociological development and in its corporate connection with civilization.[8]

One response to this problem was the Social Gospel of 1865-1915. In America this was the assertion of Christian responsibility in the face of industrialization and urbanization. Paul Abrecht has summarized the basic presuppositions of this movement.[9] The immanence of God was affirmed as men were summoned to work with him in the realization of his kingdom. Static concepts of man and society were challenged as men became aware of the need to change social structures and institutions. A more organic conception of society was set over against atomistic individualism, corresponding to a new concern for the importance of environment in shaping men's lives. Sin was defined in social as well as individual terms, with new emphasis upon human solidarity and equal opportunity. The focus was on the world of work, but in dealing with economics men turned to a more positive understanding of the role of the state.

Challenge to the Social Gospel. According to Abrecht, the Stockholm Conference of 1925 gave ecumenical endorsement to these ideas. But the experience of World War I had already set in motion challenges to the Social Gospel. The challenges came to a climax with the crisis theology, or Neo-Orthodoxy, or Barth and Brunner. Looking back from 1959. Walter Muelder was able to list eight protests made by the new theology against these Social Gospel emphases:

1. A zeal and idealism . . . which ignores the givenness of human existence.

2. A misunderstanding of history derived from a failure to grasp the limits and possibilities of human nature.
3. A tendency to over-emphasize the initiative of man.
4. A utopian faith in the role of government.
5. An overevaluation of the role and power of reason.
6. An accent on the immanence of God . . . and on inevitable human progress.
7. The loss of the eschatological understanding of history.
8. The failure to note the need for continuing redemption . . . since the struggle for power and the motivations of self-interest are unceasing.

Muelder adds that one judges a theology not by the hindsight it offers on earlier formulations, "but whether it grasps the problems of its own time and deals with them in the light of the whole gospel." [10]

Whether these were ecumenically endorsed achievements or items of theological protest, they do reflect certain underlying problems for social ethical thought at the start of the 1930s. The focus was on the application of an ethic either received or derived theologically. The religious concern was more with continuity and equilibrium than with change and conflict. The type case was assumed to be a homogeneous society with at least nominal consensus on values, rather than a pluralistic society with minorities contending for influence. The churches were just becoming aware of their minority status and groping to find ways to exert influence on social policies rather than to exercise presumed moral control (what came to be called the post-Constantinian awareness). There was a continuing struggle with individualism, which found ambiguous expression in a crusade for Prohibition on one hand and in the assertion, on the other, that racial patterns would not change until individual attitudes changed.

FOUR CRUCIAL DECADES: 1931–1971

It was at the beginning of the thirties that Reinhold Niebuhr, in *Moral Man and Immoral Society,* set the fundamental problematic for social ethics for at least four decades.[11] He inveighed against individual piety which ignored social injustice, castigated illusions and utopias, yet insisted upon the necessity of some illusions such as "that the collective life of mankind can achieve perfect justice." [12] But the persistent impact of his thought was to contrast the possibility of individual moral achievement with the overwhelming difficulty of doing more in social morality than balancing contesting forces, meeting power with power, and qualifying a brute struggle. It was in the mid-thirties that John C. Bennett wrote *Social Salvation* to insist that, if "social conditions do not of themselves save souls," they "do of themselves damn souls." [13] In 1929 H. Richard Niebuhr had written *The Social Sources of Denominationalism,* demonstrating how factors other than theology condition and imprison the churches themselves. The churches which should be free servants of God (responsible *for* society *to* God) are rather agents of class, racial and national loyalties. [14]

The crisis theology, which spread from the European continent to America in the thirties, not only portrayed an internal theological dialectic but also was a portent of crises or threats to come — depression, Nazism and Fascism, war, Stalinism, and severe challenges within Western democracies. James Gustafson, reviewing H. Richard Niebuhr's ethical thought, noted: "The problems change, and with them ethical reflection must change." [15] Problems seem to have required redefinition, both in nature and scope, as well as reinterpretation of responsibility.

Race and Color. This was true in problems related to race and color. In the 1930s the problem was thought to center on Negroes in the South, and the concern was to deal with such evils as lynching and the poll tax within a system of segregation. It appeared to require World War II, with Hitler's open espousal of the ideology of racism and the movement of Negroes into cities as well as into the armed services, to force reinterpretation. Then came the challenge to segregation itself (the denial of "separate but equal"), the affirmation of the goal of integration, and the assertion of Black Power. Slowly the realization came that the problem was not southern, but national, with worldwide dimensions; not a Negro problem, but a problem of black — white relationships, requiring attention to majority attitudes and, finally, to institutional racism. Remedial efforts moved from the courts to legislation to direct action. Some of the most bitter opposition came when in early 1967 Martin Luther King, Jr. emphasized the stake of the civil rights movement in peace.

Economics. Economic concerns in the 1930s centered on the right of labor to organize for collective bargaining and the use of government power to deal with big business, i.e., on the political control of economics. Church criticism of the economic order found its most vigorous expression about 1936, with serious questions about the profit motive and about the fundamental viability of the capitalist system.[16] By 1960, warnings about the military-industrial complex were manifestly directed at the dangers of war, but the latent question was whether economic problems had been solved only by resort to the arms race. By 1970 we became aware of the growth of multinational corporations. Robert Heilbroner, among others, has called attention to the *"internationalization of production itself,"* a process in which nations affect each other by producing goods directly within each other's borders. Such corporations have an obvious effect on development, for they desire order rather than revolutionary upheavals, even where change may be required for modernization. The struggle is not simply that of the rights of labor, as in the thirties, but whether there can be any effective political control of international economic entities which are larger than many nation-states.[17]

The corporation itself has become a battlefield. More and more consumers are organizing to ask who pays the social costs of problems arising from industries, such as pollution. Questions are being raised, particularly in churches, about the social responsibility of investment. The first appeal was for divestment, getting rid of funds invested in war-related enterprises. Now there is more reflective effort to combine church board and university portfolios in order to exercise influence on a broad range of corporate decisions.[18]

War and Violence. Historic responses of the churches to war and violence were challenged by the advent of nuclear weapons and by the resort to guerilla tactics. Some pacifists came to acknowledge the necessity for limited police powers in an agency such as the United

Nations. Non-pacifists had to rethink the adequacy of just-war doctrines. Could any war which was potentially nuclear be an instrument of justice? Does the criterion of legitimate authority have any meaning in an age of revolution?[19] Can war as an outbreak of conflict be distinguished from the endemic conflict characteristic in a world of deterrence? And, finally, do both nuclear weapons and guerilla tactics render impossible any protection of noncombatants—and thus no longer viable the criterion of just means, as well as that of proportionality of good achieved to evil done? A further question is raised as some critics have pondered the "violence of order," asking whether the responsibility for violence can always be placed on those who seek to challenge the system.

The four decades saw the waxing and waning of the importance of ideologies. The thirties began with a vast American ignorance of Marxism and communism.[20] World War II became a period of uneasy collaboration with Russia under the threat of nazism and fascism, brought to a halt in the Berlin crisis and the fall of China. All too often the churches were uncritically supportive of anticommunism, because of communist atheism and totalitarianism. Only in the sixties was any genuine contact made, through the Christian Peace Conference and the World Council of Churches. The Christian-Marxist dialogue focused attention on the common problems of churches in secular societies, the concept of transcendence, and the openness of history. Church leaders who sought contacts as well as peace across ideological divisions disavowed anticommunism but became increasingly frustrated as political maneuvers of governments interfered with church affairs, especially following the Czechoslovakian crisis of 1968.

There were, of course, other issues. The ecology movement was a response to a threatened life-support system; it was also a challenge to the biblical injunction to subdue the earth. At the end of the sixties there was great concern with medical ethics, organ transplants, and genetic manipulation. Many discussions in this area focused on the individual decision of the doctor rather than on the social-policy issues of utilization of resources for the public health.[21]

Redefinition of Problems. What do these changes in perceptions and definitions of the problems of race, economics, and war mean for the discipline of social ethics? First, the problems with which ethicists must deal are less localized and more universal (or at least national) than they were perceived to be forty years ago. Second, the problems and solutions are larger, more complex, and more interrelated than they were earlier thought to be. The problems are too big for appeals to individual conscience; in some cases they are too big for state action as conceived in the 1930s. And the nation-state itself is seen as part of the problem (or enemy), especially in the issue of war. Third, the problems seem more urgent. In the thirties there was a sense that time was on our side; now we sense that time is running out and doomsday approaches. This mood is especially prevalent in parts of the youth culture. Fourth, we are less sure that we can learn the required answers from history. Thus there is a new attempt, however fumbling, to take seriously the theological dimensions of problems. This means more than pointing to a doctrine of man; as, for example, is being done in ecology literature where new attention is paid to creation. It also means doing theological work other than writing prefaces to position papers.

If the problems have been redefined, certain issues — having to do with coercion and conflict, individualism, and the responsibility of the church — have remained central. Part of the legacy of Reinhold Niebuhr has been preoccupation with coercion — its legitimation or its avoidance and limits. This preoccupation is partly due to the unresolved individualism of Protestant ethics, a holdover of the social-contract theory as over against a more organic conception of man and society. Niebuhr was sure that national cohesion depended in large part on force (or the threat of force) and emotion rather than on ideas and consensus as to values. Walter Muelder is more of a consensus theorist, following Robert M. MacIver and insisting that "community is written into the constitution of man." [22] Debate about coercion often reflects an unwillingness to hold in tension ethical responsibility for conflict as well as for resolution of conflict. Failure to resolve the issue of coercion also reflects a peculiarly American unwillingness to believe that America can do wrong or should not be trusted. Robert N. Bellah has pointed to our proneness to divide all things into categories of good and evil, identifying our land with the good, and then assuming that "the good, being good, can do no evil. Any action taken against groups seen to be evil is justified, for the good can have only good ends in view." [23] It is not unknown in Christian history for coercion to be justified as necessary to deal with unredeemed evil; but in the late sixties this justification came under increasing challenge. Still, in a strange way, some of the most extreme critics of the war in Indochina (e.g., the Weathermen) justified their own violent acts by reference to the greater violence of the war. And some critics have made a serious attempt to distinguish between violence against property and violence against persons.

The Role of the Church. There is yet another factor of importance for social ethics. In 1965 Saul Alinsky, community organizer and "professional radical," commented that "The biggest change I've seen in the twenty years or so that I've been involved in social action is in the role the churches are playing." [24] There was a growing awareness of the corporate responsibility of the church — in its own life and as a social institution — as resource for and obstacle to change, as well as itself being an object of change. [25] At one level the Church has demonstrated its transnational character, albeit hesitantly and erratically. In such meetings as the 1966 World Conference on Church and Society there have been candid exchanges on social issues from widely different perspectives, all asserted within the Christian framework. For many Americans this was the first realization that the Viet Nam conflict had a racist character in the eyes of many non-Westerners. At another level, "ecumenical" came to have an expanded meaning with the papacy of John XXIII, the election of John F. Kennedy as President, the issuing of such encyclicals as *Pacem in Terris* and *Mater et Magister,* and joint enterprises such as SODEPAX (Committee on Society, Development and Peace of the World Council of Churches and the Vatican).

But at another level the churches discovered, particularly during the civil rights movement, that they were voluntary associations and had to maintain the loyalty of their constituents — sometimes in conflict with the claims of ethics and mission. At the same time that churchmen were exploring the idea of ministry of the laity, there became apparent a growing gap between socially involved clergy and more conservative laymen.[26] The effects of this gap were seen in unusually high departures from the ministry and in threats to the budgets of social-action agencies and conciliar movements. The situation was not helped by the pietistic individualism of such evangelicals as Billy Graham, whose effect was to sanction the status quo by foregoing effective ethical criticism as well as to offer frustrated laymen an alternative and more comfortable response to social crisis.

THE INTERDISCIPLINARY CHARACTER OF SOCIAL ETHICS

Events in the society, developments in the life of the Church, theological reflection — all of these combine to give strength to the notion of social ethics as a genuinely interdisciplinary discipline. Muelder made this explicit in 1963:

Christian social ethics, being an interdisciplinary field, is difficult to define. It is not theological ethics with applications to current social questions made apart from scientific analysis. It is not — even when the problems discussed are social — general theological ethics with biblical sanctions. It is not sociology of religion. It is interdisciplinary, which means that its practitioners undertake joint theoretical and empirical studies in theology, ethics, and the behavioral and historical sciences. Most works in Christian ethics belong in either biblical theology or systematic theology. Such books, while often perceptive in regard to social questions, do not belong in the field of social ethics unless they also exhibit a knowledge of the sciences specifically relevant to empirical and situational mastery of a problem.[27]

That this is a difficult task for the discipline is illustrated by a criticism of Muelder. A Jesuit philosopher, reviewing *Moral Law in Christian Social Ethics,* agrees with the interdisciplinary approach but does not think Muelder has faced up to the implications of such an approach. Father Blanchette argues that social philosophy and sociological theories are left "in a sort of extrinsic juxtaposition" rather than being made integral or interpenetrating. Many students of Muelder will find the critic's questions surprising about their teacher, but understandable about most social ethics: "Can we go on talking as if the moral dimension came from the interior of individuals first and then had to be extended outward to embrace society only afterward, as it were, as if the social were not already moral in its own right?"[28]

The persistent problem bequeathed by Niebuhr is not settled. Some avoid an interdisciplinary social ethic by attempting to keep the decision on secular grounds. It is strange to find a scholar such as Kenneth W. Thompson seeming to take such a position: "Christians as humanists are constantly tempted to find religious justifications for necessary or inevitable choices that are wholly secular."[29] The crudest expression of such a position is the justification of U.S. continuation of the Viet Nam war by arguing "We are there." Another, and perhaps complementary, avoidance is the requirement that ethics be a deductive discipline from Christian theology. For Paul Ramsey, "the question is whether and how far judgments (on social and political questions) may be deduced or adduced — or in any other way entailed — by the shared affirmation of *Christian* social ethics *as such.*"[30]

One unfortunate consequence of such avoidance — or failure of an interdisciplinary ethic — is that much social ethics debate is nonpolitical. Stanley Hoffman illustrates this in his discussion of principles in the formulation of U.S. foreign policy. The emphasis on principles

brings about a peculiar vicious circle of wrong questions. It makes the formulators of foreign policy decide issues in such a way that the solution will answer the question: "Which dogma, which assumption is relevant here?" When a debate breaks out over the decision, its defenders and its critics find themselves locked in a dialogue of the deaf. . . . One side's emphasis on motive provokes the other side to apply an equally formal, if different, yardstick. . . . One side upholds an ethic of intentions, the other an ethic of absolutes; both confuse the ethics of political action with the ethics of conviction, and both project into the international world a view shaped by Christian ethics as applied in a homogeneous society where questions tend to be treated as psychological rather than social.[31]

32

Contributions of the Disciplines. In this interdisciplinary exchange, what may each expect from the other, or, better, what may social ethics expect from its contributing disciplines? The first contribution of theology and philosophy might be termed "illumination" through historically derived loyalties, traditions, insights, and categories of interpretation. They should also contribute categories and procedures of logical consistency and rational coherence. They provide reminders and intimations of transcendent perspectives and ultimate context in the light of which all political and social judgments are made provisional and no institution receives final sanction or uncritical loyalty. Finally, theology and philosophy deal with sources of motivation and concern and with the grounds of hope.

For many ethicists to learn from social science they would have to get beyond caricatures that are only partially accurate, such as the notion that social science is retrospective, reductionist, and concerned only with man-as-object. Alvin W. Gouldner, in contrast, proposes a reflexive sociology, which no longer divides men into "subjects and objects, sociologists who study and 'laymen' who are studied."[32] The first contribution of the social sciences is aid in understanding the facts of the case. Significant facts are not easy to come by, perhaps because isolated facts are too easy to come by. Thomas L. Hughes writes that "in a sense the facts of foreign policy are not facts, or if they are, they are highly slippery and manipulable." He goes on to say that there "are so many just plain facts," some more relative than others, so that patterns of interpretation are required.[33] Thus the more important contribution is that of concepts, frames of reference, structures of interpretation. Social sciences can also aid in the previsioning of alternative consequences of choices. Thus Gibson Winter writes: "Social ethics translates the discerned regularities with which the social sciences clarify the human project into the practical context of societal responsibility."[34] The contributions are both received and used critically. Gouldner opens his volume with this statement: "The criticism and transformation of society can be divorced only at our peril from the criticism and transformation of theories about society."[35] I am not sure that it is either possible or desirable to reconcile social ethics and social science as Winter proposes. It is better to keep alive the dialectical tension and mutual criticism and correction. Winter himself later counsels "critical appreciation of the human sciences."[36]

Theory, Research, and Practice. As important as correction from contributing disciplines is the self-correction possible when there is interplay between theory, research, and practice in social ethics. Years ago Robert K. Merton pointed to the ways in which sociological theory and empirical research inform and correct one another. He noted that research (1) reveals consequences unanticipated in the theory; (2) exerts pressure for the recasting of theory; (3) brings new items into theoretical focus; and (4) makes possible the clarification of concepts by illustrative materials.[37] One can see the possibilities for similar learnings from practice in ethics, for morality must be lived both before and after it is formulated. Roger Shinn has stressed obedience to truth as a requisite to further ethical knowledge. And, in a famous essay "On Practice," Mao Tse-tung wrote: "Man's knowledge becomes verified only when, in the process of social practice . . . he achieves the anticipated results. Knowledge starts with practice, reaches the theoretical plane via practice, and then has to return to practice."[38] There are, of course, differences in the processes of argument and appeal between theory and practice. Rhetoric and slogans used to arouse groups to action often obscure the deeper issues and prevent a coherent view.[39]

James Gustafson has written of "The Burden of the Ethical" as involving this same "dialectic between disinterestedness and involvement" or theory and practice. The burden lies on us because we are at once moral agents and scholars of ethics.[40] The theory/disinterest edness side of the dichotomy stresses analysis, objectivity, coolness, abstraction, detachment, deliberation, reflection — usually post hoc — self-criticism of one's commitments (which Gustafson contrasts with wholeheartedness), and more concern with the ways in which decisions are made than with actual results. The other side, practice/ involvement, puts emphasis on engagement, commitment, passion, depth of feeling, urgency, concern for results. We may achieve far more self-understanding through involvement. I am not sure that

Gustafson is correct in thinking that only ethicists are inhibited from wholeheartedness, for all ethically-sensitive persons ought to be self-critical about goals and methods and ought to weigh actions strategically rather than with unalloyed enthusiasm. It is surely true that many ethicists have tended to "choose up sides" as either action-oriented or theory-oriented, rather than pursue a principle of alternation. It is also true that we do not yet know enough about how to evaluate our involvement and learn from it, testing effectiveness of strategy as well as hypotheses.[41]

LEVELS OF MORAL REFLECTION AND DISCOURSE

A number of social ethicists have incorporated into their own theoretical writings the levels of moral discourse formulated by Henry David Aiken. The four levels proposed are (1) the expressive or unreflective, (2) moral rules, or "What ought I to do?" (3) ethical principles, or reflections on how rules can be justified, and (4) the post-ethical, which faces the question of why one should be moral.[42]

Pre-ethical Reflection. I want first to explore the meaning of Aiken's first level of discourse for the discipline of social ethics and then to consider a further level — the social. Aiken describes the expressive level as unreflective, spontaneous, primarily "conventional expressions of personal feelings" of pleasure or displeasure. Whether these expressions are at the level of *discourse* is an implicit question in Aiken's statement: "To challenge them or to raise questions of 'truth' or 'validity' with respect to them would be pointless. They do not solicit agreement or invite reply."[43] Discourse would seem to involve reply and either agreement or disagreement. I am not sure whether the pre-ethical dimension of ethical reflection includes the expressive level or is distinct from it.

At any rate, it is important to recognize as factors affecting ethical reflection at Aiken's other three levels (and a fourth to be treated below) *persistent* — rather than spontaneous — *internalized* — either consciously or unconsciously—taken-for-granted bents of mind and habits of thought. These pre-ethical factors exercise a lasting and almost irresistible influence on the style of doing ethics as well as upon a given decision. Roger Shinn, reviewing Paul Ramsey's account of the Conference on Church and Society, notes how Geneva brought into encounter Christians with different cultural histories, a contribution as important to social ethics as refined analytic precision: "Christian ethics needs far greater intellectual attention to the sociology of knowledge and the modes of human perception. The most conscientious work of ethical analysis is usually inadequate because it works from skewed perceptions." [44]

These skewed perceptions occur in the ethicist himself, as H. Richard Niebuhr noted in describing his own theological pilgrimage: "No matter how much all of us work out our thoughts . . . it is in every case the highly personal, not to say private, experiences that most immediately affect the basic form and formulation of our faith." [45] These pre-ethical factors may affect perception, judgment, and discourse most when they have not been brought to the level of consciousness. When the ethicist becomes aware of the influences, he may be better able to take account of his bias, both in his own reflection and in seeking correction within a community of shared loyalty but more diverse experience and perspective. [46]

The pre-ethical factors, especially when hidden, also affect the debate over social policy, as persons become defensive of a position already taken (perhaps on non-rational grounds), of loyalties which cannot be betrayed (or at times acknowledged), and of commitments which interfere with even hearing opposing views — much less understanding them or seeking agreement.

It is one of the most crucial tasks of social ethics to work to improve the quality and clarity of public dialogue and debate over ethical decisions. A first roadblock to such debate is the difficulty in determining what official policy is. This is true of any institution, but especially government. Sam Brown suggests that people's feeling of alienation and powerlessness arises not only from their inability to change policy, but more fundamentally from "the inability to even determine what the policy is." [47] In mid-1971 there occurred a "leak" of the Pentagon Papers, documents and interpretation hitherto secret, on the origins and development of U.S. involvement in Viet

Nam. James Reston lamented that "the available record shows almost no protest among the President's closest advisors against what they knew to be deceptions of the American people." Reported questions from within the government seemed to focus more on the pragmatic dimensions of policies rather than on moral issues.[48]

Interests and Values. Leaders in church and in government (opposition as well as those in power) tend to assume that it is more important to win a vote or an election than to risk defeat by the kind of open debate which might contribute to public awareness and informed opinion. Thus, there is a vicious circle which reinforces the ignorance, apathy, and confusion which themselves are invoked to justify the deception or appeal to slogans in the first instance. William Arrowsmith, a classicist, deplores the "new illiteracy" which he sees as the result of the intellectuals' pride "in which the assertion of the self involves a godlike denial of the other" and which makes the elite "almost unteachable." The essence of pride is the "distrust of the audience," the habit of believing that the audience is not up to what he has to say and therefore ending up inferior to the potential of his audience.[49]

One form of the distrust is the appeal to interests instead of values, justified as the only way to sway the masses. In part, of course, this reflects a bias of theory, as Sister Marie Augusta points out. In functional terms "values are perceived as setting limits on the interests that can be expressed," while conflict theory perceives interests "as generating values or manipulating existing values as a means to legitimate group-member behavior." She does go on to distinguish more objectively values as "widely shared conceptions of the good" from interests as "desires for special advantages for the self or for groups with which one is identified."[50]

Alinsky unabashedly accepts this appeal to interests as a strategy, stressing the need for polarization by threats to self-interest. "People and organizations inevitably do the right thing for the wrong reasons. Then they dredge up the right reasons and those become the rationalization for why they did the right thing." Alinsky makes the concern for ethics, if not ethics itself, a function of interest: "One's concern with the ethics of means and ends varies inversely with the degree of one's personal vested interest in the issue." The question is "pragmatic," asking of ends "only whether they are achievable and worth the cost; of means only whether they will work." There may be a joker in the reference to *cost,* but Alinsky's perspective is probably aptly expressed when he puts in italics: *"The means-and-end moralists, or non-doers, always wind up on their ends without any means."* [51]

There are both empirical and theoretical criticisms of interest theories. Many, if not all, persons think — and want others to think — that their appeal to values is genuine; thus, hypocrisy is the homage vice pays to virtue. And tolerable social order would not be possible were there not widely shared conceptions of the good which provide *some* limits in the expression of interests. Gibson Winter points out that the theoretical "difficulty with interest theories . . . is that their recognition of the struggle for power readily elevates that struggle to a final principle." [52] There would seem to be some situational requirement for the assertion of the public interest when special or private interests get out of hand. It is the task, then, of the ethicist to escalate the moral discourse from the pre-ethical or expressive level, through that of moral rules, and into reflection on how the moral rules are justified (or unjustified), as well as why one should be moral.

The Social Dimension of Moral Discourse. There is a further, social, dimension of moral discourse, already implicit in the above, which comes with the necessary transposition of reflection and discussion from personal decision to group decision and public policy. Aiken's levels still seem to leave the discourse preoccupied with the subjective and individual. Warren generalizes from his New England studies: "Much of the falsity of the Protestant ethics lies in just what—whether in its popular or its philosophic form—it has prided itself on: its concern with self and subjectivity. Concern with *my* motives, *my* intentions, *my* conscience is always in danger of becoming more concerned with me than with God and my neighbor, with that whole vast other world. Egoism — refined subjectivity — is morally more dangerous partly because more subtle, than plain frank egotism or selfishness." [53] Gustafson's discussion of moral discernment leaves implicit or undeveloped the acknowledgement that such discernment should involve "some appeals to reason and principle both to help one discern and *to defend* what one discerns." [54] It is not only to defend but to set forth the terms of debate, the grounds for appeal — factual or normative — on the basis of which one might be willing to yield, to change, to compromise. The point here is that the very individualistic cast of ethics lends itself to defensiveness and rebuttal rather than to listening and to resolving conflicts within and between groups.

One result of the above is that we, as ethicists and citizens, do not take sufficient advantage of our differences, our pluralism, as an aid to critical reflection, to discovery of truth beyond the present truth, to confronting other ways. Thus separated, we tend also to use our past as justification for the present, as "cultural reinforcement," learning "how we became what we are," rather than exploring what we might be. [55] Ethical reflection can become ideological rather than critical; nonetheless, Joseph Stamey's statement of tendency is not altogether correct, for there have been challenges to privilege, and there has been a stream of more universal, more prophetic, more critical ethical thought. Stamey writes: "every concretely specified ethic of the past has tended to function as an ideology rather than as an instrument of critical ethical reflection. Ethical reasoning has functioned not only to translate universal ethical principles into concretely specified situational duties; it has served to validate and perpetuate the (unjustifiable) privileges of a limited segment of the human community." [56]

Charles West sees in this ideological clash "the problem of ethics today." In his view, the world conflict of two experiences has become "internal to theological ethics itself": "two fundamentally opposed experiences of life confront each other in the modern world: the one of experienced peace and freedom, with the hope that it may be preserved and developed; the other of rejection, frustration, and alienation with the hope of revolution." The problem, if ethics is to do more than justify given positions, is for ethics to achieve a more universal, critical, self-corrective, and thus reconciling spirit. West's hope is that the Christian community might gather up the social conflicts and perform some service of reconciliation. He sees the Church as "the place where men and social forces are confronted with one another in a way from which there is no escape by the usual methods — coercion, stereotyping, apathy, and the like — so that they must take their own convictions with final seriousness, the seriousness that consists in readiness to convert or be converted." [57]

The Political Conscience. This seeming digression began with an emphasis on the individualism of most moral discourse and on the typical focus on examination and expression of conscience rather than the responsibility for advancing ethical considerations through social policy. Hannah Arendt defines conscience as "unpolitical . . . not primarily interested in the world . . . or in the consequences." She notes how, in Christian philosophy, conscience was taken to mean "the voice of God" ("Obey God rather than men") and was thus self-validating. It is for this reason that recognition of conscientious objector status has only with difficulty been extended to those who do not appeal to a supreme being or hold membership in a religious community whose teachings support the objection. Arendt makes her distinction between conscientious objection and civil disobedience turn on this matter of civil disobedients becoming "organized minorities, bound together by their decision to take a stand against an assumed majority." This action in the name of a group focuses attention on social policy. [58]

But the difference is not only in the expression of one group or movement; it involves a moral criticism and appeal to the social conscience of the majority as well. It is not an attempt to simply translate individual ethics into collective terms, but to wrestle with the corporate dimensions of ethical responsibility. Troeltsch acknowledged that, because of diffused responsibility and complexity of issues, "Moral regulation is certainly much more difficult of accomplishment for a group than it is for individuals"; but he held that "in principle we have to do with the same demands of justice and of kindness, of recognition and of education, of respect and of support." [59] T. E. Jessop proposed in 1952 that we begin the construction of a social ethic by working on four levels of decision and action: (1) personal; (2) membership-action, *within* a group; (3) group-action, expressing the consensus of the group *outside* the group; and (4) representative action by individuals who speak or act on behalf of a group consensus.[60] Attention to such distinctions and levels of responsibility can help us move beyond the dichotomy of "moral man and immoral society."

A still unresolved problem is why a person, group member, or representative might change his mind in regard to a policy. To what appeals is one—and should one be—responsive and responsible? Does change come because of pressure or threats, or because of moral reasoning, or due to new facts, to seeing facts in new frames of reference, or to the shock of consequences or the experience of incongruity? Study of such changes should be related to the ways in which we ourselves learn from our involvement.

THE POSSIBILITY OF A DISCIPLINE

Implicit in much of the preceding is the suspicion that the development of a discipline of social ethics is impeded by its lack of a social problematic. Llewellyn Gross opens his inquiry into the possibility of a sociological theory by referring to Horace Kallen's comments on the meaning of "problem." Problems in philosophy and the social sciences, according to Kallen, "seem to follow from their solutions," rather than solutions from problems. A problem "designates the formal or systematic elaboration of the unproblematical." Gross proposes a more Socratic approach as preferable to system-building, with the focus to be on "dialogue and inquiry, conflict and controversy, dialectic and dilemma."[61] I have been expecting for some time the emergence of social ethics as a cumulative, methodologically precise, unified discipline, but the time is not yet. Surely social ethics must become more systematic and rigorous in clarifying definitions, employing more adequate concepts, and testing generalizations and theoretical probes. But the preliminary requirement is the refinement of the statement of the problem of the proposed discipline.

Ethicists share a responsibility to continue reexamining previous paradigms or models of work. This is most likely to come through sustained dialectic of inquiry, criticism of problems as stated, and collaboration regarding methods—within a framework of critical attention to institutionalized goals, policies, and procedures of the larger society. Such reflection on social issues, testing concepts in application and practice, may enrich the discipline more than the methodological preoccupation of the past decade. Sheldon Wolin, writing of political theory, insists that great theories have come in response to global crises, inspiring new ways of looking at the world, proposing new criteria of significance, and specifying new norms of what can count as an answer.[62]

The movement toward such a discipline would seem to involve at least the following: (1) a self-conscious community of inquiry and exchange, with a continuing attempt to focus on commonly defined problems; (2) an interdisciplinary effort to work out the understanding of what constitutes an ethical issue in a social policy; (3) an evolving body of knowledge, with principles of evaluation; and (4) a reflective alternation between detachment—with attention to theory—and involvement—with concern for practice. Thus conceived social ethics becomes a shared attempt

1) to reflect carefully and systematically about the choices of goods and the appropriate means which inhere in responsible social policy;

2) to use that reflection in guidance concerning substantive issues, procedures in decisionmaking, and critical evaluation of the results;

3) to learn from the consequences of the policy decision and of the decision process;

4) to continue to seek to translate the modes of ethical reflection into terms applicable in the more inclusive community, thus setting a framework for argument regarding ends, means, decisions, results.

There is, of course, the danger that even such a discipline might become arrogant, elitist, prescriptive (to focus on norms is not necessarily to prescribe policies). Such a warning comes hard for one whose professional efforts have been directed toward stimulating and disciplining social action in and by the churches. But the call is not "For God's sake, do *something!*" when something means anything. It is the *something* which requires analysis.

Early in the 1930s there occurred the only published exchange between Reinhold and H. Richard Niebuhr. This was invoked by the latter's response, entitled "The Grace of Doing Nothing," to proposed United States military intervention in the Sino-Japanese conflict. H. Richard Niebuhr confronted the dilemma of being anxious to do something when there seemed nothing constructive to do. As came to be his habit, he restated the problem as "that of choice between kinds of inactivity rather than of choice between action and inaction." He listed the inactivity of the pessimist, of the conservative, of the frustrated who finally explode in the necessity of "one more war to end war," of the Communist, coming finally to the inactivity which is "profoundly active in rigid self-analysis" and which will prepare for the future by creating the conditions for genuine reconstruction. The implicit moral is that activists should not make later good choices impossible by rushing into present choices of the lesser evil. The method is clearing the path by repentance. And the approach, he concludes, "is valid for societies as well as for individuals." [63] This is at least a healthy antidote to Bellah's understanding of America's belief that the good can do no evil.

But it is most interesting and instructive to find the director of intelligence and research of the Department of State, thirty-five years after Niebuhr's essay, putting the case for a comparable restraint. Thomas L. Hughes distinguishes the "community of hardware orientation" from that of "human orientation." The former links the physical sciences with industry, defense, and intelligence; it is concerned with determining factors, scenarios, realistic policies. The "software" community is more concerned with such intangibles as "motivation, conviction, identification, participation, loyalty, persistence," social cohesion, ethics, and democratic leadership. Hughes holds that the two communities are in polar tension, but he puts the case for the human orientation in these words:

Thinking people in the second culture long ago accustomed themselves to living with contradiction, to having faith in skepticism, to advancing toward the solution of a problem by admitting as a possibility what few but the greatest among the scientists, soldiers, and game-theorists of the first culture admit — namely that the problem may be insoluble. In terms of practical politics in a nuclear era, that is a viewpoint which we discard at our peril. For we live in an age which constantly presents us with impossible alternatives — none of which appears to lead us where we want to go.[64]

The discipline of social ethics will require concern for coherence, commitment, strategy, and practice. But it must avoid becoming doctrinaire, refuse to capitulate to the demand for more clarity in theory than exists in the situation, and deny the attempts to over-determine policy ideologically. Its health, and usefulness, will depend upon its keeping alive its sense of problem, its sensitivity to changing dimensions of problems, its refusal to establish a canon, its ability to maintain a critical capacity — both concerning itself and its setting — and its determination to listen to voices from the past and from outside its own community. By so doing it may well improve the quality of its own dialogue and, in turn, frame the issues and procedures for public resolution of ethical problems.

NOTES

1. Austin Warren, *The New England Conscience* (Ann Arbor: University of Michigan Press, 1966), p. 12.

2. Thomas Jefferson wrote in an 1816 letter: "Some men look at the Constitution with sanctimonious reverence, and deem it like the ark of the covenant, too sacred to be touched. They ascribe to the men of the preceding age a wisdom more than human, and suppose what they did to be beyond amendment. I knew that age well; I belonged to it, and labored with it. It was very like the present, but without the experience of the present; and forty years of experience in government is worth a century of bookreading; and this they would say themselves, were they to rise from the dead." Quoted in William O. Douglas, *We The Judges* (Garden City: Doubleday and Co., 1956), p. 430. Men may, of course, refuse to learn from experience. On the usefulness of history for social ethics, see chap. 2, below.

3. Eric Sevareid, C.B.S. Evening News, August, 1970.

4. James Gustafson, "Context versus Principles: A Misplaced Debate in Christian Ethics," *Harvard Theological Review* 58 (April 1965):171–202.

5. Max L. Stackhouse, "Technical Data and Ethical Norms: Some Theoretical Considerations," *Journal for the Scientific Study of Religion* 2 (Spring 1966): 191–203.

6. Beverly Harrison "Earnest Ethics," *The Tower*, Union Theological Seminary (Spring 1969), p. 4. "Ethics," "social ethics," and "Christian ethics" seem to be used interchangeably in this piece.

7. Gibson Winter, *Elements for a Social Ethic* (New York: Macmillan Co., 1966), p. xiii.

8. Ernst Troeltsch, *The Social Teaching of the Christian Churches*, Olive Wyon, trans. (New York: Macmillan Co., 1931), 2:815. 819–20.

9. Paul Abrecht, "The Development of Ecumenical Social Ethics," in John C. Bennett, ed., *Christian Social Ethics in a Changing World* (New York: Association Press, 1966), p. 155.

10. Walter G. Muelder, "The New Theology and the Old Social Gospel" (unpublished manuscript, 1959).

11. The choice of these four decades, 1931–1971, for review is not altogether arbitrary. Walter G. Muelder finished his doctoral dissertation on Ernst Troeltsch in 1933 and his professional career spans these decades. There are other social ethicists whose careers lie in whole or in large part in this period — John C. Bennett, James Luther Adams, Joseph Fletcher, H. Richard Niebuhr and Reinhold Niebuhr, and Paul Ramsey, to name only a few Americans. These men have helped to shape the American Protestant tradition in social ethics; they and their students have contributed substantially to the emergence of a self-conscious field of study, a professional society, and the expansion of social ethics as a subject of study in seminaries.

12. Reinhold Niebuhr, *Moral Man and Immoral Society* (New York: Charles Scribner's Sons, 1932), p. 277.

13. John C. Bennett, *Social Salvation* (New York: Charles Scribner's Sons, 1935), p. vii. See also chap. 4, below, for further reference to this volume.

14. H. Richard Niebuhr, *The Social Sources of Denominationalism* (New York: Henry Holt and Co., 1929). In 1937 Niebuhr wrote *The Kingdom of God in America* (New York: Harper and Brothers) to express his dissatisfaction with a sociological orientation that failed to account for the religious movement itself; yet he never really repudiated the sociological study. In it he had set the stage for the later World Council of Churches Commission on Institutionalism, which was chaired by Walter Muelder. Some of the commission's studies were published in Nils Ehrenstrom and Walter G. Muelder, eds., *Institutionalism and Church Unity* (New York: Association Press, 1966).

15. James Gustafson, "Christian Ethics and Social Policy," in Paul Ramsey, ed., *Faith and Ethics* (New York: Harper and Row, 1957), p. 122.

16. See Walter G. Muelder, *Methodism and Society in the Twentieth Century* (New York: Abingdon Press, 1961), especially chap. 5, "The Social Creed in the Great Depression."

17. Robert L. Heilbroner, "The Multinational Corporation and the Nation-State," *The New York Review of Books,* 11 February 1971, pp. 20–25.

18. See Philip I. Blumberg, "Introduction to the Politicalization of the Corporation," *The Record* of the Association of the Bar of the City of New York, vol. 26, no. 5, (May 1971); and "Corporate Responsibility and the Social Crisis," *Boston University Law Review,* vol. 50, no. 2 (Spring 1970).

19. See chap. 8, below, for Joseph Stamey's discussion of the problematic character of sovereignty in this regard.

20. Among the informed critics of Marxism should be counted Reinhold Niebuhr and Walter G. Muelder, especially in the latter's "A Personalistic Critique of Marxism" (unpublished, undated), a remarkably balanced argument.

21. See Walter G. Muelder, "The Ecological Era," especially the second lecture on "Man in the Bio-technical Revolution," *The Foundation,* Gammon Theological Seminary, 67 (Summer 1970):3–26.

22. Walter G. Muelder, "Power, Anomie, and Personality," in L. Bryson, L. Finkelstein, and R. M. MacIver, eds., *Perspectives on a Troubled Decade* (New York: Harper, 1950), pp. 477–93, especially pp. 478 and 484.

23. Robert N. Bellah, "Evil and the American Ethos" (unpublished paper from a 22 February 1970 San Francisco conference on The Legitimation of Evil), p. 9. Bellah comments on the way the conflict over Viet Nam has made this assumption a matter of public debate, especially among the younger generation.

24. Saul Alinsky, "A Professional Radical Moves in on Rochester," *Harper's,* July 1965, p. 52.

25. See Herbert E. Stotts and Paul Deats, Jr., *Methodism and Society: Guidelines for*

Strategy (New York: Abingdon Press, 1962), pt. 2; J. Milton Yinger, *The Scientific Study of Religion* (New York: Macmillan Co., 1970), chaps. 21 and 22.

26. See J. K. Hadden, *The Gathering Storm in the Church* (Garden City: Doubleday, 1967); E. Q. Campbell and Thomas Pettigrew, *Christians in Racial Crisis* (Washington: Public Affairs Press, 1959).

27. Walter G. Muelder, "Christian Social Ethics Bookshelf," *The Christian Century,* 30 October 1963, p. 1336.

28. Oliva Blanchette, S.J., "Law and Morality," *Nexus* (Boston University School of Theology) 10 (May 1967): 12, 35; see also Muelder, "Theology and Social Science," in Bennett, ed., *Christian Social Ethics,* pp. 330–47.

29. Kenneth W. Thompson, "Forgiveness and Foreign Policy," *Christian Advocate,* 29 September 1960, p. 15.

30. Paul Ramsey, *Who Speaks for the Church?* (New York: Abingdon Press, 1967), p. 18; see also Wilhelm Korff, "Empirical Social Study and Ethics," *Concilium* 5 (May 1968): 5–13.

31. Stanley Hoffman, *Gulliver's Troubles* (New York: McGraw-Hill Book Co., 1968), pp. 126–27. The principles given by Hoffman are self-determination and peaceful change (rather than by force). He insists that he is not pitting idealism versus realism or moralism versus power, and that "ideals are a proper and ineradicable part of reality" (p. 125).

32. Alvin W. Gouldner, *The Coming Crisis of Western Sociology* (New York: Basic Books, 1970), pp. 489, 491.

33. Thomas L. Hughes, "Policy-Making in a World Turned Upside Down," *Foreign Affairs* 45 (January 1967): 203–04.

34. Winter *Elements,* pp. 166–67.

35. Gouldner, *Coming Crisis,* p. 3. He goes on to argue that politics is by itself insufficient for social transformation. "For the old society is not held together merely by force and violence or expedience and prudence. The old society maintains itself also through theories and ideologies. . . . It will be impossible either to emancipate men from the old society or to build a humane new one, without . . . new social theories . . . without a critique of the social theories dominant today," (p. 5).

36. Winter, *Elements,* pp. xv, 201.

37. Robert K. Merton, *Social Theory and Social Structure* (rev. ed., Glencoe: The Free Press, 1957), pp. 85–117.

38. Roger Shinn, "Some Ethical Foundations of Christian Theology," *Union Seminary Quarterly Review* 15 (January 1960): 102; *Mao Tse-tung: An Anthology of his Writings,* Anne Fremantle, ed. (New York: Mentor Books, 1962), pp. 201, 209; cf. A. N. Whitehead, *Process and Reality* (New York: Macmillan Co., 1929), pp. 8, 12.

39. Marion J. Levy, Jr. has some skeptical observations on the kind of thinking characteristic of reformers in "Levy's Nine Laws of the Disillusionment of the True Liberal," *Midway* 10 (Winter 1970): 81–92. His fourth law reads: "Always pray that your opposition be wicked. In wickedness there is a strong strain toward rationality. Therefore, there is always the possibility, in theory, of handling the wicked by outthinking them. Corollary 1: Good intentions randomize behavior. Subcorollary 1: Good intentions are far more difficult to cope with than malicious behavior. Corollary 2: If good intentions are combined with stupidity, it is impossible to outthink them."

40. James Gustafson, "The Burden of the Ethical," *The Foundation* (Gammon Theological Seminary) 46 (Winter 1970): 8–15.

41. Gouldner, *Coming Crisis,* p. 499, sees reflexive sociology as calling into question a value-free sociology while remaining aware of the dangers of a value-committed sociology. See also Ralph Potter's discussion of "Temptations to 'Relevance,' " in his *War and Moral Discourse* (Richmond: John Knox Press, 1969), pp. 15-22. The use of the word *temptation* seems to suggest that the proper approach to doing ethics is disinterestedness. This may be a reason why some groups in the youth culture find so little help in traditional ethics. These groups go to the opposite extreme, with emphasis on immediacy — NOW, trusting only

personal experience as authoritative and displaying an almost puritanical ability to focus on a single issue. See my "Youth Revolution?" in *Religion in Life* (Winter, 1971).

42. H. D. Aiken, *Reason and Conduct* (New York: Alfred A. Knopf, 1962), pp. 65–87. Aiken notes that moral discourse typically shifts from level to level, that the connections are pragmatic rather than logical, and that there are a variety of modes of justification. Both James Gustafson and Ralph Potter are indebted to Aiken.

43. Ibid., pp. 68–69.

44. Roger L. Shinn, "Paul Ramsey's Challenge to Ecumenical Ethics," *Christianity and Crisis* 27 (30 October 1967): 245.

45. H. Richard Niebuhr, "Reformation: Continuing Imperative," *The Christian Century* 77 (2 March 1960): 248.

46. My colleague, Leroy S. Rouner, raises the question of "whether these presystematic or prereflective elements are regarded as limitations (only) or a common uniting resource." He agrees that "the 'pre-ethical' presents problems for coherence and for consensus on what . . . a social ethic is all about." He elaborates: "My question is whether or not the 'pre-ethical' may not also provide areas of common experience, concern, and insight. Indeed . . . one might even argue that it is in the pre-reflective sense of what is good that hope for a common ethical discipline and . . . consensus really lies. Part of my argument . . . hinges on the question whether reason *discovers* the good, or only analyzes it. [Rather than] arguing that we can find out what the good is if we reason carefully enough . . . my conviction is that the good which reason discovers is usually the good which was already hidden in the original intuition, or, if you will, the 'pre-ethical' level of 'conscience.' (Personal letter, 24 June 1971).

47. Sam Brown, "The Same Old Gang Turns Up in Washington," *Life*, 29 January 1971, p. 2.

48. James Reston, in "News of the Week in Review," *New York Times*, 13 June 1971, p. E 13. The focus on pragmatic questions should not be a surprise, given the choices noted in the second paragraph of this essay.

49. William Arrowsmith, "Teaching and the Liberal Arts: Notes Towards an Old Frontier" (mimeographed, undated), p. 11.

50. Sister Marie Augusta Neal, *Values and Interests in Social Policy* (Englewood Cliffs: Prentice-Hall, Inc., 1965), pp. 7, 9.

51. Stephen C. Rose, "Discerning Power Realities: An interview with Saul Alinsky," *The Christian Century* 88 (19 May 1971): 624; "Of Ends and Means," *Union Seminary Quarterly Review* 22 (January 1967): 109, 107, 108.

52. Winter, *Elements*, p. 193; see also I. M. Crombie, "Moral Principles," in Ian T. Ramsey, ed., *Christian Ethics and Contemporary Philosophy* (London: SCM Press, 1966), pp. 234–61.

53. Warren, *New England Conscience*, p. 19.

54. Gustafson, "Moral Discernment," p. 25, italics added.

55. Arrowsmith, "Teaching and Liberal Arts," p. 4.

56. Joseph Stamey, "The Emerging Ethic: Religious, Non-Religious, or Anti-Religious?" (unpublished paper), p. 15. Jorge I. Dominguez of Harvard distinguishes "ideological" ethics as used to justify established positions from "prophetic" or critical ethics embodying broad statements of general principle, (unpublished memorandum, March, 1971).

57. Charles C. West, "The Problem of Ethics Today," *Theology Today* 25 (October 1968): 342, 365; see also West, "Theology and Technical Change," *Anticipation* 5 (December 1970): 10.

58. Hannah Arendt, "Civil Disobedience," *The New Yorker*, 12 September 1970, pp. 72, 76, 78, 86.

59. Ernst Troeltsch, *Christian Thought*, Friedrich von Hügel, ed. (New York: Meridian Books, 1957), p. 83.

60. T. E. Jessop, *Social Ethics: Christian and Natural* (London: Epworth Press, 1952), pp. 40–41. O. H. v. d. Gablentz distinguishes between the responsibility of a trustee, who acts

in the name of a body, and an agent, whose responsibility is limited by instruction. He argues that democratic society invalidates the distinction. "Responsibility," *International Encyclopedia of the Social Sciences,* 16 vols. (New York: Macmillan Co., 1968), 13:449.

61. Llewellyn Gross, "Sociological Theory: Questions and Problems," in L. Gross, ed., *Sociological Theory: Inquiries and Paridigms* (New York: Harper and Row, 1967), pp. 3, 5; the Kallen quotation is from his *Modernity and Liberty,* University of Buffalo Studies 18 (March 1947): 73.

62. Sheldon S. Wolin, "Paradigms and Political Theories," in P. King and B. C. Parekh, eds., *Politics and Experience* (Cambridge: Cambridge University Press, 1968), pp. 140–48.

63. H. Richard Niebuhr, "The Grace of Doing Nothing," *The Christian Century,* 23 March 1932; and id., "The Only Way into the Kingdom of God," 6 April 1932. The references are to the *Christian Century Reader,* H. E. Fey and M. Frakes, eds. (New York: Association Press, 1962), pp. 216–21, 231.

64. Hughes, "Policy-Making," pp. 205, 208ff.

2 The Relevance of Historical
Understanding   *James M. Gustafson*

STUDENTS of ethics, whether Christian ethics or other sorts, have a strong inclination to neglect history. Critical moral philosophy, almost by definition, is concerned with formal questions — with the structure of arguments, with issues of logical consistency and precision of thought. As the New Critics in literature counselled their students to go to the texts rather than to the biographies of authors or to the study of their times, so the students of ethics have also tended to study texts as if they were not conditioned by the life history of their authors and the social conditions under which they were written. How many articles does one read on the just-war theory, for example, which do not consider the political and military situations in which the theorists existed when they wrote? To be sure, there is a weightier pressure on the practical moralist to consider the contemporary historical conditions about which he makes judgments and in which he counsels certain forms of action; but even such writers sometimes are limited by the lack of awareness that these moral issues, or similar ones, have been addressed in particular historical contexts in the past.

An intellectual giant now dead for half a century, namely Ernst Troeltsch, made clear to his readers that historical understanding was important for the study of ethics, and particularly the study of Christian ethics. This great historian, philosopher, and theologian had more impact on Christian ethical thought in America than he did in his native Germany. One looks in vain for a successor to Troeltsch in German theological and social ethics; that is, one does not find in the German literature anyone whose major efforts were directed toward assessing the interactions between cultural developments, historical circumstances and events, theology, ecclesiology, and ethical teachings. The reasons for this would make an interesting investigation, but would take us far afield.

In the United States the impact of Troeltsch has continued through the influence of some of the most important teachers of Christian theology and ethics during the past fifty years. H. Richard Niebuhr at Yale and Walter Muelder at Boston University both wrote dissertations on Troeltsch, and both were teachers of many persons working in the field of Christian ethics today.[1] Troeltsch's impact on their writings was persistent; for both, the socio-historical matrix of Christian ethical thought was kept in view, although each of them resolved the Troeltschian theological problematic in a different way. James Luther Adams, at the University of Chicago and at Harvard University, led many students, including this author, into serious encounters with Troeltsch and his patterns of thought, not only in *The Social Teaching of the Christian Churches,* but also in important essays in the other volumes of the *Gesammelte Schriften*.[2] Adams' own interests and scope have been as broad as Troeltsch's, and he has sponsored English translations of many of Troeltsch's essays. Wilhelm Pauck, the only one mentioned here who was actually a student in Troeltsch's classes — at Chicago and at Union Seminary in New York — always made it clear that he stood for the historical rather than the dogmatic method in theology and had many students read Troeltsch on that issue. His classroom claim during the height of the influence of Karl Barth — that Barth failed to come to grips with Troeltsch's problematic — is probably borne out by recent developments in theology.

The purpose of this essay, however, is not to discuss Troeltsch or his influence on American theology and ethics. Rather, it is to look at the continuing importance of the Troeltschian perspective, namely the relevance of historical understanding for scholarly work in Christian ethics. Three aspects of this relevance are attended to in this essay: (1) the importance of knowing the historical context in which religious ethical ideas were formulated in order properly to understand them; (2) the importance of, and difficulties in, using historical analogies in formulating constructive ethical positions; and (3) the freedom to be historically situated and aware of the press of historical circumstances on one's own ethical judgments.

THE IMPORTANCE OF HISTORICAL SETTINGS

Historical studies of themes in Christian ethics are lamentably few in number and do not begin to attend to all the facets that are interesting and important. Studies of teachings about particular moral problems are a case in point. There are useful studies, for example, a volume edited by Joseph Fletcher on property, the work of Roland Bainton on war, religious liberty, and sex, Schillebeeck's study of marriage, the treatments of usury by Benjamin Nelson and John Noonan, Noonan's work on contraception and abortion, and others.[3] But with occasional significant exceptions, these are sketchy treatments, and the range of topics by no means exhausts the possibilities for research. Studies of theological ethical themes are also few in number, and none of them is very recent: Anders Nygren's *Agape and Eros,* Newton Flew's *The Idea of Perfection,* K. E. Kirk's *The Vision of God,* and N. P. Williams' *The Ideas of the Fall and Original Sin,* are perhaps most prominent.[4] But many comprehensive studies are lacking; for example, there is no first-rate history of natural-law theory available in English.

Many of these books are written in the mode of the history of ideas; indeed, they are literary histories of ideas, histories which study documents but do not set the documents in the historical contexts out of which they emerged. While some of them engage in the historian's task of analyzing the influences of antecedent texts upon subsequent ones, others are more clearly ideal-typical in method. No demeaning of the significance of these approaches is intended by observing that they might lead to seriously mistaken impressions: for example, that a theologian's writings about love, or property, were not reactions to events in his time as well as to other writings of his time; or that one can understand teachings about war or property without understanding the sorts of wars and the economic conditions that existed when the teachings were articulated. Many of these studies need supplementation from the Troeltschian point of view that ethical ideas are formulated in a complex historical matrix —a culture, a society, historical events, theological polemics, an ecclesiological and ecclesiastical setting, philosophical currents, and other matters. Ethical thinkers, perhaps by predilection oriented toward abstract ideas, are prone to deal with texts as if the historical context is of little significance for understanding them.[5] A reader may know, for example, that St. Augustine's *The City of God* was written while the Roman Empire was under its most severe threat; but he probably does not know much about those historical events or what their import is for accurately understanding that classic in Christian theology and ethics.

Two important studies of the ethics of birth control are illustrative of our concern: David M. Feldman's *Birth Control and Jewish Law* and John Noonan's *Contraception*.[6] In some respects it is unfair to compare these two. Feldman's method is the *halahḳic* one, and is appropriate to both the subject matter of Jewish law and to his own profession as a rabbi. Noonan's work is a study of the Christian Catholic tradition by a historian of law. But they do invite comparison for a number of reasons: birth control is their common subject, the Western religious traditions have a common root, and the role of law — Jewish and canon — is central to both. Each has made an indispensable contribution to our knowledge of the historical background of matters of contemporary importance. But there are differences in their uses of historical contexts which illustrate our concern.

Both Noonan and Feldman have texts as their basic data. The extended subtitle of the Jewish study is: "Marital Relations, Contraception, and Abortion as set forth in the classic texts of Jewish Law.

An examination of the relevant precepts of the Talmud, Codes, Commentaries, and, especially, rabbinic Responsa through the present day, with comparative reference to the Christian exegetical tradition." Noonan's briefer subtitle is: "A History of Its Treatment by Catholic Theologians and Canonists." Both are clearly literary histories. It is the difference in approaches to literary history that is important to note; a richer and more intensive use of a broader historical context characterizes Noonan's work, and thus enables the reader to understand not only what particular canonists and theologians said, but the reasons for saying what they did at the time that they said it.

Perhaps Feldman assumed that the reader, or at least the Jewish reader, of his book was familiar with the detailed contexts in which the writers he cites produced their works; and thus the issue is not the character of the writing, but the ignorance of the reader. Perhaps also Feldman works within an accepted and acceptable tradition of Jewish scholarship; nonetheless, this reader consistently finds himself puzzling about issues not explicitly dealt with. Feldman is generally careful about identifying the dates and places of rabbis he quotes: for example, at the end of a chapter on non-Jews and the Commandments he introduces R. Yehiel M. Epstein and informs the reader that he lived in Navarrodok, Russia, and died in 1908 (p. 58). Rabbi Epstein's contribution was made in a restatement of the *Shulhan Arukh,* the great code of Joseph Karo. This information entices the reader. Why did a nineteenth-century rabbi restate a great fifteenth century code? Granting a great degree of continuity in Jewish religious life, were there nineteenth-century currents of thought which prompted a restatement of the code? Particularly, were there reactions to Gentile communities at that time which prompted the particular passage that Feldman quotes? Among the currents of East European Judaism of the nineteenth century, was Rabbi Epstein particularly influenced by one of them? Over and over again, given his own ignorance and the absence of an explication of the historical context of the writing, the reader is uncertain of whether he comprehends the particularities of the contribution acutely and properly.

To be sure, it would not be possible for an author who has as much material at his command as Feldman uses to satisfy the questions of the reader at each point. And it is clear that the rabbis themselves worked within a literary tradition which was composed largely of responses to previous texts received as authoritative and important to varying degrees. Within the tradition itself the historical conditions under which certain texts were written were not judged to be as important as modern curiosity finds them to be. But it is apparent that one would have a different, and presumably better, understanding of the texts and the moral teachings if one knew a great deal about the historical background of the authors and their times.[7]

Noonan's work, by comparison, is more in a Troeltschian spirit, although there is no explicit reliance on the great German for authority or inspiration. For example, in Part 2, which covers the years 450–1450, he establishes many reference points by which the reader can orient himself to the intent of specific teachings. One finds accounts of the means of contraception used during the period, descriptions of the motives of those who used them, the views of heretical and other groups on the issue of contraception, the state of sexual morals, and the ecclesiastical situation in which teachings were established, as well as the theological warrants for them. The moral teachings, under Noonan's historical examination, are seen to be not only later responses to earlier texts, but also responses to a variety of conditions. The reasons given for the teachings of a particular person or for a certain period of the Church's history are many, and the reader is able to read the texts as quoted in a much more penetrating light. A better grasp of the author's meaning is thereby possible.

Of course, recognition must be given to the different cultural and historical situations of Christianity and Judaism and to the different internal traditions of the two streams of biblical religion, in looking at the differences between the works of Feldman and Noonan. Indeed, there are theological differences as well as historical ones that require a different sort of historical writing: Jewish ethical teaching is, with reference to specific issues like contraception, developed in a legal tradition; Christian teaching came from more speculative theology, from the penitential concerns of the Church, as well as from canon law. Historical precedent has a more important function in the Jewish tradition, although it is of great significance in the Christian as well. Granting these, and other conditions, it remains possible, at least for the modern reader, to read more accurately the ethical teachings of the past when they are set within the wider historical context.

The issues here are not, of course, confined to the best way to read religious ethical texts; they are present wherever historical texts of any sort are used by scholars. The problem is that of understanding and interpretation; it is the hermeneutical problem. What is the significance of a biographical and historical context for the proper understanding of a text? Does one have to know Gnosticism and Hellenistic Judaism in order to understand the texts of the New Testament? Does one have to know Luther's biography and the political and social conditions of the sixteenth century in order accurately to understand Luther's teachings? We are beginning to scratch against the thorny hedge of both the formal and material problems of historical literary scholarship, where general theories compete with each other at levels of ideological abstraction and where practitioners disclose different aspects of meaning from different perspectives. Abjuring such discussion will be excused, I hope, in order only to make a modest claim pertinent to the study of Christian ethics. Religious ethical texts, and more particularly the material moral teachings of the churches, have arisen within complex religious and cultural circumstances. In order properly to understand these texts and teachings, it is necessary to understand the circumstances. As trivial as this sounds, as often as one has heard it since his first course in history, it bears repetition, if only to encourage more studies in a Troeltschian mode. Perhaps historians are to be admonished as much as scholars of ethics; the professional group to blame is a matter of indifference.

THE USES OF HISTORICAL ANALOGIES

In popular moral exhortation, as well as in certain more sophisticated Christian ethics, historical comparisons are often made in order to convince the reader or hearer of a moral point. Vivid recollections come to my mind of a conference on ethics sponsored by the World Council of Churches in June 1960. Anti-Gaullist French Protestants were passionately comparing the situation in France at that time to the situation in Germany in 1932. The parallels that they drew were political, cultural, spiritual, and moral. One speaker indicated that the sermons and other discourses of Christian resistance that appeared early in the Nazi period in Germany had a particular ring of authenticity when read in the light of the events in France in 1960. Contemporary prophetic and moral discourse in the United States abounds with similar formal comparisons. The American situation is like situation *x* in the past; we can see in retrospect what moral actions should have been done in situation *x;* we ought to engage, because of the similarities of our situation with situation *x,* in such actions now. Thus the argument goes.

A different use of historical analogy occurs in Christian social ethics. Its fundamental premise is that certain historical events are normative, or revelatory, for Christian interpretations of the meaning of history, including contemporary history. The Old Testament accounts of certain events in the history of the people of Israel have come to function in this way in recent decades. For example, in the exodus of the Hebrew people from bondage in Egypt there is a revelation of God's activity as a liberating force; there is thus a theological authorization for liberation as a social moral value. Where liberation is going on in the world, God is at work, and men ought to join in those activities which foster that social moral value.[8] The critical questions that can be raised about this procedure are many. Which historical events, and which accounts of these historical events are theologically and ethically normative? What justifications would be made for the choice of one event over another, or one account over another? Would one give a theological ethical reason, for example, to show that the exodus account is normative but the conquest of the people of Canaan is not? Is the theme of liberation more consistent with Christian theology and ethics than the theme of conquest? How does one proceed to apply the normative account of a normative event to a present-day event? What aspects of the historical and social situations of the present are similar enough to those of the past to give some warrant for the analogy? Answers to these questions are assumed, often uncritically, in all normative uses of historical events, and readers need to be alerted to the importance of teasing them out. (A complete argument about how they can best be answered lies outside the bounds set for this essay.)

Whether done as a popular exhortation or with scholarly sophistication, the use of historical analogies for the purpose of clarifying how one ought to do ethics and what one ought to do in the present situation at least presupposes a continuity in history, a significant similarity between the past and the present. Such a presupposition need not entail a high level of theory of history, such as a cyclical one. If such a theory were accepted, one could presumably read present events about which there is moral consternation as the return to the fundamental order of previous events; thus one could act to conform to the inevitabilities of such recurrences. Nor does one need to presuppose a natural moral order imbedded in the structures of being which takes on historical manifestations of similar sorts from time to time in order to make comparisons that would shed light on contemporary issues. It is quite possible to eschew speculative philosophies and theologies of history and, in the interests of practical moral reasoning within the Christian community, to reason directly from history. Indeed, most persons who engage in such practical uses of historical analogies would be surprised to be pressed into a clarification of their assumptions about the fundamental nature of history.

These are, however, significant issues for the theologian of social ethics, and there are arguments which suggest that where one stands on the map of theologies of history makes a difference in how one functions in practical moral discourse. As we shall see, the issues are more complex than some theologians of history and political theologians seem to realize; they also involve the question of what the practical task of the theologian addressing social issues, or of the social ethicist, is. Jürgen Moltmann's essay, "The Understanding of History in Christian Social Ethics," provides a basis for adumbrating some of these concerns.

Moltmann's concern is to develop the proper theological understanding of history and briefly to indicate what its consequences are for the social ethics of the Christian community. The first assumption in his argument is that one will find out what reality is by looking to the Scriptures. Within the Scriptures, "the reality of man is understood through an eschatological disclosure to be 'history.'" The familiar polemic against "Greek" views of time and history from the standpoint of biblical views is at the heart of the matter. God's action is not seen in natural eternal laws, but "in the unique and unrepeatable quality of temporal contingency." The "Israelite-Christian man . . . experiences a truly 'open,' namely an eschatologically open, world and he experiences his reality as a history which is unique and unrepeatable, irreversable [sic] and oriented towards a goal; he does not experience his reality as eternal nature which always remains the same in the cyclical pattern of its process." Such a view would, on the face of it, preclude significant use of historical analogies in moral reasoning, for in Moltmann's view to be human is to have a history and not a nature, and to have a history is to be involved in the unique and unrepeatable.[9]

While Moltmann is concerned to undercut "Greek" views and the social ethics that come from them, he is also concerned to define his position against remnants of that position in the theologies of orders of creation, the idea of spheres, mandates, etc. But he must also define his position against views in which contingency and uniqueness preclude any sense of what one ought to do in the eschatological openness, that is, from views in which there are no bases for identity and continuity in historical and personal experience. Indeed, in the passage quoted above, the phrase "oriented toward a goal" already qualifies the sense of contingency, which other terms Moltmann uses lead one to believe are more important for him. Such continuity, identity, and "determination" stem from eschatology, as readers of Moltmann's other writings are aware. "Theologically, we may say that man is an eschatologically determined being and that his history is controlled by eschatological transcendence in its unique aspect. Determined by eschatological revelation, he experiences the future of truth as history. . . . Consequently, nothing can be acquired from Christian faith for the stabilizing of normative conceptions of order in an unstable world. There is, however, the wider horizon, an eschaton of all history which is itself historical and yet no longer historical. There is no security in history, though there is an eschatological horizon for all historical processes."[10]

In order to develop a social ethic which in any sense proposes, however modestly, to render moral judgments about the ways in which events are carrying mankind or about the ends and purposes of social action, that horizon of the future must be given some material content, some substance. Moltmann recognizes this when he writes: "If, however, the future is not to be made unreal as empty openness for the arbitrary character of every new plan, one must talk about a concrete future."[11] What makes the future concrete? How do the moments of ethical particularity achieve continuity? How does one come to some understanding of a process of history within the discrete events? Moltmann's answer to these questions is more psychological than ethical or theological. It is that "definite hopes arouse definite remembrances" and that "traditions are alive when hopes are aroused." So hopes arouse memories and traditions. But, for Moltmann, there is a normative history that is remembered; it is not that hope can justify any tradition or any memory. The history to be remembered is "the history of the promise." Thus, if any historical analogies are to be used in making moral judgments about contemporary events or in giving direction to contemporary activity, it would appear to be those biblical accounts of a promise.

What Moltmann derives from this rather elaborate theology of history for social ethics confirms the impression that there is little of positive and constructive significance in making practical and material moral judgments about particular conditions. The people of God who "travel in hope" become a "source of eschatological unrest" in society. They bear witness to the openness of the social process when the culture would seek to close it in various ways. Moltmann, however, wishes to claim more, namely that the people of God also provide a directive for the society, which otherwise seems to sink into "the trauma of resignation in the face of meaningless determinism." There is an appalling paucity of content to that directive; in the end it functions in a way similar to the "eschatological impatience"; namely, it shows that "social institutions can be made obsolete by being questioned about their final purpose and their eschatological justification." In sum, it appears that the social ethics which comes from this theological interpretation of history and of hope rest primarily, if not exclusively, in the provision of a stance for a prophetic critical response to institutions or movements which seek to absolutize themselves or to foreclose the future. Even Moltmann's essay on "Hope and Planning"[12] becomes another occasion for elaborating a theology of history and of hope, and functions more to counsel an attitude than to provide the basis for moral reflection about what plans might be in accord with the Christian hope.

In introducing this excursus on Moltmann, it was noted that one issue that had to be raised was the practical task of the theologian who addresses social issues, or the question of what social ethics is. One answer to that question is that the social ethicist's vocation includes the obligation to make particular moral judgments about particular social proposals and to suggest optional courses of moral action which might be judged morally approvable. This has been at the heart of the American social ethical tradition. The most valid criticism against this answer is that often such a definition of the task has led to premature acceptance of the institutional frameworks within which particular issues are raised, and thus the sharper prophetic criticism of the institutions themselves gets blunted. That is not necessarily the case, nor has it actually always been the case.

Troeltsch's understanding of the relativity of all historical movements in relation to the Absolute probably contributed to the capacity of some Christian ethicians to keep two points in mind. First, that given the historical character of ethical issues, no values involved can be absolutized. Thus there are grounds for the sorts of radical critiques of politics, religion, and morals such as one finds in H. Richard Niebuhr's *Radical Monotheism and Western Culture*. Indeed, Niebuhr's unrest with established institutions is as deep as Moltmann's, but is developed from a Troeltschian base rather than from a theology of hope. Second, that at the same time, Troeltsch's ethics of social and cultural responsibility within historically relative institutions and movements have led those who learned from him to be deeply concerned with the moral requirements of specific and concrete circumstances. Niebuhr's ethics of the "fitting response" is a case in point.[13] Walter Muelder's work taken as a whole is another example of the readiness to make more fundamental criticisms while at the same time dealing with particular problems in a constructive way.

Theologies of history and hope and of politics, such as are currently being proposed from Europe and by Americans who take their cues from the continent, attempt to move from theology to history or to politics without going through a stage of more careful ethical reflection—both about why certain things are judged to be bad and about what concrete proposals are necessary to make them better—that characterizes the social ethical tradition in America.

There are, no doubt, different theologies of history involved in different conceptions of social ethics. In characteristic German fashion, Moltmann and others begin with the big ideological issue—the proper theology of history—and move from that to social ethics. The more pragmatic mentality of much American ethics often leaves the big issues implicit rather than explicit and does not feel an obligation fully to expose and expound what are considered prior questions from another point of view. And it may be that when persons from the two traditions work together to resolve practical issues, the ideological differences will appear to be of little significance. The use of historical analogies in ethics in the ways suggested in the first paragraphs of this section, however, does presuppose the existence of historical continuities in events and experience and presupposes that there are significant similarities, as well as differences, between the events of one time and the events of another. If the exodus of the Hebrew people is to be used to indicate the theological ethical direction for Black Americans today, there must be similarities between the conditions under which the Hebrew people lived in Egypt and those in which black people live in America. If liberation, as a social moral value that has a particular theological justification, was an end under the conditions of slavery in Egypt, the conditions must be similar today if it is to be judged to be God's moral purpose for suppressed people.

Indeed, a case could probably be made on biblical grounds (if one feels compelled to look to Scripture in order to understand reality rightly) that such continuities and similarities of historical experience are assumed in the Bible. Without denying the eschatological expectations present in many parts of the Bible, one can also note that frequently recollection of a past event provides a clue to the understanding of God's purposes (including his moral purposes) in contemporary events. While the uses of remembrances do not take a precise analogical form (stating that present conditions are similar, for example, to the exodus conditions in ways *a, b,* and *c,* but differ in ways *x, y,* and *z,* and therefore what was applicable under the exodus conditions would appear to be applicable in certain limited ways to present conditions), nonetheless the past events are used to interpret the significance of present events and to shed light on what men ought to do. This seemed to be possible without defining a consistent theory of history. It is, after all, systematizers who push for consistent theories of history and seek to justify them either biblically or philosophically.

Does the use of historical analogies beg a prior question of some continuities in human nature? Does it suppose that man has a nature as well as a history? Or at least that there are universals in human experience, which, while not denying the uniqueness and precise unrepeatability of events, nonetheless are a ground for continuities? These are questions raised by the natural law tradition, and a full answer to them would require a critical account of that movement. Suffice it to say that I believe that uses of historical analogies, given their tenuous character and expressing the caution that is required in using them, do assume continuities of experience which presuppose that man has a nature as well as a history. One cannot dispose of such continuities by appealing to the authority of Scripture as the source of the proper understanding of reality. Other evidences and arguments than scriptural ones are required to settle issues as complex as this.

Historical analogies about contemporary events are often used in Christian ethical reflection with less than proper awareness of the perils of such an enterprise. What appears to be rhetorically persuasive does not always stand up under rigorous scrutiny with regard to the assumed similarities of circumstances and the rectitude (or fault) of actions taken under past circumstances deemed to be similar. Nonetheless, there is limited but important value in such efforts. If under the past circumstances, conscientious, religious men, Jewish or Christian, perceived God's purposes to be of a certain character, it is certainly worth considering whether under similar circumstances his purposes might not be similar today. If in past circumstances men misjudged the purposes of God in a disastrous way, under the present circumstances the same course of action might also be a disastrous mistake. At least the discipline of such historical reflection will help one to avoid the error of assuming that every occasion is unique in all its respects and, therefore, that the ways in which men have thought in the past are of no significance in the present. The assumption of absolute novelty in history is at least as great a mistake as the assumption that history flows in cycles, or that inexorable laws govern the development of history.

THE FREEDOM TO BE HISTORICALLY SITUATED

A sense of man as historical being, and of the way in which ethical ideas are related to particular historical conditions, can lead to quite different attitudes, depending to some extent upon one's personal background. For example, one finds that writers in Roman Catholic ethics, both fundamental and practical, have become freshly aware of historical as against ontological ways of thinking. One response to the discovery of man as a historical being is an attack upon all moral absolutes. The older, "manual" moral theology assumed the immutable and eternal moral order and trusted the inferences drawn from it for all sorts of issues without taking the historicity of man adequately into account; so the charge goes. When one sees that man is better understood as a historical, psychological, and social being, a new way of ethical thinking emerges which avoids entanglement in moral absolutes.[14] Ethical arguments begin to rely more heavily upon the historical and empirical elements in man and his circumstances than they do upon principles or values judged to have been enduring, if not eternal and immutable.

Another response in Catholic theology is more moderate; it seeks to incorporate into fundamental moral theology a more historical understanding of natural law, without giving up the interest in lining out the ontological structures of human nature. This is done in part by emphasizing in natural-law theory the dynamic and personalistic aspects of man; aspects which, it is sometimes argued, are present in the work of St. Thomas himself but were lost through a static and absolutistic interpretation. The point is to find in human nature a dynamic aspect which is historically developed. Bernard Häring is an important moral theologian who has sought to make this turn. He has written: "The rationalistic understanding of natural law started with abstract principles; and, finding that these principles remain always the same 'truths,' this understanding admitted variety only in different 'applications' according to the varying 'circumstances.' Our approach starts with the real man, as a historical being, with his real capacity for understanding himself in his essential relationship to his fellow men, to the world around himself, and to God." In this way Häring and others have sought to overcome the "physicalist" bias of the tradition in favor of a view that understands the nature of man more in terms of his personal and historical being than his physical being.[15]

Persons from traditional Catholic backgrounds who have tasted the wines of historical understanding in one way or another, then, find themselves directed toward overcoming static absolutism. The excesses of moral certitude, of depersonalized rationalism, of rigid mentalities, and of ecclesiastical authoritarianisms built upon such foundations, are the objects of criticism. From a modern Protestant background, however, which has assumed the historical stance for some generations, the response can often be quite different. While there are Protestants who take historical understanding to provide license for radical relativism, there are others for whom the task of constructive ethics is overcoming historical relativism, at least in part. We have noted that Moltmann, whose theology of history (except for the insertion of history's orientation toward a goal) would seem to lead to radical relativism in ethics, has a way of giving some closure to the openness, some identity and continuity to that which is also claimed to be unique and unrepeatable. The work of Paul Ramsey during the past decade, beginning with his *War and the Christian Conscience* (in which he announces that he is seeking to overcome the "wastelands of relativism"), has been increasingly directed toward the development of unexceptionable moral principles.[16]

As Walter Muelder and others note, the relativism of much contemporary Protestant ethics is not grounded in historicism alone; but there are ways in which Christian theology itself is formulated which provide a warrant for relativism. Muelder breaks through the relativism in his *Moral Law in Christian Social Ethics* by developing further the moral laws stated by E. S. Brightman and L. Harold DeWolf, following the tradition of personalistic idealism in philosophy. The development of these laws does not move one away from concerns for the concrete and the historical, as Muelder works them out; indeed, his sixth law, "The Law of Specification," moves one toward "concrete relevance. . . . It states: *'All persons ought, in any given situation, to develop the value or values specifically relevant to that situation.'* . . . This law is a corrective against abstract laws, against mere idealism. It is a law that recognizes the unique and unrepeatable in social process. . . . [it] forbids escape from existential decision." The classical doctrine of prudence is invoked as necessary in its application; one discerns what is fitting in the historical circumstances. But by making this one law among fifteen, a great deal of general guidance is provided in coming to that discernment.[17]

An understanding of both the historical aspects of persons and of circumstances — whether hedged by the development of moral laws or by other devices — does provide a freedom to work within the particular historical situation in order to provide constructive proposals or relevant principles for dealing with the moral issues which arise in one's own time and place. This is the warrant for the sorts of continuing commentary on the political and social events that have characterized Christian social journalism in this country, such as one finds in *The Christian Century, Christianity and Crisis,* and *Commonweal.* It is also the warrant for more systematic investigation of one's historical situation through the uses of the social and behavioral sciences. Muelder's work is again instructive, for he has consistently insisted that social ethics is an interdisciplinary task which requires the uses of economics, political science, and sociology. The task of Christian ethics in its "applied" forms (as well as in its constructive theory) demands intelligent and thorough immersion in the data of the problems that one seeks to address.

Risks are involved in exercising this freedom. Of least significance is the fact that within a short time what one has written may be outdated; one's successors can look back with critical derision and assert that the author was timebound and culturebound. The risks of being bound to time and context are sometimes more formidable than the risks of irrelevant abstraction, and they are more formidable in certain periods than in others; in the very determination of the historical situation to be addressed there are often errors of short-sightedness, limitations of vision with reference both to problems emerging on the historical horizon and to persistent and deeper issues imbedded and nearly hidden in the data of a focal concern. The practical moral theologian is forced also to make judgments that have heavy empirical weight, judgments about precisely what the historical situation is in which he is counselling some form of policy or action. Since often the experts do not agree on what the historical situation is, the social ethicist finds himself assuming the burden of giving the empirical dimensions of the problem a configuration which makes it an identifiable object of thought and action. And clearly, if he feels the obligation to make specific moral judgments about a historical situation, he has no guarantee that they will turn out to be right in the light of future developments.

The freedom to be historically situated does not, as Muelder and others remind us, mean that there are no continuities in history, persons, and experience. Nor does it entail the stance of an existentialism which abjures serious critical reflection and serious empirical inquiry. The awareness of the individuality of historical occasions does not rule out the necessity for serious study of ethical traditions. Yet it does free one from the paralyzing effects of excessive scrupulosity, from the emasculated idealism that retreats to the eternal verities and universal values and principles in order to avoid the possibility of being culturebound or mistaken in a particular judgment.

For some persons who discover the insights of historical understanding, particularly if they are in reaction against an absolutist tradition, they issue in an extreme relativism. If, for example, one is persuaded that the truth or validity of an ethical teaching is bound to the biography of its author and the historical context of his life, what the Church has taught about contraception, or war, or any other matter is valid only for a particular author, or for his time and place in history. The warrants for historical analogies are weak because of a persuasion that historical individualities are more dissimilar than similar. What one is left with is only the third aspect of this article, namely the freedom to be historically situated. Often this leads to a severe weakening of any objective moral discourse and to an acceptance of whatever moral standards prevail. But such relativists respond to different present circumstances in different ways. They do not uniformly accept what currently is to be the "ought." They operate with hidden criteria. While they may affirm the "sexual revolution," they deny the legitimacy of the current war. In our time a principle of humanization, generally not developed with precision, often is appealed to in order to justify the distinctions between what they accept and what they reject in the present historical situation.

The story is often different for those who have lived with the insights of historical understanding for a long time. Troeltsch's own intellectual biography is a case in point; toward the end of his life he was almost plaintively seeking a framework for greater universality.[18] The task of theological and ethical work becomes that of finding justification both for religious belief and for moral decisions which do not deny the relativities of history, but which provide an objectivity short of absolute claims. In ethics the task is to find some degree of order, continuity, and structure within historical change. If the absolutist has morality conforming to an immutable order and thus has difficulty in coping with historical change, the relativist has an openness to change but a difficulty in developing the criteria of purpose and action to guide choices and give direction to moral activities.

Some activities of historical understanding are useful in the relativist's pursuit. To see how moral questions were framed in the past, and why they were framed as they were, provides insight into his present situation in which the same general issue arises. He can see not only what is valid in the teaching, for example, about contraception, but also what was mistaken and how present conditions alter our understanding of the problem. He can carefully formulate analogies between present and past and gain insight into what might now be required.

But larger philosophical and theological issues remain. In a sense the debate between realists and nominalists continues, and the question for the relativist is how to retain universality in the context of historicity. This surely is the question at the heart of the ethical thought of Catholics like Karl Rahner and Bernard Häring; and it is the issue under debate in both popular and scholarly Protestant treatises. Does man have a nature? Or only a history? Are there abiding moral principles and rules? Unexceptionable ones? Or only individual intuitions of the ethical demand in particular circumstances?

The work of Walter Muelder, like that of many others who write theological ethics, can be read as dealing with these questions. We have inherited Troeltsch's problematic; we find some value in his dealing with it. But the debates and discussions continue and will for the foreseeable future.

NOTES

1. H. Richard Niebuhr, "Ernst Troeltsch's Philosophy of Religion," (Ph.D. diss., Yale University, 1924); Walter Muelder, "Individual Totalities in Ernst Troeltsch's Philosophy of History," (Ph.D. diss., Boston University, 1933).

2. The most readily available materials by Troeltsch in English are *The Social Teaching of the Christian Churches,* 2 vols., trans. Olive Wyon (New York: Meridian Books, 1957); and *Protestantism and Progress,* trans. W. Montgomery (Boston: Beacon Press, 1958). *Gesammelte Schriften* was published in four volumes (Tübingen: Verlag von J. C. B. Mohr, 1912–1925).

3. Joseph Fletcher, ed. *Christianity and Property* (Philadelphia: Westminster Press, 1947); Roland Bainton, *Christian Attitudes toward War and Peace* (New York: Abingdon Press, 1960); id., *The Travail of Religious Liberty* (Philadelphia: Westminster Press, 1951); id., *What Christianity Says about Sex, Love and Marriage* (New York: Association Press, 1957); E. Schillebeeck, O.P., *Marriage: Secular Reality and Saving Mystery,* 2 vols. (London: Sheed and Ward, 1965); Benjamin Nelson, *The Idea of Usury,* 2nd ed., (Chicago: University of Chicago Press, 1969); John Noonan, *The Scholastic Analysis of Usury* (Cambridge: Harvard University Press, 1965); id., *Contraception* (Cambridge: Harvard University Press, 1965); id., ed., *The Morality of Abortion* (Cambridge: Harvard University Press, 1970).

4. Anders Nygren, *Agape and Eros* (London: S.P.C.K., 1953); R. Newton Flew, *The Idea of Perfection in Christian Theology* (London: Oxford University Press, 1934); K. E. Kirk, *The Vision of God* (London: Longmans, Green, 1931); N. P. Williams, *The Idea of the Fall and Original Sin* (London: Longmans, Green, 1927).

5. Max Stackhouse properly criticizes my *Christ and the Moral Life* on these grounds in his review in *Interpretation* 23 (July 1969): 333–37.

6. David M. Feldman, *Birth Control and Jewish Law* (New York: New York University Press, 1968); John T. Noonan. Jr., *Contraception* (Cambridge: Harvard University Press, 1965).

7. I have chosen briefly to compare Feldman's work with Noonan's because they are recent studies and because Feldman explicitly refers to Noonan. My point could also be made, however, with reference to the issue of war. One could, for example, get the impression that the historical context in which St. Thomas's ideas of just war were developed is of no significance for understanding them precisely. Yet a study of the political struggles, the involvement of St. Thomas's family in them, the specific crusades, the military technology, and other aspects of thirteenth-century history illuminates our understanding of his theory. One sees more clearly how it was applicable in its day and why certain aspects are accented and others (non-combatant immunity, for example) are undeveloped. Further developments in the just-war tradition must be seen against the backgrounds of their times and places. See the excellent dissertation written in the mode of Troeltsch and, more particularly, Noonan, by LeRoy B. Walters, "Five Classic Just-War Theories," Yale University, 1971.

8. For more extensive discussion of the use of Scripture in this way, see J. M. Gustafson, "The Place of Scripture in Christian Ethics: A Methodological Study," in *Interpretation* 24 (1970): 430–55.

9. Jürgen Moltmann, *Hope and Planning,* trans. Margaret Clarkson (New York: Harper and Row, 1971), pp. 101–29, passim, esp. pp. 103–04.

10. Ibid., pp. 107–08.

11. Ibid., p. 122.

12. Ibid, pp. 124, 125, 178–99.

13. H. Richard Niebuhr, *Radical Monotheism and Western Culture* (New York: Harper and Row, 1960), esp. pp. 24–89; idem, *The Responsible Self* (New York: Harper and Row, 1963), esp. pp. 47–68.

14. This is the basic stance of John Giles Milhaven's essays collected in *Toward a New Catholic Morality* (Garden City, N.Y.: Doubleday, 1970). See, for example, his contrasts between "classical" and "modern" mentalities, pp. 72–82.

15. Bernard Häring, "Dynamism and Continuity in a Personalistic Approach to Natural Law," in G. H. Outka and Paul Ramsey, eds., *Norm and Context in Christian Ethics* (New York: Scribners, 1968), p. 202. Karl Rahner works out a similar intention in a variety of essays, perhaps the most important of which is "On the Question of a Formal Existential Ethics," in *Theological Investigations,* 5 vols., trans. Karl-H. Kruger (Baltimore: Helicon Press, 1963), 3:217–34. See the persistent criticism of the "physicalist" bias in Charles Curran, ed., *Absolutes in Moral Theology?* (Washington: Corpus Books, 1968).

16. Paul Ramsey, *War and the Christian Conscience* (Durham, N.C.: Duke University Press, 1961), chap. 1.

17. Walter G. Muelder, *Moral Law in Christian Social Ethics* (Richmond, Va.: John Knox Press, 1966), pp. 90–94.

18. See Troeltsch's essay, "The Ideas of Natural Law and Humanity in World Politics," app. 1, in Otto Gierke, *Natural Law and the Theory of Society* (Boston: Beacon Press, 1957), pp. 201–22.

3　The Struggle for Political

Consciousness　*Alan F. Geyer*

IN Robert Penn Warren's tragic novel of public morality, *All the King's Men,* the Huey Long-like boss, Willie Stark, declares to a man of rather tender sensitivities: "Politics is not like Easter week in a nunnery."

Given recent changes in the styles of nuns and nunneries, that statement needs more careful elucidation in the 1970s than it required in the 1930s or the 1940s. But many selfstyled saints within the Church continue to share Willie Stark's cynical estimate as to what politics is like and what it is all about. There is a kind of unwitting — and sometimes witting — conspiracy between the most unprincipled politicians and the most uninvolved Christians to keep religion fenced off on a reservation, as remote as possible from the struggle for power and purpose which is the raw stuff of politics. In the United States, the legitimate but static principle of separation of church and state is perniciously invoked to rationalize the retreat of Christian action from the dynamic arena of political conflict. On the reverse side of this rationalization is the fog of phoniness which chronically shrouds the Church's own very lively internal political life.

A much more adequate ethical perspective on the significance of politics for Christianity is that of the late Archbishop William Temple who affirmed: "To religion the sphere of politics is never neutral ground. The state is an exposed sector of that mysterious struggle between *civitas Dei* and *civitas diaboli,* which is the central issue in world history." [1]

This disposition to see politics as a central reality in the action of religious history is as old as the ancient Hebrew prophets. It is paralleled by the classic Greek notion, summed up in Aristotle, that man is fundamentally a political creature who finds his highest fulfillment in common service through politics. While some New Testament scholars have, in effect, depoliticized the Christian Gospel, Oscar Cullmann views political ethics as the penultimate concern of the New Testament. Cullman rejects, however, the religiopolitical monism of both Hebrew and Greek traditions in favor of a "chronological dualism." In Christ, the end of history is already fulfilled, yet its consummation remains in the future. Politics finds its meaning in this historical dualism: "Because the Gospel presents itself as the *'politeuma,'* the community of the coming age, it must accordingly see as its most intrinsic concern its disposition toward the present *'polis'* the secular state." [2] And so the state cannot be regarded as something final and definitive: it is accepted for its necessary but temporal and provisional character.

Christian ethicists have varied considerably in their appeals to prophetic, philosophical, and Gospel valuations of politics. But few major twentieth century ethicists have lapsed into the apolitical individualism of earlier periods, doubtless because ours has been preeminently the century of "politicization" [3] in which all other institutions have been penetrated by the concerns of government. At the very time the religious agenda was being liberally extended to touch the whole of human life, the political agenda was being spread out over the same domain. The comprehensive scope, in principle, of both prophetic and classical political ethics has been experienced existentially in the modern state system, with its pretensions to omnicompetence. Yet popular religious thinking about politics has continued to wallow in the sentimentalities of individualism and compartmentalization.

Most recently, such ethicists as Paul Lehmann, Harvey Cox, Rubem Alves, and Richard Shaull have portrayed God's essential action in history as political and have asserted that the language of the Bible itself is fundamentally political. These assertions indicate that the very words *religion* and *politics* are caught up in an unprecedented definitional struggle. We may tentatively define politics as the social struggle over the exercise of power by governmental and other organizations. Politics is characterized by group conflict and usually by public controversy, tempered by processes of cooperation and consensus. If issues concerning authority and coercion are not immediately present in every political action, they are bound to emerge in every form of public and private government. Some political scientists, like some dictionaries, simply settle for the notion that politics and government should be taken as equivalent terms. But that politics is a many-sided activity, which cannot be fenced off by a definition any more than religion can, is an assumption of this chapter.

THE WHOLENESS OF MUELDERIAN ETHICS

The writer of this chapter is primarily indebted to two eminent Christian ethicists for helping to direct his lifelong quest for religious perspectives on politics. No one can do serious work in this field without coming to terms with the incredibly rich contributions of Reinhold Niebuhr to political understanding. Niebuhr's biblical and historical realism provided the most important link between continental theology and the American cultural situation; he has been at once neoorthodox and pragmatically liberal. Niebuhr has also provided the most prophetic versions of dialectical thought in the realm of political analysis. But there are problems and limitations in

73

Niebuhrian realism. For all his brilliant insights, Niebuhr's lack of sustained and thorough attention to the social sciences has deprived his system of empirical credibility at a number of points. His dogmas about the nature of man have tended to dull an appreciation for the variety of creative human responses to political conflict. His lack of philosophical clarity has caused serious confusion even among those most disposed to follow his lead.

If it cannot be said that Walter Muelder has matched Niebuhr's influence as a political ethicist, Muelder's overriding interests have, in fact, been in other areas. It is nevertheless important to appreciate that Muelder's general approach to social ethics is a powerful complement to Niebuhr's more particularly elaborated political ethics. Muelder's hospitality to empirical analysis, even while insisting upon well-ordered moral doctrine, provides in some respects a more satisfactory foundation for the person who tries to maintain a relationship of integrity with both political science and Christian theology. Where Niebuhr is sharp in pointing up paradoxes and ambiguities, Muelder is synoptic in providing integral perspectives, in focusing all the relevant streams of data, and in opening up the possibilities of redemptive action.

For purposes of this brief discussion of the pervasiveness of politics, it is good to begin with a favorite Muelder-word: *ubiquity*. Government is a ubiquitous human phenomenon, a function of all social groups. It is not therefore some separate realm of existence. Related and characteristic Muelderian emphases are: the sociocultural foundations of law and politics; the provisional character of the state historically; the analytical and moral importance of small groups, local governments, and intermediate associations of all kinds.

On the principles side, Muelder makes much of these themes: (1) the distinction between state and community; (2) the priority of moral consensus over sheer force in maintaining the integrity of the state; (3) the state's legitimate monopoly of the ultimate forms of coercion; (4) the moral priority of the state, as the most synoptic form of social organization, over the economic order; (5) the subordination of the state to the claims of mankind as a whole; (6) the insistence that no particular form of political order is sacrosanct to the Christian; and (7) the importance of politics as vocation in terms of both responsible and critical participation. These may not be original emphases, but they are extremely significant ones.

If there are problems in Muelder's political ethics, they have mostly to do with the underdevelopment of such themes. His prior commitments in economic ethics, the sociology of religion, moral philosophy, and ecumenics have kept him from exploiting more fully the political implications of his distinctive approach; yet those very same commitments have also brought important secondary contributions to political ethics. Similarly, Muelder stresses the need for Protestantism to develop a positive view of the state, but he does not himself go very far in articulating a constructive ideology of the political community. Dean Muelder has always borne a very heavy extracurricular load of involvement in ecclesiastical and other affairs — a practical exposure which has provided a continual flow of supplementary insight into the behavior of all human institutions. However, he has characteristically maintained a semi-detachment from the politics of parties and movements, an important laboratory for an increasing number of social ethicists. At times, Muelder's comments about government and public issues seem to suffer from an inconstant appreciation of the vitality of social conflict, and here Niebuhr's grasp may be surer. Yet Muelder's seminars and writings have been studded with treasures of political acumen; the conscious and unconscious indebtedness of his students for such treasures is very heavy indeed. As one who studied with him during the first Eisenhower-Nixon campaign of 1952, I cannot forget Muelder's instant analysis of public relations and image manipulation in the electronics media prompted by the Nixon "Checkers" broadcast—an analysis which, lamentably, anticipated more pronounced trends and systematic studies of later years.

Perhaps Dean Muelder's most salutary contribution to political ethics is in the fundamentals of his general style of social ethics, with its rigorous demand for honest analysis, integrating descriptive and normative studies, and philosophical clarity. Finally, no one faithful to "Muelderism" can remain an entirely academic man: he must constantly work at the development of both the interior life of the spirit and the institutional life of action. Muelder is the most mature and thoughtful institutionalist in the experience of all who know him well. It is the wholeness of both the person Walter Muelder and the system of social ethics he has nurtured which has had such a liberating impact upon those who have been privileged to sit at his feet and stand at his side.

POLITICIZATION AND ITS ENEMIES

Because politics tends to be viewed by middle-class Americans as the befouling enemy of almost every basic human activity, politicization is bound to be met by fiercely moralized defenses. In those defenses, secular interests and religious sentiments are likely to become closely allied. In one realm after another, the theme remains the same: "Politics and you-name-it should not mix." The variations upon that theme are almost infinite; all of them derive from the lack of an integral view of society and its governance or from a willful effort to keep self-aggrandizement licentiously free from political interference.

Beyond reconstructing relationships between politics and institutional religion, the Christian ethicist has a much wider responsibility to participate radically in the reconstruction of lateral relationships between politics and other fields. The vitality of freedom, justice, peace, and other precious values depends very heavily on this lateral reconstruction. Practically, the churches must sustain a serious effort to engage the laity in diverse vocational strategies of political responsibility. That task has hardly begun in earnest.

When the Christian ethicist confronts the characteristic prejudice of a business civilization that "business should not mix with politics," he should unmask the primitive conceptions of self-interest and social irresponsibility behind such a prejudice.

When the ethicist encounters the ideological rationalizations of organized medicine which for a generation has been fighting against a humane national health policy — on the grounds that "politics and health don't mix" or that a national health insurance program would be "socialized medicine"—he should not be surprised at the entrepreneurial aggressiveness which underlies such slogans.

When the ethicist hears that "politics and art shouldn't mix," he must question whether any civic order which fails to celebrate and advance the fine arts and the performing arts can ever lift itself above a mean spirit and a gross materialism. He must also ask whether the artist himself may not have some special political obligations. Pablo Casals, whose brilliant career as cellist, conductor, and composer has been heroically intertwined with some of the most momentous political events of this century, has testified that for him "the question is whether art is to be a pastime, a toy for man to play with, or if it should have a deep and human meaning. . . . It would be too easy, under the pretext of artistic neutrality, to [withdraw] instead of fighting injustice. I have shown to you my conception of all art, which should elevate and not degrade us." [4]

When the ethicist reads that "the Supreme Court shouldn't mix in politics," he must be prepared to assert that a judicial system without an independent capacity to affect the political order can hardly serve the ends of human rights and civic justice. This is hardly a new phenomenon: Alexis de Tocqueville in 1832 noted that "scarcely any *political* question arises in the United States that is not resolved sooner or later into a *judicial* question" (italics added). Two decades ago, Justice Robert H. Jackson, in a lecture prepared just before his death and never delivered, wrote: "Not only has the Supreme Court been the center of bitter debate itself, but its decisions have played some part in nearly every great political issue that has vexed our people." [5]

When dissenters are told that "politics should stop at the water's edge" and "shouldn't mix with foreign policy," the ethicist must insist that foreign policy is political and controversial by its very nature as the response of a people to international conflict.

When benevolent Christians persist in believing that their charities and philanthropies around the world demonstrate the full measure of their good will, the ethicist must help them to understand that they are escaping from the politics of the world economy which largely determines whether the poor and the malnourished and the chronically diseased and the illiterate will ever be liberated from their dehumanized condition. For some years now, the churches have unleashed many resolutions and study documents on the subject of world poverty and development; but the churches' own structures and programs are not yet oriented toward engagement with the issues of public policy in international economics, such as U.S. trade policy toward the third world. The redressing of injustices in the world-market structure requires governmental action in such matters as commodity agreements, liberalized tariffs for third-world products, positive trade assistance, the untying of purchasing restrictions tied to U.S. aid, and the development of shipping by third world countries to lessen their dependence upon the West's shipping monopolies. The churches of the United States, if they were seriously attentive to such prophetic Christians as Dom Helder Camara of Brazil and Samuel Parmar of India, would already be profoundly engaged in creating an informed and politically active constituency in world trade as just about their highest priority in defining their mission toward the third world. But such a concern is not yet apparent in either the missions or social-action operations of the American churches.

When a great power seeks by massive military force to control a revolutionary situation in a smaller country where the struggle for nationhood demands social justice above all things—but disdains responsibility for "internal politics"—the Christian ethicist must affirm the primacy of the political. Roger Hilsman resigned his post as assistant secretary of state for the Far East in the Johnson administration in 1964 because of what he regarded as the militarization of an essentially political struggle in Viet Nam:

I was deeply convinced that the political approach was the wiser course. The human costs of a military approach to Viet Nam, both for Americans and Vietnamese, would be much greater, in my judgment, and success less likely — especially in the permanent sense of achieving a politically viable outcome. A military course of action in Viet Nam would impede also the slow but significant movement toward a *détente* with the Soviet Union that President Kennedy had set in motion with the test ban treaty following the Cuban missile crisis. And a military approach would put enormous obstacles in the way of working toward a more realistic, "open door" policy toward Communist China, as we had planned.[6]

When critics of strategic nuclear weapons programs are met with the intimidating claim that such programs are technical matters which should be kept out of politics and left to the experts, the Christian ethicist must declare that international security and arms control are highly political subjects which cannot simply be contracted out to technicians. McGeorge Bundy, former White House assistant for national security affairs, has concluded that the nuclear arms race is now almost completely irrelevant to the real problems of international politics, given the circumstances of nuclear stalemate and mutual terror. The difficulty, says Bundy, is that the political issues of security have become captive to the spurious momentum of military technology, even when political leaders themselves know better. Strategic discussion, however, tends to be shaped by "think-tank analysts" who function in "an unreal world"—a world divorced from political responsibility.[7] To make strategic military and disarmament issues political and not simply technological is to insist on maintaining the capacity to grapple with human realities. Here again, to be political is to hold open the opportunity for human fulfillment.

In all these and many other fields, a positive valuation of the political is the beginning of proper ethical analysis. Bernard Crick's little book, *In Defence of Politics* (especially the last chapter titled "In Praise of Politics"), is an almost lyrical non-theological statement of what is at stake in this positive valuation of politics. Crick views politics as "a bold prudence, a diverse unity, an armed conciliation, a natural artifice, a creative compromise, and a serious game on which free civilization depends; it is a reforming conserver, a sceptical believer, and a pluralistic moralist; it has a lively sobriety, a complex simplicity, an untidy eloquence, a rough civility, and an everlasting immediacy; it is conflict become discussion; and it sets us a humane task on a human scale. And there is no end to the dangers it faces: there are so many reasons that sound so plausible for rejecting the responsibility and uncertainty of freedom." [8]

But the Christian ethicist must, again, do much more than establish the legitimacy of religious concern for politics. He must enter into the infinitely more complex and more difficult task of interpreting the moral issues at stake in the lateral relationships between politics and economics, between politics and health, between politics and art, between politics and social development, and between politics and military technology.

To define an issue as political does not, of course, guarantee anything about how policy decisions will be made. In the most forthright political conflicts, where clashing interests and influential personalities are clearly visible and contrasting opinions are thoughtfully formed, serious mistakes and even tragic blunders will be committed. A virtuous method in either politics or theology is no insurance of salubrious decisions or consequences.

Still, there is much more at stake in establishing the legitimacy of political methods of dealing with human problems than most churchmen and moralists suppose. Essentially, the basic rights of participation in decisions affecting the well-being of one's self, family, and community are at stake. Politics, again, has to do with the struggle for power, which is a very necessary, certainly inevitable, sometimes redeeming, and terribly dangerous fact of life as the Creator has ordained it.

At the heart of the rising demand for *empowerment* by minority groups in our time is the insistence that power is the distinctive mark of a man's humanity — or a woman's. To be powerless is to be dehumanized by definition. To be apolitical, or antipolitical, is not simply a matter of personal taste: it is to be considerably less than the creative actors we were born to be. Empowerment is admission to legitimate participation in decisions affecting personal and group interests. It is making things political for me and mine.

CAMPUS GOVERNANCE

The escalating demand for empowerment has done much to focus analytical energies on the ubiquity of political structures and processes, particularly in nongovernmental organizations. College and university campuses have provided perhaps the most spectacular displays of this phenomenon, some institutions being nearly destroyed in the process.

It can be very misleading to describe student protest as the politicization of the university if that characterization assumes that the university was a clinically academic, nonpolitical institution prior to such protest. In fact, of course, governance has been going on all the time; even governance interacting with public governmental authority has been going on all the time. What recent campus conflict has demonstrated is the need for a more constructively self-conscious, open, and honest approach to the pervasive exercise of power in the university. Too many administrators, trustees, and faculties have not had any very clear notions of representation, due process, grievance procedures, and the like. Student rage has done terrible things, including the destroying of lives and careers, and the future of higher education is troubled at many points. But the new seriousness and honesty toward the problem of campus governance is a positive ethical gain.

PROFESSIONAL GOVERNANCE

Most professional organizations have also been going through a painful process of political awakening for several years. Both academic and nonacademic professions have been hit with the phenomena of activist caucuses. These have been pressing for goals such as: (1) open competition and campaigning for leadership, rather than cut-and-dried elections; (2) augmented representation of blacks, women, and other minorities; (3) styles of program and procedure which are more informal and dialogical, and less authority-oriented; (4) affirmation of the profession's social responsibilities and renunciation of its pretenses to ethical neutrality; and (5) resolutions on specific controversial issues, such as the Indochina War, racial justice, and environmental health.

Intraprofessional conflict over such goals has become rather ferocious in both the physical sciences and the social sciences. Disputes over the value commitments of the sciences have been complicated by extensive federal research contracts related to military programs. One critic of government largesse to intellectuals speaks of "a new kind of *condottieri*," who serve as mercenaries of science and scholarship making studies tailored to contract specifications. Observers differ in their use of the term *politicization* in this connection: some denoting thereby the government-educational complex itself, others reserving *politicization* for the process of critical awareness and controversy over the emergence of such a complex.

It is not surprising that the political science profession should be peculiarly torn by such conflicts. The dominant behaviorism of a generation has come under sharp assault from those who would hold teaching and research in the field of government to a high ethical standard of political self-consciousness. Hans Morgenthau, a senior scholar of prestige, has been followed by a large company of younger scholars in deploring political science's "retreat into the trivial, the formal, the methodological, the purely theoretical, the remotely historical — in short, the politically irrelevant." There is no sharp separation between ethics and politics for Morgenthau, who speaks of the moral commitment of political science in "telling the truth about the political world . . . telling society things it does not want to hear. The truth of political science is the truth about power, its manifestations, its configurations, its limitations, its implications, its laws. Yet, on the other hand, one of the main purposes of society is to conceal these truths from its members. That concealment, that elaborate and subtle and purposeful misunderstanding of the nature of political man and of political society, is one of the cornerstones upon which all societies are founded." The myths and prejudices of any political system are threatened by this moral commitment. Political science at its very best "cannot help being a subversive and revolutionary force with regard to certain vested interests — intellectual, political, economic, and social in general: for it must sit in continuous judgment upon political man and political society, measuring their truth . . . by its own."[9]

Where the national leadership of nonacademic professions has become monopolized by conservative and aged persons — as in the medical and legal professions — caucuses have become not only instruments of attack by the young upon the establishments, they have also become positive agencies of service to the dissenters and the disinherited of American society. Providing health care for ghetto dwellers and victims of "police riots" (to use the Walker Commission's description of Chicago's official response to demonstrations during the 1968 Democratic Convention) or offering them legal aid, youthful professionals have seen themselves as a new social and political force, testifying to the awakening of a humanistic consciousness. The Medical Committee for Human Rights and Nader's Raiders are conspicuous examples of this new militancy of younger professionals. Such groups have another positive function not sufficiently appreciated by the antagonized: they provide a kind of sectarian solidarity and self-respect for some early careerists who might otherwise leave the professions.

The antipolitical disposition of the American business community has been modified in recent years by groups as divergent as the U.S. Chamber of Commerce (with its corporate responsibility drive) and Business Executives Move for Vietnam Peace. Of course, American business has never been seriously inhibited from seeking to influence government policy. What laissez faire ideology and the Protestant ethos have long done for business, however, has been to perpetuate two moral disabilities of the most serious kind: (1) an excessively narrow and self-interested view of the responsibilities of government; and (2) an artificial separation of government from politics which has undermined the businessman's receptiveness to politics as a vocation.

While Chicago economist Milton Friedman continues to declare that profit-making is the only social responsibility of business, others have taken a much more organic view of business interests. Richard S. Gordon, a Monsanto Chemical vice-president, says that the chances for survival of a socially irresponsible industry are now as dim as those of a person who measures his performance solely in terms of his physical health. In a time of growing urban congestion and municipal interdependence, a business must learn to share limited space and scarce resources. Many corporations have come to realize that they share a "closed biosphere" and depend on all kinds of other institutions for specialized services in the common good.

Even though businessmen during the past two decades have come increasingly to possess a sense of public service, the specifically political demands of public policy-making often remain beyond their tastes and talents. While foreign policy has tended to dominate governmental affairs more and more, the business elite continues to exhibit a trained incapacity for the tasks of foreign policy. Not long before going to the White House to toil for an administration which takes a disproportionate share of its cues from Wall Street and Madison Avenue, Henry Kissinger made this observation:

> The special skill of the executive is thought to consist in coordinating well-defined functions rather than in challenging them. The procedure is relatively effective in the business world, where the executive can often substitute decisiveness, long experience, and a wide range of personal acquaintance for reflectiveness. In international affairs, however — especially in a revolutionary situation — the strong will which is one of our business executives' notable traits may produce essentially arbitrary choices . . . The business elite is even less able or willing than the lawyer to recognize that the formulation of an issue, not the technical remedy, is usually the central problem.[10]

For the churches, one baneful reflex of the political hangups of the business elite is to be seen in the governance of congregations and ecclesiastical boards and bodies dominated by that elite — a subject to which we shall return. Not only the impulse to political action in the world but the demand for empowerment within the churches — instead of being perceived as a potentially liberating force — is too often greeted by religious institutions as simply a negation of sacred institutional values. Once again, it is felt to be a religious obligation to repress or escape the process of politicization.

On the whole, organized labor has been much less inhibited than business and other professions in engaging in open political conflict. That fact is largely a consequence of labor's long struggle from powerlessness to legitimacy to establishment. An upward struggle sharpens a social movement's political sensitivities in ways which more securely established groups find difficult to match. It is true that there has been an unending controversy among labor leaders as to whether union politics should be neutral or partisan; both neutrality and partisanship impose their own peculiar restraints and inhibitions. But union leaders have been oriented by their history and experience to think in terms of power and conflict, bargaining and compromise—the very stuff of politics—and not to hide from themselves and others what the struggle is all about.

In recent years, however, the political consciousness of labor has been somewhat dimmed by the attainment of establishmentarian success. It has begun to vacillate between preoccupation with vested union interests and idealistic attention to the wider political agenda of social and international affairs, the latter personified in the increasingly lonely crusades of Walter Reuther. Resistance to that wider agenda has come from many blue-collar workers who feel that their stake in the system, which emerged in the 1930s, is threatened by automation, a growing proportion of white-collar employment, the black invasion of jobs and neighborhoods, and the rebellion of their own college-educated children. This new apprehension of powerlessness on the part of blue-collar workers will perhaps continue to generate reactionary political tendencies for some years. Mainstream Protestantism, unfortunately, is now so feebly rooted in blue-collar America that it is almost by definition incapable of relating itself to labor's very painful identity crisis.

POLITICAL CONSCIOUSNESS AND CHURCH GOVERNANCE

Whatever the deficiencies of secular institutions and professions in facing the facts of political life, the Christian churches have long been conspicuously robed in the pretense of nonpoliticalness. At the 1968 Fourth Assembly of the World Council of Churches in Uppsala, Sweden, one presiding officer greeted a flurry of controversy on the floor with this fatuous rebuke: "This is not a political meeting! We are here, by the grace of God, to strengthen the unity and mission of the church." The almost irresistible urge among churchmen to substitute sanctimonious language for the human reality of the church-at-work was particularly out of place at Uppsala. The healthiest thing about that assembly was the lifting up of institutional issues to the light of political visibility. It was the severely underrepresented minorities — laymen, women, black Americans, third worlders, youth — who caucused and forced the assembly to see itself honestly in political terms, and who became the prime catalysts to the renewal of W.C.C. structures and procedures. These minority activists found special inspiration in an address by James Baldwin who spoke of "the lies the church has always told itself, to itself, about itself." It was just because of these lies, warned Baldwin, that "the destruction of the Christian church as it is presently constituted may not only be desirable but may be necessary."

If politics is seen as that action by which human beings achieve their highest common fulfillment, the denial of politics in the church becomes the denial of humanization of the church. The surge of political self-consciousness so apparent at Uppsala hit the triennial assembly of the National Council of Churches in Detroit in early December 1969. Unfortunately, despite heroic individual performances by some N.C.C. officers (especially Council President Arthur S. Flemming), it was clear from the beginning that the council's over-bureaucratized and under-politicized structure simply could not cope with the rage of the underrepresented. One minority after another — blacks, Indians, Chicanos, women, youth — unloaded its grievances upon an increasingly shellshocked gathering overpopulated with aging white male clerics. At this writing, the N.C.C. has yet to recover from that event, which traumatized not only council staff but the nation's denominational leaders. During 1970 and 1971 denominational assemblies barely survived similar ordeals of politicization.

The emergence of black caucuses within predominantly white church bodies has had these very positive values: (1) both white leadership and other minorities have been catalyzed into a keener awareness of power as an institutional reality; (2) the pattern of institutional racism, which has tended to be invisible to whites, has been made more visible; (3) black leadership has been more intensively recruited for service to the whole church; (4) the issue of priorities has been sharpened for the whole church; (5) a new appreciation of the treasures of black religious experience has been encouraged; and (6) extremist excesses have been moderated in the caucuses' concerns for strategy.

The worst possible response to this upsurge of political sensitivity in the churches is to seek to repress it or to deny its legitimacy. In the long run, institutional maturity and creativity absolutely require a capacity to accept the turbulence of group conflict which may be unleashed by the rage of the disinherited. Of course, the original responsibility for provoking such upheavals almost always rests, as in most revolutionary circumstances, with those regimes which have been too slow or too self-serving to respond to the dehumanizing experience of powerlessness. Recent experience in church governance suggests that many ecclesiastical potentates exhibit a trained incapacity to cope with the sudden and open intrusion of political conflict into precincts they thought were providentially immune to such goings-on. Their incapacity is not traceable solely to inadequate professional education or to moralistic illusions about power; it is compounded by the uncritical transfer of secular organizational models into notions of church polity. This disability has been conspicuous in recent efforts at restructuring national and regional church bodies. Notwithstanding a great deal of radical rhetoric concerning institutional change, these efforts have typically surrendered to the antipolitical mythologies of managerial consultants who bring with them the organizational biases of the business elite. A premium is put upon bureaucratic virtues such as efficiency and coordination rather than on the essential political capacity to cope with conflict and give moral purpose to controversial decisions.

Keith Bridston's *Church Politics* is a welcome introduction to what he variously calls "the political pathology" of church leaders, the reality of "the church as a power complex," the "camouflage of political processes" in the church, and "ecclesiastical tycoonery." [11] But Bridston's concerns need to be advanced by thorough empirical analysis. The sociologists of religion, who have not adequately portrayed the political phenomena of religious organizations, should be joined by a new breed of political scientists of religion, whose specialty would be the investigation of power complexes, party systems, lobbies, filibusters, gerrymanders, rotten boroughs, slush funds, propaganda mills, intelligence operations, colonial empires, and the like; for all these things are indeed to be found in the churches. There can be no wholeness in the churches until these realities are openly acknowledged and ethically appraised.

On the positive side, some churches and church bodies are experiencing a new kind of Pentecostal vitality in which the drive for political self-consciousness is celebrated as a gift of the Holy Spirit.

HUMANISM AND POLITICAL IMAGINATION

The demand for empowerment, as a revolutionary slogan, is subject to all the romanticism of false hopes which revolutionary sentiments generate. Such a slogan is no substitute for the painfully creative formation and reformation of political processes which actually serve the goals of freedom, justice, and peace. Empowerment in a highly technicized, urbanized society certainly does not mean mass referenda on every policy decision. Dozens must still represent millions; the loneliness of the solitary decision-maker remains an inescapable feature of modern government. The challenge is to build responsive and humanizing features into the systems of decision-making and policy-implementing — features which make trust and representation palpable realities.

If the main emphasis of this chapter has been upon a positive valuation of the political, it is nonetheless important to stress the highly personal values of creative development, of individual expression, of private reflection and intimate communication which a totalitarian state destroys. For life, after all, is more than politics: it has to do with love and leisure, with personal devotion and achievement, and with many private joys and sorrows where no apparatus of government should intrude.

Yet even here we see that resolute political action is often necessary to preserve these enclaves of individuality in a politicized world. For it is not only in totalitarian states that governments ruthlessly

88

assault personal values. Whenever the law enforcement, national security, and intelligence machinery of a government invades an essentially private domain — even while mustering a righteous resistance to dissenters who protest that invasion — political means must be used to serve the ends of privacy. Whenever governmental priorities and social policies permit subhuman living conditions to persist so that the capacity to love or to develop healthfully or to enjoy privacy is virtually denied by the inequities of the social system, such personal issues must be made more political, not less so.

C. Wright Mills's essay, *The Sociological Imagination,* makes a helpful distinction between the *troubles* of an individual in his private world and the *issues* of society in a public world. The artist, the novelist, the dramatist, the poet may offer a more imaginative insight into the relationship between *troubles* and *issues* than the social scientist who fails to close the gap between science and the humanities. Yet, says Mills, it is the "*political* task of the social scientist — as of any liberal educator — continually to translate personal troubles into public issues, and public issues into the terms of their human meaning for a variety of individuals." [12]

If such a task can be charged to the social scientist, surely the Christian ethicist must be a humanist with political imagination. From such a dialectical perspective, politics will never be reduced to the fatuous judgments of a purely private morality, nor will the rights of the person ever be legitimately swallowed up in the functions of statehood.

IDEOLOGY AND POLITICAL CONSCIOUSNESS

Finally, it may be the most serious mistake in contemporary political analysis to assume that politicization is synonymous with government control. To recognize the pervasiveness of political influence upon the full range of human affairs is not necessarily to settle for any particular ideological view as to who holds the preponderance of power in American society — or who should hold it. The ethicist should be aware of the remarkable variety of current perceptions as to who governs the United States.

On Left and Right alike, there are constricted if not conspiratorial models of political control. C. Wright Mills saw a power elite of business, political, and military chieftains. G. William Domhoff sees continuing control by an upper-class aristocracy. Sidney Lens has taken President Eisenhower's "military-industrial complex" to be the dominant system. John Kenneth Galbraith describes a "new industrial state" of de facto planning by large corporations. Michael Harrington writes of the "social-industrial complex" based on the "knowledge industry." Noam Chomsky zeroes in on a liberal tech-nocracy of "new Mandarins." From the Right, it variously appears that intellectuals or bureaucrats or the Eastern Establishment or the Supreme Court or socialists or communists or the media or some other group really runs the country.

Centrist liberals often retain the rational harmony of an eighteenth century pluralistic vision of how society is and ought to be governed. Many social scientists are enamored of equilibrium models such as the principle of "countervailing power." Radicals at both extremes say that such a pluralistic model is a myth, that the system doesn't actually function in response to countervailing power but is manip-ulated by some more limited group. If radicals could only agree as to just what that group is!

The true view (which we shall modestly call "the Geyer view") is, of course, that nobody is in effective control of the politicization process. Over against leftist, rightist, and pluralist models alike, let us risk the judgment that American society has arrived at a state of practical anarchy in the affairs that matter most. It is possible that, apart from the brief and eccentric 1933–1938 period of the New Deal, political institutions in the United States have virtually lost the ca-pacity to govern responsibly and effectively. It is possible that our antipolitical, antigovernmental traditions and prejudices (embedded in such irresponsible anachronisms as Congressional procedures) have never really been overcome by a coherent modern view of gov-ernment and of power in society. (Any student of Walter Muelder must conclude with an appeal for coherence!) There is support for this not altogether original lament in Robert Paul Wolff's observa-tion that "the most significant fact about the distribution of power in America is not who makes such decisions as are made, but rather how many matters of the greatest social importance are not objects of anyone's decision at all." [13]

There is a dangerously debilitating contradiction in the American situation just now: the age of politicization is not the age of super-government but the age of no government at all. Conservative Americans, rebellious Americans, and Middle Americans are astonishingly alike in regressing to antipolitical sentiments very similar to those of earlier generations. They resent government and all its works and are not willing to entrust it with the power or the resources required to cope with the nation's most grievous problems. Disaffection with both major parties is growing and is hastening the decline of regular party organization; in most cases, this has meant that the individual assumes the more withdrawn posture of "independence." The Viet Nam War and the succession of shocks related to race and the cities have seemingly exhausted citizen capacity to deal with national and international issues. The illusions of the romantic localism-and-decentralism ideas (so similar to our traditional agrarian fundamentalism) have at least temporarily monopolized the energies of many activists. The campus scene, so politically alive in the late 1960s and the spring of 1970, in 1971 is suddenly and almost inexplicably caught up in an intense new ardor for privatization. While such mercurial currents may change direction again very soon, the underlying problem of sustaining vocations and structures of political action beyond episodic and ad hoc fits cannot be quickly solved.

The next stage of political consciousness in America may belong, not to the pragmatists and the technicians of a political system which has seldom if ever functioned with systemic wholeness, but to the ideologues who have been so regularly despised by both our politicians and our ethicists. If that is the case, the Christian churches of the land may well find their mission in helping to generate new visions of political community which are powerful enough to transform both chronic prejudices and inherited institutions — and humane enough to be authentically liberating.

NOTES

1. Quoted in Alden D. Kelley, *Christianity and Political Responsibility* (Philadelphia: Westminster Press, 1961), p. 28.

2. Oscar Cullmann, *The State in the New Testament* (New York: Charles Scribner's Sons, 1956), pp. 4–5.

3. *Politicization* is used in this chapter as the substantive form of the verb *politicize,* especially in the second and third meanings given in *Webster's Third New International Dictionary:* "to give a political character to; to bring within the realm of politics." This use is contrasted with *politicalization,* which has a more totalistic reference, implying all of society (arts, etc.) being politicalized.

4. J. Ma Corredor, *Conversations with Casals* (New York: E. P. Dutton and Co., 1956), pp. 212–13.

5. Alexis de Tocqueville, *Democracy in America,* 2 vols. (New York: Vintage Books, 1956), 1:290; Robert H. Jackson, *The Supreme Court in the American System of Government* (Cambridge: Harvard University Press, 1955), p. 22.

6. Roger Hilsman, *To Move a Nation* (Garden City, N.J.: Doubleday and Co., 1967), p. 535.

7. McGeorge Bundy, "To Cap the Volcano," *Foreign Affairs* 48 (October 1969): 10.

8. Bernard Crick, *In Defence of Politics* (Baltimore, Md.: Penguin Books, 1964; Revised Pelican Edition), p. 161.

9. Hans Morgenthau, "The Purpose of Political Science," in *A Design for Political Science: Scope, Objectives, and Methods,* James C. Charlesworth, ed. (Philadelphia: The American Academy of Political and Social Science, 1966), pp. 69–73.

10. Henry A. Kissinger, *American Foreign Policy* (New York: W. W. Norton and Co., 1969), p. 32.

11. Keith Bridston, *Church Politics* (New York: World Publishing Co., 1969).

12. C. Wright Mills, *The Sociological Imagination* (New York: Oxford University Press, 1959), p. 187.

13. Robert Paul Wolff, *The Poverty of Liberalism* (Boston: Beacon Press, 1968), p. 118.

4 The Logic of Moral Argument

Ralph B. Potter, Jr.

Among professional practitioners of Christian Social Ethics in the United States today there is relatively little agreement concerning the nature of their discipline, the intellectual tools necessary to perform it, and the scope of their responsibility for the guidance and stimulation of Christian social action. Some accentuate the qualifier, "Christian"; others place stress upon the second modifier, "social." There are those who emphasize that Christian Social Ethics is a subfield of the general philosophical discipline of ethics.

Social ethics, according to the definition of Gibson Winter, "deals with issues of social order — good, right, and ought in the organization of human communities and the shaping of social policies. Hence the subject matter of social ethics is moral rightness and goodness in the shaping of human society."[1] Walter Muelder has been constant in preaching and practicing a view of the field which binds these three emphases of *Christian, social,* and *ethics* together. For him, "Christian social ethics is an interdisciplinary field . . . which commits its practitioners to undertake joint, supplementary, or complementary theoretical and empirical studies in theology, philosophical ethics, behavioral and historical sciences."[2] Unlike most of the contributors to this volume, I have not studied directly under Walter Muelder and have not been steeped thoroughly in his thought through days of contact in classroom and hallways. Nevertheless, as one who has profited from countless more indirect ways from his leadership in the profession, I would like to do him honor by trying to grapple with the central issue of the nature and scope of the practice of Christian social ethics, a question of obvious import for the field to which Walter Muelder has contributed so much.

Those who would refer to themselves as Christian social ethicists generally agree that their field is a practical discipline; that is, it is concerned not only with the definition or determination of what is good, right, just, feasible, appropriate, or obedient but also with the performance of acts which can be characterized by such terms. Ethics is concerned not only with knowing, but also with doing. It is a matter not only of the intellect, but also of the will. The concern of the Christian social ethicist extends beyond inquiry into what men ought to do to the consideration of how they may be enabled to do what they ought to do. To say that ethics is a practical discipline is to say that those who are concerned with the subject are interested in shaping behavior, not simply in prescribing what it ought to be or in describing how it comes to be. The practical concern requires knowledge both of the direction action should take and of the capacity of individuals and groups to influence behavior in particular circumstances.

Within this underlying consensus, there are divergent views concerning how the practical concerns can best be served. A broad view of the field of Christian social ethics would, in effect, make the ethicist responsible for guiding the thought and action of the Church with respect to every factor that could significantly affect direction and performance in every stage of Christian social action. I wish to argue that this broad view leads to a lack of focus, a dispersion of effort, a failure of discipline, and a neglect of the specific contribution that practitioners of a more carefully defined version of Christian social ethics might make in relieving the perplexity of churchmen and citizens confronted with baffling choices of policy. I shall propose a narrower definition of the field. The first task is to show, by a consideration of what is entailed in the doing of Christian social ethics under the broad definition, that such an undertaking is unhelpful and, indeed, impossible in practice. The second assignment is to indicate how a narrower conception of the field may make it possible to contribute more by trying to do one thing well.

THE DANGERS OF DILETTANTISM

The broad concept of Christian social ethics makes the practitioner in the field directly concerned for the entire process of Christian social action. Almost every dimension of human life and thought must be considered to fall within the scope of his professional responsibility when the field is so conceived. Walter Muelder states that "a qualified Christian social ethicist ought to be well grounded in Bible and theology, in philosophy, in history, and in the behavioral sciences. Science, philosophy, and theology interpenetrate and converge in the methods of social ethics."[3] The intellectual demands of this broad view of the field are clearly immense. They are also imprecise.

A more detailed specification of the concerns of Christian social ethics might be derived by converting Kenneth Kirk's definition of the scope of moral theology from an exclusively individually oriented to a socially oriented scheme. Kirk provides the following outline in his book entitled *Some Principles of Moral Theology*.

The aim of moral theology is therefore to accumulate from every available source whatever information will be of use to the priest for his task of shepherding individual souls. Its scope therefore must comprise the following subjects:

(a) The natural endowments of the human soul and the laws of responsible action.

(b) The ideal of character to which God desires each man to conform.

(c) The means by which God enables the soul to progress towards that ideal.

(d) The means by which the priest can co-operate with God in stimulating or fostering such progress.

(e) The hindrances, natural or acquired, to spiritual progress, and the means by which they can be eradicated or their influence counteracted.

To these should be added:

(f) A discussion of the principles by which actions whose legitimacy or morality is doubtful, or which do not seem to be referable to any rules of morality at all, are to be regulated.

(g) The qualification demanded of the priest in his capacity as a spiritual director, or guide of souls.[4]

Christian social ethics must, under the broad definition, do all this and more. Adapting his scheme to their own field, advocates of the broad view might rephrase Kirk to observe that "The aim of Christian social ethics is to accumulate from every available source whatever information will be of use to participants in Christian social action for their task of deliberating concerning policies to be pursued by individuals and groups in matters relating to social order." They would then add a social dimension under each of Kirk's headings to establish something like the following outline, which would be of direct and immediate relevance to the conscientious social ethicist:

I. The natural endowments of man, the nature of society, and the reciprocal relationship of individual and society.
   A. The individual
      1. Philosophical and theological anthropology
      2. Psychology
   B. Society
      1. Sociology
      2. Social and cultural anthropology
   C. The reciprocal relationship between individual and society

II. The Christian ideal of character
   A. For the individual
      1. Christology
      2. History of Christian ethics

B. For society
1. History of Christian social thought
2. Political philosophy

III. The means by which individuals and congregations are motivated to practice love and seek justice.
A. Individual
1. Theology of grace and sacrament
2. Ascetical and mystical theology and Christian biography
3. Religious psychology
B. Society: Theories of social change

IV. Resources for leadership in Christian social action
A. Individual
1. Pastoral theology
2. Christian education
B. Society
1. Ecclesiology
2. Theories of voluntary associations

V. Hindrances to progress and the means of their overcoming
A. Individual: Penitential theology
B. Society: Social pathology

VI. Principles by which actions whose legitimacy or morality is doubtful are to be regulated: Casuistry

The seventh requirement, corresponding to Kirk's point (g) having to do with "the qualifications demanded of the Christian social ethicist in his capacity as guide and implementer of Christian social action," would, presumably, be met by successful completion of a curriculum requiring demonstration of proficiency in each of the above areas.

This specification of what it might mean for a "qualified social ethicist . . . to be well grounded in Bible and theology, in philosophy, history, and in the behavioral sciences" remains crude. I have no inclination to define it for use as the basis of a curriculum of study since I believe that such a broad definition of the field results in an immodest stance within the Church and a ridiculous appearance within the academic community. These two unhappy effects are linked in their common origin in the failure to define carefully the specific contribution that Christian social ethics, more narrowly defined as a subfield of the discipline of ethics, might make to the very complex process of stimulating, directing and implementing Christian social action.

The broad definition of the field leads to an unfocused pattern of training and practice that makes those who pursue its impossible demands appear within the academic community to be ridiculous dabblers and dilettantes, eager for interdisciplinary work but unable to define their own discipline. Even the most talented or brazen recruit would find it presumptuous to suppose that he could make an original contribution to knowledge in each of the disciplines he is told he must master to qualify as a Christian social ethicist. In order to avoid being dismissed as a marginal, peripheral hanger-on in each field, he might decide to select one or two in which to labor intensively, narrowing his focus to gain depth and mastery. But he would thereby forfeit his identity under the broad definition of Christian social ethics. He might find shelter in one or another of the specialized fields well established in the academic world, but he would be lost to the field of Christian social ethics.

Faced with the challenge of contending day by day with talented men and women who are willing to specialize in a single discipline and thereby gain, in their own bailiwick, a detailed command of the subject that the thinly spread ethicist can never attain, it would be possible to moderate the demands for competence. One might settle for second- or third-rate performance in the specialized disciplines and rephrase the requirements to suggest that the aspiring ethicist need merely "be conversant with" the several fields that impinge upon the conduct of Christian social action. But such a formula would add little to the traditional mark of the liberally educated man. Colleagues in related fields, sharing a commitment to liberal arts education, may be very tolerant of undergraduates wishing to sample work in various fields in order to be conversant with the wide range of human knowledge. But if a scattered pattern of sampling fields persists into and beyond graduate training, it may become difficult to evoke serious interdisciplinary conversation. How would the ethicist uphold his end of such a conversation? More bluntly, what would he have to offer? What expertise could he contribute that sociologists could not get more reliably by speaking directly, for example, to biblical scholars, social philosophers, or psychologists? Of what distinctive body of knowledge of general cultural interest and import is he the master? How can his mastery be assessed in relation to some definable standard? What community of scholars can vouch for his competence and explain and criticize his contribution?

The unfortunate consequence then of the broad definition of Christian social ethics is the hindrance to the creation of a community of scholars sharing a similar perception of a field of study and able to criticize and counsel one another in the generation, preservation, and refinement of a cumulative body of knowledge and wisdom. The broad definition imposes an ideal of the qualified practitioner that is impossible of realization. In response to their inevitable inability to realize the extravagant ideal, those trained in Christian social ethics are forced to create their own idiosyncratic form of specialization. The field is so immense and the number of possible combinations of interest so large that seldom does there exist a critical mass of scholarly competence and interest necessary for the fusion that brings both heat and light to a subject area. Three main alternative forms of specialization present themselves. All result in the impoverishment of the field.

Many students enter graduate programs in social ethics in order to become more effective leaders in the ministry of the Church in the world. Most frequently, they have been trained for a particular office in the Church, and, under the pressures of the impossible diffuseness of the broad definition of Christian social ethics, they tend to specialize in the analysis of problems of practice encountered by incumbents of particular roles in the conduct of the social ministry. Thus, they may write a dissertation on "The Role of the Pastor in the Quest for Fair Housing." When such work is well done it is difficult to distinguish from what might be contributed by a secular student of the sociology of religion. Indeed, the authors of such dissertations not infrequently become teachers of the sociology of religion and closely related subjects. They preserve interest in the *social* dimension of the subject but forswear deep concern with that which is indicated by the terms *Christian* and *ethics*.

A second pattern of adjustment is to select a single topic of considerable immediate relevance and attempt to explore every conceivable dimension of the issue, carrying over the eclectic methodological implications of the broad definition of Christian social ethics but confining study to a specific issue. Thus, one might offer a dissertation on "Christian Faith and Race Relations," or "International Relations in Christian Perspective." The authors of such treatises are forced to rely on specialized authorities in each of the several fields on which they touch. University examination committees, if they are made up of representatives from the departments in which the candidate has sought out necessary specialized expertise, are likely to be in a quandary if the material in each individual part of the dissertation falls somewhat short of the work done in that field by more narrowly focused scholars. Is there any way that second- or third-rate work in four or five special fields can be alchemized into first-rate work in Christian social ethics? Those who take this route of topical specialization may become prominent bureaucrats or leaders in social action or teachers; but seldom do they establish themselves as men to whom anyone concerned for their topic must listen for a distinctive and penetrating exposition. More often, they attain the rank of translator of more original work into terms and formats palatable for wider popular audiences. They tend to retain a *Christian* orientation but have a second- or third-hand acquaintance with the *social* dimensions and give little systematic attention to *ethics*.

A third way of coping with the impossible demands laid upon the qualified Christian social ethicist is to retreat into abstraction and generality and rest content with the provisions of "guidelines" and "middle axioms." By eschewing all requests for specific guidance in relation to immediate, concrete perplexities, the ethicist may avoid for some time the exposure of his relatively poor grasp of the detailed information necessary for a truly expert judgment on particular issues of social policy. If he ever comes down to earth he will be badly outmanned by those who have laid claim to specialized tracts in the landscape of human knowledge. It is safer to drift in midair, to offer advice at a level of abstraction far above the down-to-earth level at which churchmen must act in their daily efforts to be faithful disciples. Those who ask for immediate help in clarifying the reasoning by which they might choose between contending courses of policy are abandoned and left dangling by those who would offer them "guidelines" and "middle axioms" as the outcome of a procedure such as that sketched by Walter Muelder in the following passage.

The process of finding fruitful guidelines in Christian social action is sometimes like this: (1) identify the problem or crisis; (2) indicate why it is important for Christians; (3) amplify the analysis of the situation by all the tools available; (4) show what the resources are in the Christian faith which bear on the issue, including ultimate concepts; (5) indicate the middle axioms that can mediate between these ultimates and the particular situation; (6) formulate guidelines for action; (7) recommend these for study and appropriate action by Christians and Churches in the situations in which they find themselves, reminding them always of their mission as servants of Jesus Christ in his ministry of reconciliation in the world.[5]

The interesting and demanding work peculiar to the field of ethics is here eased off onto others. The excitement begins after the local churchmen have received the "middle axioms" and "guidelines" and settle down to the task of determining what exactly is the "appropriate action" in their situation. It is at that moment that perplexity is likely to be sharpest and the supposed skills of the ethicist most welcome. But proponents of the broad definition of Christian social ethics, having exhausted themselves elsewhere, are seldom available to help overcome very specific onslaughts of perplexity over immediate decisions. What is left undone by purveyors of middle axioms constitutes a sin of omission that makes the situational or contextual brands of Christian ethics, which Muelder finds implausible, appear plausible to believers when they discover that the elaborate interdisciplinary apparatus constructed in seminary classrooms can yield so little guidance on how to span the gap from guideline to appropriate action.

The mediating position that gives middle axioms their airborne quality is described in Muelder's summary:

> In ecumenical social ethics responsible work has found it useful to formulate not only statements of ultimate faith but also "middle axioms." A middle axiom is a general ethical concept which provides guidelines and norms for ethical evaluation and action, but which is not as abstract or general as are ultimate theological principles on the one hand nor as specific and concrete as prescriptions in empirical decisions on the other hand. The idea of "the responsible society" is one such fruitful middle axiom.[6]

Noting the gaps in reasoning that yawn on either side of every middle axiom, Paul Ramsey has asked the question likely to occur to curious Christians, eager to proceed to "appropriate action" but left to wonder, "How do we get there from here?" "What stands between a 'universal ethical principle' and a 'middle axiom' or between one of these and specific plans for action? Surely not another 'middle axiom.' "[7]

Middle axioms would seem to be so unhelpful, or at least so inadequate to most situations that Christians would encounter in the immediacy of practical involvements today, that one is moved to ask in what situation would middle axioms be helpful to sober, conscientious, and talented practitioners of Christian social ethics? The answer appears to be that if Christians of diverse denominational loyalties, long estranged, with strikingly different traditions concerning the responsibility of the Church in relation to civil power and authority, were seeking to come together in face of vivid threats to social order and to the very life of the churches, they might find middle axioms to be a helpful means of reducing the dimensions of disagreement and improving prospects for united action. Such a circumstance existed within the ecumenical movement in the two decades prior to World War II; it was then that middle axioms enjoyed their strongest appeal. In that particular historical setting the approach may have served to mobilize the dispersed forces of western churches for more attentive concern for Christian social action.

It was a mistake, however, for Christian social ethicists to confuse an approach that may have been momentarily useful in a particular historical and institutional circumstance with the definition of the major task and technique of their discipline. In an emergency it may be necessary for every churchman to contribute to the mobilization of the energies of Christians by extending the scope of his activities beyond the confines of the calling for which he has been specially trained. He may take on the responsibility of other offices. The cost is always a relative neglect of his specific function within the fellowship of believers and the community at large. In assuming responsibility for the investigation of *all* factors that impinge on the effectiveness of Christian social action, ethicists have lost sight of their specific function: to aid the reflection of the Christian community by relieving perplexity about decisions with significant bearing on the public good. The assumption of the broad responsibility for oversight of the entire course of Christian social action has forced the ethicist to assume an immodest stance within the Church, a stance which suggests both a lack of faith in the performance of men and women called to other offices which contribute to the effectiveness of social action and an intimation of the pride of the philosopher-king.

Christian social ethicists are properly concerned for effective Christian social action. But within the Church, it is not their specific task to stimulate and direct the entire course of such action. Action on behalf of a just society is the responsibility of the entire body of Christians and each office within the Church must make its own distinctive contribution to its initiation, guidance, and accomplishment. The creation of a reservoir of actors is accomplished by preachers and evangelists who declare the Word and draw men into the fellowship. Christian educators instill categories of thought that enable believers to make discriminating judgments. Prophets take the initiative in redefining certain actions and states of affairs as problematic for Christian conscience. Priests help to form character and conscience by superintending the means of grace. Those adept in Christian rhetoric stir congregations and excite them to action on particular occasions. Bureaucrats provide the organizational resources that facilitate action. Activists exemplify and lead in the immediate performance of needful tasks. It is only when the way ahead is uncertain, when conflicting senses of "ought" engender perplexity concerning the propriety and priority of actions, that the specific skill of the ethicist comes into play as a response to an immediate need and as a service to the Christian community.

Under the broad definition the distinctive contribution Christian social ethicists might make suffers neglect, and there is little that they actually do that someone else in the academic community and in the Church does not do better. Ethicists are reduced to juggling the elements of other men's specialties into new forms and packages. But only rarely do they hit upon just the right combination of second-hand ingredients that will captivate and bring new insight to readers. For the most part, consumers of the works of Christian social ethicists can safely bypass their products and piece together their own studies with a good bibliography and scissors and paste. Practitioners in the field are, for the most part, ignored by the public at large, by the intellectual community, and by fellow churchmen. They are not infrequently bright and diligent. Unfortunately, they are misdirected in their adherence to a vision of the field that dooms them to mediocrity and frustration.

Departments of social ethics often seem to provide the only suitable context within which those who are puzzled about problems of action in relation to the social order can pursue their interests within the seminary and university settings. But the structure and curriculum of most departments can be accounted for only by series of historical happenstances and not by a logic imposed by a clear account of the requirements of a well-defined discipline of study. Our predecessors within the field of Christian social ethics gave immense stimulus to the development of the infant social sciences. But the nature of the field has not been thoroughly thought through in response to the maturation of the specialized branches of the social sciences and the impact of the knowledge explosion in all those related fields in which adherents of the broad definition must seek to be well-grounded if they are to aspire to the title of "qualified social ethicist."

A much more narrow view of the primary setting and responsibility of Christian social ethics is clearly needed. The Christian social ethicist should seek to specialize in the critical analysis and justification of the logic of moral discourse employed by Christians, past and present, in reflecting upon the conditions necessary to attain for all men an existence which may be called decent and human in light of the knowledge of Christ. The material which constitutes the starting point of such a discipline is the discourse of Christians concerning right and wrong with respect to actions that have significant public consequences. There can be, in the narrowly defined version of the field, a focus, a starting point, an identifiable task, appropriate tests, a critical colleagueship, a manageable set of requisite skills, and an outcome of potential benefit to a specific audience.

The Christian social ethicist must be at the disposal of those who are perplexed. His proper task is to aid reflection upon action, to assist believers and citizens in overcoming perplexity concerning issues bearing upon social order and the shaping of the human community. Reflection is occasioned by perplexity. Perplexity is marked by lack of a response adequate to a situation.[8] It is, along with indecision and helplessness, a species of the phenomenon of not-knowing-what-to-do. The nature and cause of perplexity may differ significantly from group to group and from time to time. Different circumstances and different sets of moral beliefs give rise to different forms of perplexity. In order to be of assistance, the ethicist must be able to understand the course of deliberation. He must first listen attentively to grasp the quandary in which his fellow Christians find themselves at any given moment. His awareness must be perennially renewed. His starting point must be the immediate, specific, existential perplexities of those who, perhaps already in receipt of broad guidelines and middle axioms, still do not know what to do in order to perform the "appropriate action." The ethicist, as ethicist, has, in effect, no independent, self-initiating task within the Church. His professional skills are called for only when there is a breakdown in the course of Christian social action, when there is an interruption of confidence in the selection of policies. He is a trouble-shooter trained to do the very specific job of untangling conflicting "oughts." His task is secondary. It requires both the involvement necessary to attune one's ear and to grasp the urgency of the pending decision and also the detachment necessary for the periodic refurbishing of skills and the critical distance essential for original and precise thought.

Perplexity is linked to practice and is specific to pending decisions. The decisions may have greater or lesser import, wider or narrower ramifications. But the ethicist must begin with individual cases, with topics of immediate bearing for those he would serve. His starting point should be the ordinary language of Christian men and women as they discuss what they should do. Not what they should do in general, or in ideal circumstances, or in some future time and distant place; but what they should do here and now in response to the varied demands and temptations and opportunities confronting them. There is no way an ethicist faithful to his calling can make a lasting contribution to his field except by setting an example of one who is modest enough to labor patiently at the detailed work of disentangling particular puzzles at a timely moment on behalf of specific groups, even in the knowledge that new circumstances will occasion new perplexities and render his earlier work outdated and disregarded. There is no reason why the ethicist should aspire to escape the "scandal of particularity" exemplified by One who made Himself incarnate in an obscure time and place in order to fulfill his vocation.

In seeking to fulfill his distinctive calling through aiding reflection on perplexing problems of social import, the Christian social ethicist bears a particular responsibility for helping to maintain the apparatus of moral discourse. He must seek both to promote and to resolve moral arguments. His concern to promote moral argument is rooted in the conviction that debate concerning right and wrong is the most peaceable way of settling disputes and exerting influence on others. The more that can be accomplished in moral debate the less remains to be settled by more brutal means. Hence, the ethicist will try to reinforce respect for the conventions of argument that demand that reasons be given in support of moral judgments and that principles appealed to be capable of being universalized. These conventions make it possible to draw into the universe of moral discourse matters about which someone feels strongly enough to wish to make them the subject of contention. It is to the common advantage to have this contention take the form of moral debate rather than forcible means. The British philosopher, W. D. Hudson, comments upon the function of these conventions of moral argument: "Why, then, are there these conventions of reason-giving and universalisability so far as moral judgments are concerned? The answer lies in the fact that these conventions make it, on the one hand, *possible always to open* an argument, when someone has delivered a moral judgment; and, on the other hand, impossible to *refuse to join in argument,* once one has delivered a moral judgment oneself." [9]

The utility of giving and demanding reasons for actions and testing principles for their universalizability does not rest upon a super-rationalistic view that sees all men as decisively influenced by logic or by duty to the common good. It is not necessary to hold that all men are reasonable, nor that reason is the exclusive or dominant determinant of action, in order to make the clarification of moral discourse — with all its subterfuges and rationalizations — a worthwhile contribution to the public weal. As Henry Sidgwick observed: "though we do not conceive that it is by reason alone that men are influenced to act rightly, we still hold that appeals to the reason are an essential part of all moral persuasion, and that part which concerns the moralist or moral philosopher as distinct from the preacher or moral rhetorician." [10] In certain circumstances moral persuasion may be ineffective; but it is still to the common advantage to have it potent and unpolluted as a vital resource of the common life. It is the responsibility of the ethicist to help preserve that resource against abuse and disrepair.

The Christian social ethicist's concern to promote resort to ethical discourse will be advanced only to the extent that moral debate proves in practice to be an effective means of guiding behavior and reconciling conflicts. He must therefore direct his energy and skill to the resolution of actual confusions and controversies as they occur in the lives of individuals and groups engaged in deliberation and justification of behavior. He can assist those who find themselves confused in the midst of deliberation by helping to sort out and assess conflicting senses of "ought" that may flow from conflicts of duties derived from special statuses, from obligations incurred by previous actions, promises or contracts, or from adherence to moral principles.[11]

In cases of controversy between parties contending for alternative courses of policy, the ethicist may assist by attempting to ferret out the sources of disagreement and bringing them clearly to view. In this enterprise a range of considerations nearly as broad as that of direct concern to adherents of the broad definition of Christian social ethics comes to be of indirect interest to the practitioner of the narrow version of the field. But, in the narrower view, the diverse, separate elements fit into procedures for performing a discrete and doable task of analysis of the logic of moral discourse and the origins of disagreement. The ethicist may proceed by isolating the major elements of a comprehensive argument and examining each one in detail as a potential source of difference in the course of reasoning carried on by the various participants in debate. Disagreement may have its sources in alternative understandings of at least four elements of moral argument which are always at least implicit in deliberation upon policy issues.

1. Disagreement may sometimes originate in alternative readings of the empirical facts of the situation. When discrepancies are located it may be possible to agree upon procedures for testing and correcting judgments in relation to explicit criteria.

2. But disagreement may also be rooted in the "facts" of the non-empirical theological or quasi-theological realm which determines the wider context of understanding within which men define and ponder their options. Procedures for settling disputes in this realm are clearly more difficult to construct.

3. A third source of variation stems from differences in decisions regarding the fundamental loyalties of disputants. Men may

invest meaning and give themselves over to a great variety of groups and causes. The identity of that which gives them their own identity and purpose is a most important determinant of moral reasoning, which can best be explored with the tools of social psychology, reference group theory, the analysis of ideologies, and descriptive ethics. The close attention moral philosophers have given to the examination of the reasons people give in the justification of conduct and the power of certain reasons to excite and motivate some but not others has led to a sharpening awareness that there is a great "diversity in what people count as a moral reason" and that "what can and what cannot count as a reason is determined by the communities to which they belong." [12] The study of the relation between loyalties to particular groups and causes and the prevalence of various patterns of moral reasoning represents an exciting intersection between social psychology and ethical theory, but it does not constitute the proper task of the Christian social ethicist as ethicist.

4. It is the fourth potential source of disagreement, which may be characterized as the "mode of ethical reasoning" concerned with the procedures for defining relevant considerations and alloting them appropriate weight, that should be the subject of the ethicist's expertise. The difficulties of defining the field of Christian social ethics and determining the skills necessary for those who would practice it become more evident when it is noted that common usage tolerates an ambiguous use of the phrase, "the study of ethics." In some instances, it can refer to critical reflection on the entire process of deliberation; according to our outline, this entails the four major elements of empirical factual data, theological or quasi-theological perspectives, decisions of fundamental loyalties, and modes of ethical reasoning. But, in a narrower sense, "the study of ethics" can be limited to the task of analyzing the single ingredient of the mode of ethical reasoning — the rules and habitual patterns of defining relevant considerations and assigning weights to various factors thought to bear upon the evaluation of action.

Close focus on the various modes of ethical reasoning employed by contestants in controversy may greatly aid the attempt to over-come disagreement at the level of policy recommendations. That is, the performance of the narrower task may facilitate, or may even prove indispensable to the broader interest in "casuistry" or the de-termination of right action in particular cases. Detailed study of the reasoning employed by American Christians in debating questions of nuclear arms policies from 1958 to 1963 has suggested that four distinctive styles of ethical reasoning are prevalent within the churches.[13] These alternative patterns of moral thinking differ sig-nificantly — in the style used to express ethical evaluations; direc-tives given concerning the proper starting point and priorities of policy discussion; the sense of what constitutes a good reason for arriving at a particular evaluation or directive; the related disciplines relied upon in the consideration of issues; the faculty or source of knowledge considered most indispensable for ethical reflection; how disagreement is to be understood and dealt with; the degree of spe-cificity provided in prescriptions for conduct; the tendency to en-courage or foreclose debate upon issues; and the range of potential participants considered competent to contribute to the deliberative process.

These four alternative styles of moral reasoning do not coincide with traditional, Christian theological, or denominational distinc-tions. All four types may coexist and contend within a single denom-ination creating an exceedingly complex pattern of disagreement that can only be sorted out by minute attention to actual moral dis-course on decisions of public import. To conduct such patient study in the hope of aiding reflection in the face of moral perplexity is the modest but useful task of the Christian social ethicist under the nar-row definition of his discipline.

A TRULY DISCIPLINED DISCIPLINE

Christian social ethics is a practical discipline concerned with shap-ing behavior. Those who tend toward what we have labelled the "broad definition of the field" leave the Christian social ethicist in the embarrassing and impossible position of being directly and equally responsible for understanding and influencing all the factors which shape or misshape the behavior of men in political communities. In face of the overwhelming demands of such an enterprise, they fail to provide a clear basis for determining which aspect of this immense task is most essential to their peculiar calling and which may be pared away, abandoned, or left to others as the ethicist comes to realize that he cannot master all that the broad definition would require of the qualified Christian social ethicist.

Our argument for a narrower definition of the field rests upon the recognition that the ethicist lives in an age of expanded awareness of the determinants of human behavior and increased specialization in the study of them. He cannot hope to do well all that might be required of one called on to illuminate all the factors that shape behavior. Since he can't do everything he might logically seem committed to do, he needs some basis for deciding which skills he should develop, which topics he should treat, which conversation partners he should seek out, etc.

Such decisions concerning the daily course of labor should be rooted in reflection upon the resources and unmet needs existing within ecclesiastical, academic, and political communities. Given the demands of the decision-making process, what necessary intellectual tasks would not be well provided for in the absence of the practice of Christian social ethicists? Theologians exist to criticize underlying theological beliefs. Social scientists abound to trace the impact of loyalties upon perception, evaluation and action. Specialists of all sorts immerse themselves in the detailed empirical data relating to particular issues of policy. The ethicist need not pose as an expert in one or another of these roles or hope to supersede the labors of those who have devoted themselves to such undertakings. What he needs to do is to engage these specialists in public debate on matters of public policy in a manner which affords each one the opportunity to bring his expertise to bear within the complex chain of policy thought that encompasses each of their respective specialties.

In order to draw these specialists into broad conversation, the ethicist must himself be prepared to offer a quid pro quo, he must have something to contribute that is not just a rehash of what one or another of his interlocutors knows better than he. What the ethicist can hope to know best and offer as his contribution within the division of labor which marks the communities in which he lives has to do with the understanding of the structure of the logic of moral arguments. Through repeated participation and reflection upon moral debate the ethicist may develop a capacity to foresee the moves open to defenders of particular views, to discern implications that will later unfold, to imagine counter-cases that test the consistency and coherence of values invoked, and to draw upon the experience and wisdom of forebears to design a "map" charting the pitfalls encountered along various paths of reasoning. His participation in the conversation carried on among experts for the guidance of complex decisions regarding public policy will be welcome as long as he can bring to even the most critical circle a capacity to aid others in perceiving and bringing to scrutiny the habits of thought they employ in the ubiquitous activity of evaluating choices. For the sake of his broad mission of facilitating debate upon issues of policy, the ethicist must perfect and offer up his narrower skill as an analyst of the single ingredient of moral reasoning.

The common core of a lively field of Christian social ethics must be the analysis of the logic of moral reasoning. Particular practitioners may combine expertise in this realm with interests and attainments in any one or several of the immense range of related fields that have significant bearing upon the understanding and influencing of human behavior. But what makes Christian social ethics *ethics* is its concern for the analysis of patterns of thinking about right and wrong, good and bad, just and unjust. One who calls himself a Christian social ethicist is free to spend his energies in solving theological problems, investigating empirical questions, or perfecting the skills of the social scientist. There is surely no need to prevent his making a contribution to related fields if he is able. It is simply odd to refer to what he would then be doing as Christian social ethics. It is, moreover, lamentable if, in his eagerness to be helpful, he should leave undone the distinctive task which fellow Christians, scholars, and citizens might wish him to offer as his contribution to the division of labor within the communities which have nurtured and equipped him to fulfill a calling of potential utility to all.

Reflection upon the communal setting of the vocation of the Christian social ethicist is indispensable for the definition and the performance of his task. In the theoretical definition of his field and in the practical performance of it, the ethicist must acknowledge a division of labor through which the total capacity of the network of specialties is enhanced by the willingness of each to do his task well in the confidence that others will be called and equipped to do their complementary chores. The training of Christian social ethicists can best take place within a divinity faculty located within a university; for the arena within which men are trained for the field should be the arena of public debate, of encounter among the several specialties. There should be constant conversation in which those whose minds are of a particular philosophical, or historical, or empirical, or theological, or practical bent are made to contend with others who impose upon them the habit of considering what may at first have little resonance or appeal to their habitual mode of thinking. Out of such conversation may come the mutual correction of partial perspectives and an awareness that in every turn of argument one is invading a region defended by experts prone to jealous defense of their territory. One becomes accustomed to the rules of fair trade by which one must have something of distinctive value to give in conversation in order to receive that which has cost another great effort.

There is no way the Christian social ethicist can escape the difficulties imposed by the ambiguity of the phrase, "the study of ethics." He can best proceed by a pattern of alternating focus, moving from topical attention upon a particular problem of casuistry (in which he is forced to try to comprehend the relevance of all of the elements of the decision-making paradigm) to a focus on the intense study of the logic of moral discourse that has flourished among students of philosophical ethics. Hopefully, such an alternation may lead to a spiraling effect by which each new assault upon a topical area would bring a consciousness of heightened capacity for insight into the nuances of reasoning that underlie contending policy views. The alternation would allow the ethicist to serve the community by aiding reflection, first through relieving perplexity over specific issues of policy in his topical phase, and then through the application of the specific skills honed more sharply in his philosophical phase. He may thus hope to avoid becoming a withdrawn intellectual recluse mulling over abstract questions no one else ever thought of asking while also reducing the likelihood of looking ridiculous in treating others to garbled accounts of the ABC's of their own fields. In this way, there may be some chance for the Christian social ethicist to enter into interdisciplinary discussion as a member of a truly disciplined discipline.

NOTES

1. Gibson Winter, "Introduction," *Social Ethics: Issues in Ethics and Society,* Gibson Winter, ed. (New York: Harper and Row, 1968), p. 6.
2. Walter Muelder, *Moral Law in Christian Social Ethics* (Richmond, Virginia: John Knox Press, 1966), p. 20.
3. Ibid., p. 20.
4. Kenneth Kirk, *Some Principles of Moral Theology* (London: Longmans, Green and Company, 1920), p. 8.
5. Walter Muelder, "What Has Theology to Do with Social Action?" *Nexus* X (May 1967): 8.
6. Ibid.
7. Paul Ramsey, *Basic Christian Ethics* (New York: Charles Scribner's Sons, 1954), p. 350.
8. See Peter Schwankl, "On the Phenomenon of Perplexity," *Philosophy and Phenomenological Research* XXVII (June 1967): 553–63.
9. W. D. Hudson, "On the Alleged Objectivity of Moral Judgments," *Mind* LXXI (1962): 533.
10. Henry Sidgwick, *The Methods of Ethics* (7th ed., London: Macmillan Company, 1907), available in paperback edition (New York: Dover Publications, 1966), p. 23.
11. See John Lemmon, "Moral Dilemmas," in *Christian Ethics and Contemporary Philosophy,* Ian T. Ramsey, ed. (New York: Macmillan Company, 1966), pp. 262–79, first printed in *Philosophical Review* LXXI (1962): 139–58.
12. R. W. Beardsmore, *Moral Reasoning* (New York: Schocken Books, 1969), p. 137.
13. See Ralph B. Potter, "The Structure of Certain American Christian Responses to the Nuclear Dilemma, 1958–1963" (Th.D. diss., Harvard Divinity School, 1965), pp. 360–401.

PART II

Ethics, Power, and Strategy

5 Toward a Christian Understanding
of Power   *Tex S. Sample*

Many Christians have the uncomfortable feeling that the use of power is an unbaptized activity. The position in this paper is that we cannot remove ourselves from power struggles because they present us with what William James used to call "live options." To choose *not* to choose *is* itself a choice which runs the same theological and ethical hazards as the conscious acceptance of choice. This is because we are involved in mankind and cannot extricate ourselves from the human condition and destiny. This is not true only for individual Christians; the Church itself cannot avoid the problem of power. If she chooses *not* to enter power conflicts she finds herself in complicity with the powers-that-be and thus contributes to their continuation. She may both accommodate to and challenge the power order. She may throw herself against it completely; or, of course, she may simply escape into an ecclesiastical womb, leaving the field open for those with less vulnerable stomachs. It is worth noting that this last alternative does not avoid the problem of power; it surrenders decision to others. I shall argue for a ministry of empowerment by the Church in response to God's activity in history.

Power is defined as the capacity to transact or impose control through the recognition, threat, or use of sanctions. Our definition, first of all, deals with both reciprocal and asymmetrical power. Many discussions of power deal only with asymmetrical relationships, contending, with Peter Blau, that "interdependence and mutual influence of equal strength indicate lack of power."[1] Dennis Wrong's view seems more compelling when he argues that the "asymmetry of power relations is at least immanent in the 'give-and-take' of dyadic interaction between equals, in which the control of one actor over the other's behavior is reciprocated by a responsive act of control on the part of the other." Thus asymmetry is present in each individual act-response sequence, but power shifts in the alternating initiatives of control. Wrong also points out that power may be relatively equal between parties because each has control of different spheres or scopes; thus the power of one party in a given sphere is countered by the second party in yet another sphere.[2] Hence, in this paper, transactional power shall refer to reciprocally negotiated control between two or more parties. Imposed power shall refer to relationships in which one party dominates another with the latter unable to maintain control reciprocity.

The second factor in this definition distinguishes power from influence, which is the inducement of desired behavior from others without the use of sanctions. While these can be analytically distinguished, they are inseparable and hopelessly mixed in social interaction. Thirdly, the definition includes both positive and negative sanctions. Definitions which restrict power to negative sanctions rule out massive territories of power, ignoring some of its most salient forms. Intersanctional power shall refer to the ability of each group to grant or withhold gratification or penalty to the relatively equal enrichment or detriment of the other. Finally, sanctions can be both material and normative, i.e., relating either to material interest, normative values, or both.

CREATED POWER

The God of Christian faith is one who is active in all events, and we as Christians are called to respond to Him. His activity manifests itself in three expressions as Creator, Judge, and Redeemer. He is the Creator of a good creation, the Judge of its fallen sinfulness, and the Redeemer who seeks to release it from bondage. With this understanding of God's activity I shall discuss power in three aspects: created power, corrupted power, and redeemed power.

God is the source of all there is, and nothing in existence is intrinsically evil. All of the creation is finite and dependent upon its source, but finitude and dependency are good. Power is theologically good and ethically premoral and neutral. Theologically, power is a central process of human existence. It is a gift of God and is therefore good. It is good in God's intentionality. God as revealed in Jesus Christ does not intend a world where the powerful dominate the powerless. Rather, he intends a community of mankind offering their diverse talents and skills in divisions of labor which fulfill each person and provide the greatest good for all of God's creatures. Power then is not meant to be the possession of one group and poverty the property of another; but power is intended to be shared so that all' men shape the systems of control required for finite existence and participate in the decisions which affect their welfare. Ultimately God wills that all men might be co-creators with Him in the righteous rule of His Kingdom.

From an ethical perspective, power is premoral in that choice depends upon some modicum of power if a person is to express his will in the affairs of people. To be without power is to be without the capacity to bear history, to be a history-making creature. Power is a precondition of moral decision-making; at the most fundamental level, without power one cannot be human.

Power is ethically neutral in that God's intentionality does not override man's freedom. Power is of God, but like all gifts of creation man has the freedom to misuse it, to throw his power around in such a way as to disembowel justice and cast out love. The elemental potentialities and structures of life are always threatened by the demonic simply because they are so elemental and man's misuse of freedom involves them.

God as creator has made power good, but it has also become corrupt. We must turn then to a discussion of power in its fallen condition and God's judgment upon it in alienation and broken relationships.

CORRUPTED POWER

God acts in human history as judge. When men sin and in faithlessness turn from God, they find judgment, they find "the wrath of God." E. Clinton Gardiner argues that the wrath of God "does not mean that God acts out of anger after the fashion of our purely natural impulses."[3] Rather the wrath of God symbolically conveys the self-destructive character of evil. God has willed into being a moral order and men play "fast and loose" with it at their peril; for when the created goodness of power is misused by sinful men, it becomes corrupt and the users violate and dehumanize people. Corrupt power has a self-destructive character which expresses itself in separation and alienation of people from each other and from God. In this section an interpretation of the corruption of power will be made as it relates to a conception of human nature which includes social and cultural dimensions.

Human Nature and Power. No Christian thinker in the twentieth century has had more influence on the understanding of power than Reinhold Niebuhr. His view of the nature of man and its role in power and political process has dominated Christian social ethics for almost forty years. Man, in Niebuhr's view, is a finite creature whose nature bridges animal vitalities and self-transcendence, with faith enabling him to live creatively in a tension between these two. Yet, the anxiety of his finite freedom occasions — not causes — his temptation to sin. The basic source of this temptation is man's inclination to misunderstand the contingent character of his existence either by denying his finitude and attempting to escape into pure freedom (arrogance), or by losing himself in creaturely vitalities (sloth). Dan Rhoades suggests that the "subjective root of the former would be pride, and the objective form would be idolatry. The subjective root of the latter would be sloth, and its objective form would be sensuality."[4]

This basic aspect of human nature makes corruption inevitable in human existence. In man's social and political life Niebuhr sees arrogance manifesting itself in self-love and the will-to-power, with man's egotistic inclinations compounded in group life. The group is more arrogant, hypocritical, self-centered, and ruthless in pursuit of its ends than the individual. Thus sinful pride and idolatry are inevitable concomitants of the cohesion of large political groups. Conscience and sense of guilt are immensely weakened in man's collective life, and such altruistic motives as persons have can be used — even sacrificially — in behalf of the most egotistic, arrogant ends of a race, class, or nation. The corruption of power for Niebuhr, then, grows out of the struggle between freedom and finitude in man's nature with the inevitable consequence of man's arrogance and egotism being exacerbated in collective life.[5]

In this view, a relative social justice requires a balance of power to the end of time. Short of a balance of power, justice becomes simply the will of the stronger. Thus the arrogance and egotism of groups must be checked in a balance of power. Only then will individual groups receive a hearing and stand a chance of consideration in the adjudication of the conflicting and competing claims they make.

In our view two fundamental problems mar Niebuhr's analysis. The first is the one-sided use he makes of his anthropology; he neglects sloth in his overemphasis on self-love and arrogance in analyzing political issues and power relations. John C. Raines sketches the application of sloth to both the powerless and the affluent, with emphasis on the latter. Niebuhr's "keen insight into self-love, pride and pretentiousness . . . needs to be balanced with Marx's sensitivity to the self-loss, passivity and false consciousness that seduce and vitiate mankind from the opposite direction."[6]

Niebuhr's insight needs to be completed with Marx, who saw man as a maker of things go through a reversal in which man became a thing. As a result he retreats into passivity and self-hatred.

Sloth can thus be useful in understanding the affluent. The growing privatism of American society is a case in point. Those in privileged groups in the society may not use their status for arrogant, direct exploitation of others. Rather they function uncritically within established society. They unwittingly sustain unequal power relations and social injustice, while escaping to patios, campers, summer lodges, spectator recreation and the like. Or they bury themselves in work. If life is not good, then judgment is turned in upon the self to change one's attitudes, think more positively, or to escape from unhappy thoughts in more consumption or compulsive career pursuits. Not only does this perpetuate injustice; it also avoids participation in decisions which shape the society and leaves a vacuum to be filled by those prepared to sustain and increase established injustices.

In the case of the powerless poor, sloth is expressed in the "culture of poverty." For some this means the poor are impoverished because of the values they hold — e.g., fatalism or the unwillingness to postpone immediate gratification for the sake of long range gain — which are a result of improper socialization into the dominant values of the society. This, in effect, blames poverty on the poor and frees the wider society from its responsibility. I think sloth has greater interpretive power if we understand the values of the poor as realistic adaptations to powerlessness and the structural realities they confront in society. Sloth may then be seen in the escape into apathy, depressant drugs, and violence against one's self or against one's own group. In this view, the values of the poor are not primarily learned through improper socialization but are adaptations to the constraints they face. The fault is not then in the flawed family structure of the powerless, but in the structures the family faces and cannot control. This is not to remove all accountability from the poor but to place primary responsibility where it belongs: on society rather than its victims.

Parenthetically, this raises a question as to what extent one freely chooses this kind of sloth. Does one do so simply in response to the anxiety of finitude, or is one pressed into it by the unbearable state of one's social condition? Sloth, seen simply as escape from anxiety, fails to account for the role of social factors in driving persons toward this variety of sin. It does not adequately deal with the role of the external factors which victimize people, both affluent and poor, into slothfulness. This raises the next point.

The second fundamental problem in Niebuhr's analysis is his

tendency to see political and social phenomena as the outgrowth of individual tendencies in the nature of man. By so basing his political analysis he tends to see collective groups as the individual writ large, and by treating social structures as individual reifications he over-simplifies or neglects the emergent structure and dynamics of human collectivities. For example, Niebuhr's use of the balance-of-power model falls into this category. "That is, the balance of power model is predicated upon the treatment of nations as discreet individual actors seeking their egoistic, egotistic, and prideful ends through the instrumentality of power. Then after rigidifying this structure, he insists that other actions which are the expression of other tendencies and capacities must be forced into the restrictive boundaries of this mold to be 'relevant.' " [7]

Niebuhr's concentration on arrogance and egotism and his view of human collectivities as individuals writ large are reasons for his failure to use sloth with more depth than he did. More than that it kept Niebuhr from looking at power and its role in structured social fields. Balance of power is much too imprecise, static, and simplistic to account for the complexities of power in human societies. Put bluntly, Niebuhr's political analysis is guilty of anthropological re-ductionism.

A fuller understanding of the corruption of power — and its re-demption — must take into account the socio-cultural structures in which human nature expresses itself. For one thing, human nature, individualistically conceived, cannot fully account for cohesion in human societies. How can one account for stability and order as well as change in society simply on the basis of such a view of the nature of man? A fuller understanding of power must take into account cooperating and antagonistic structures of interests and their relationship to value-informed patterns of behavior. These are levels of reality not reducible to Niebuhr's view of human nature.

In modern sociology two schools of thought are feuding over pre-cisely this point. One view, the functionalist, accounts for order and stability by means of a consensus shared by persons and groups around cultural values. People are able to cooperate and sustain soci-ety because of their basic orientation to nature, personality, and society. The other view, the conflict school, maintains that stability and order are based on coercion. Order is the result of groups and persons being constrained by other groups and persons. Society does not float on a sea of ethics (ethos), but people fulfill roles in structures oriented around interests, and change results from the antagonistic struggles of conflicting interest groups. To my mind, these two views represent different perspectives of society, and as perspectives they are accurate. Neither view is accurate alone. Both of them are needed for a fuller comprehension of human nature and the place of power in society. I shall discuss each view as it relates to the question of power and attempt a synthesis of them, toward the end that a more comprehensive understanding of the corruption of power and its redemption will emerge. Thus, a brief excursion will be necessary before we return to the corruption of power later in this section.

Human Nature and the Constraint System. Niebuhr's treatment of nations as individual actors fails to deal with the highly complex and differentiated character of what I shall call the constraint system in human society. The constraint system is the interest structure of a collectivity. It is not a monolith of shared interests but a nexus of cooperating, competing, and conflicting interest-structures stabilized by multidimensional constraints. Horizontal constraints are those exercised by groups relatively equal in power with coinciding or competing interests. Vertical constraints occur when a powerful collectivity controls another, the latter being without sufficient power to prevent or check it.

Such a complex phenomenon cannot be reduced to an individual actor because the kind of coordination or integration implied in such a reduction is a distortion. Harvey Wheeler describes modern nations as "massive, bureaucratized states composed of entrenched and institutionalized power blocs. Elites from industry, politics, the military, and science and technology furnish the internal factions of a shifting, amorphous, permeable confederation." He goes beyond this to argue that we are involved in a new kind of international politics in which one nation conducts its international affairs so as to influence the domestic policy of another nation. He illustrates this by citing President Kennedy's attempt, during the closing days of his administration, to strengthen Khrushchev's hand in the Soviet Union. "Each of the great nations is involved in the domestic politics of the other and each 'participates' in the selection of the other side's leaders and programs. Balance-of-power politics now works on an entirely new foundation. It is not states as wholes that are bargained for and against. In each of the major countries domestic power factions work to influence and control the political profile of the coalitions that rule the world." [8]

While Wheeler wishes to call this a new kind of balance-of-power politics, I think the balance-of-power concept needs to be abandoned. It seems too simplistic, too static to capture the complex phenomena Wheeler describes. Nevertheless, Wheeler's discussion does illustrate the character of the constraint system in modern society. And while less modern societies may not be so complex, I seriously question the existence of monolithic constraint systems.

In any case, it is clear that a thorough-going conception of human nature must come to terms with the constraint dimension of social life when attempting to deal with power. What such an understanding does to power analysis can be very simply illustrated. If a leader makes a decision in behalf of his nation's interest, it may or may not be the result of an arrogant will-to-power; but it will almost certainly be a brokered decision — an attempt by the leader to come to terms with the competing and contending interest-structures in his own country as well as the implications of his decision in other nations. When we attempt to define power order below, some of the implications of this understanding of the structure of interests of a collectivity will be apparent.

However, we cannot address the question of power until we have looked at the role of cultural values and normative sanctions in power analysis. Our conception of human nature must come to terms with them as well.

Human Nature and Cultural Values. Man is a valuing being. Values which he shares intersubjectively with other members of a collectivity (nation, class, race, organization) and which are expressed in certain orientations to reality, nature, and human existence, we shall call the consensus system of social cohesion. These cultural values are emergent realities of the social interaction of valuing persons. The work of Walter G. Muelder helps us extend the conception of human nature at this point because of his long interest in this field. He argues from "the assumption that cultures (also nations, states, civilizations) are social systems which constitute more or less organic wholes and that the cohesive or integrative factor in such wholes is self-enforcing (not the externally coercive or violently imposed) values and meanings." [9] His thought therefore represents a corrective of Niebuhr's too-exclusive fascination with power realities.

Moreover, this emphasis in Muelder's writing keeps before us the question of the impact of cultural ethos on the constraint system of society. The material interests of a society are informed by cultural values even as the latter reflect in part the former. This interactive relationship must be kept in mind in power analysis as we soon shall see.

My problem with Muelder's systematic work is his tendency to make cultural ethos *the* determinant of society, or at least the major determinant. While he has consistently resisted the idea of any single institutional sector — such as the economic sector — as the determinant, the implicit construction of his societal model commits him basically to a monocausal view. That is, Muelder's placement of institutional sectors in a multicausal social system which rests on a cultural ethos leaves the institutional sectors at a secondary level of causation and makes cultural values the basic determinants of society. For example, he states that "the church needs to regain its assurance that it is the ethos, the system of value-impregnated beliefs, that holds society together. This means, further, that the church must steadfastly believe that self-enforcing values in society are more basic and operationally more powerful than externally coercive measures. The church must regain its faith in and sense of responsibility for the fundamental ethos of society." [10]

What is most troublesome in the quote above and in Muelder's systematic work in general is his reliance on an implicit functional/consensus model of society. The theoretical framework of a consensus model focuses one's attention away from what I have called the constraint system of society. Moreover, the model itself fails to come adequately to terms with the intercausal relation of cultural values and material interests. Social cohesion results from both; but, empirically speaking, the cohesion may rest more on one than the other at a given time in a given setting.[11]

Thus, while we are indebted to Muelder for his important corrective in Christian social ethics, we must move to new societal models to deal more comprehensively and coherently with the question of power. The contributions of a consensus model of society and a coercive model must be brought together in a way that utilizes the salient insights of each.

Toward a New Synthesis. Gerhard E. Lenski has worked out a synthesis which I am not willing to endorse, but I find his method for doing so especially helpful. He suggests two ways of reformulating problems and concepts in the feud between consensus and conflict theories of society. The first is "the technique of *transforming categorical concepts into variable concepts.*"[12] Because categorical concepts force one into either-or thinking, the forced choice leads to acceptance of an inadequate, faulty view. Variable concepts, however, ask instead to what degree a given phenomenon is present — e.g., the constraint or the consensus system. This then leaves the question open to empirical findings with respect to a given class or society and the relative control of the constraint and consensus system. The assumption is that consensus and constraint systems exist in a given collectivity but their relative causal powers await empirical substantiation.

"The second technique involves *breaking down compound concepts into their constituent elements.*"[13] While this obviously cannot be done here in detail, I would like to illustrate this technique by an attempt at synthesis around the concept of social role. Role is a basic building block in the construction of sociological theory. A synthesis at this point could lead eventually to a resolution of the conflict between the two models of society and will enable us to discuss power with greater conceptual clarity.

A role can be diagramed geometrically as two overlapping circles. One circle represents the consensus system's delineation of expectations and the other circle the expectations of the constraint system. Each circle has an "inner space," a "free" zone where the individual may move as he will. This free zone is supported by positive sanctions, and role players are induced sanctionally and otherwise to play their roles within the free zone. The line which forms the circle, however, is a boundary. Movement beyond that boundary carries with it heavily sanctioned reprisal.

The circles overlap. Theoretically, it is logically conceivable that the circles could be in perfect congruity or in separate isolation. In any case, the overlap indicates some congruity between cultural ethos and structural interests, and lack of full congruity conveys potential or actual conflict within the role. The point is this: these concepts are variable and represent an attempt to pull together consensus and conflict models of society in a way that does not prejudice the relative power of each in determining human behavior. This question is left open to empirical verification.[14]

Moreover, this conception brings into focus at the point of social role what Alvin Gouldner calls a basic societal dilemma. "The dilemma is this: the class and power system [very close in his language to what I have called the constraint system] require, for their stability, a differentiated moral system and a rewarding prestige hierarchy; but the more 'autonomous' they become, the greater becomes the likelihood of strain between the two systems. In other words, one major source of the endemic tension between the 'ideal' and the 'actual' in social systems is that a distinct class and power system *must* create a moral system whose values oppose it."[15] Gouldner's dilemma fits well the role model suggested here. Moreover, this conception of role and Gouldner's dilemma can be applied to a person or to a collectivity such as the nation. What it does is to relate the interest structure and the cultural ethos of society to individual selves whose intersubjectivity is their precondition.

In sum, we have argued for a conception of human nature that includes Niebuhr's insight but expands it to include the constraint dimension in a more systematic and less individualized way and to include Muelder's abiding emphasis on the consensus system. Moreover, the conception of social role advanced here will enable us to come to a more comprehensive understanding of power in human societies. We shall now turn to that.

The Power Order. A banker once told me that I should quit talking about the Social Gospel and speak only about personal salvation, because that "would solve all our problems." I asked him if he regarded himself as a "saved Christian," and we both agreed that he probably was. I then asked if he, as a saved Christian, supported progressive or regressive taxation. He indicated the former. Next I asked if as an officer of the bank, he would order the lobbyists of the bank to oppose regressive measures and work for progressive ones. He informed me that I was "talking preacher talk," that any "practical man" knew that he absolutely could not do that no matter how much he wanted it. "I have to work for the interests of our investors. Why, if I did what you suggest, they'd fire me!" What I think this story illustrates is the fact that cultural values like success and achievement inform banking institutions and shape their orientations, thus forming a congruity with the interlocked interests of banks with their investors, other persons, organizations, corporations, and the like. My banker friend was right; he could not remain as a vice president and pursue the action I suggested because it led to collision with the ethos and interest structure of the bank and other groups related to it. He would have had to violate the sanctioned boundaries of his role. He could not do that and stay in the bank.

We have defined power as the ability to transact or impose control through the recognition, threat, or use of sanction. Institutionally conceived, power is power order: the organized, sanctioned control system of social cohesion. At the point of its greatest power it is both normatively and materially based. The constraint system seeks legitimation from cultural ethos and the latter seeks concreteness and relevance in the former. The continual struggle of the power order within is the matter of congruity between values and interests.

Power order is to be differentiated from power structure. Arnold

Rose's distinction between the demand and supply aspects of power is useful at this point.

We would . . . call attention to the fact that power has both a supply and a demand side. Historically most writers on power emphasized the supply side: the existence of some people or organizations which were able to control others. Recently it has become fashionable to emphasize the demand side: the requirement of all societies, or organizations, if they are to continue to exist, to have some means of ordering the relations of men to achieve at least minimal needs. Just as in economics, where supply determines price in the short run and demand determines it in the long run, so the characteristics and techniques of the power elites determine the actualities of power in the short run, but the basic culture and social structure of a society determines the actualities in the long run. Both the short run and the long run are important, as each accommodates to the other.[16]

My use of the term "power order" seeks to grasp conceptually the demand aspect of power as it relates to the structure of sanctioned control. I see power structures attempting to perform brokerage functions among the cooperating, competing, and conflicting interest structures and seeking legitimation from cultural ethos. Thus, possible decisions posed for society must go through a filtering process, percolating, as it were, through value and interest structures. The society makes demands for leadership and offers power structures filtered options. The power structure then makes decisions from among a range of alternatives constricted and shaped by the power order.

This distinction makes some sense out of the outcries by the black community and the youth culture against the power structure. Studies of community power in metropolitan centers—where most of these outcries are heard—again and again indicate the presence of pluralistic power structures, not monolithic ones. I suspect the protests of the black community against the power structure are responses to the filtered options of the institutionalized racism of the power order and not simply to some small group of decision-makers. And the youth culture too attacks a system that in its established power order simply is not now open to the options they want, nor as soon as they demand.

The Corruption of Power Order. Power order as such is good. Society must have some order or human existence is not possible. The constraint of the power order provides continuity and can function to control human caprice. Also, man's arrogant attempt to serve self and the interest-limited orientation of many organizations require containment. The problem, of course, is when the power order frustrates the conditions for community and violates authentic human existence.

For illustrative purposes I would like to select three cases of the corruption of power order which relate to the synthesis model worked out above.

First, the kind or mix of cultural values informing power order can contribute to its corruption. Cultural values may be demonic, and the values of power order may center around racism, materialism, militarism, or idolatrous nationalism. It is theoretically conceivable that inordinate inequalities of power could be equalized and yet two groups could be in an unholy deadlock of war of all against all, with values which glorify violence and chauvinism. The corruption of power may thus reside in dehumanizing cultural values.

The corruption of power order may also result from a certain mix of cultural values. In the history of the United States this can be seen in a jagged disjunction between individual freedom and the belief in equality of opportunity. The American understanding of individual freedom lacks a conception of integral justice, and equality of opportunity really means the right to "parity in competition."[17] Tocqueville captured the essence of the American's problem with freedom to achieve and equality: "The same equality that renders him independent of each of his fellow citizens, taken severally, exposes him alone and unprotected to the influence of the greater number." Then when the American "comes to survey the totality of his fellows and to place himself in contrast with so huge a body, he is instantly overwhelmed by the sense of his own insignificance and weakness." John B. Kirby sees violence in America as related directly to the aggression generated by the tension and frustration of this cultural contradiction.[18] Perhaps, however, a quote attributed to Charles Dickens — which I cannot locate — captured the contradiction in one of its most demonic expressions: "'Every man for himself and God for us all,' shouted the elephant as he danced among the chickens."

Second, power order can be corrupted in the disjunction between cultural values and the structural opportunities of the constraint system. In the United States the cultural system induces high expectations of success and achievement in the face of constricted structural opportunity for most of its population. Cultural values promote the American dream in a population where, by its own standards, less than a majority of its people have a minimal but adequate income.[19] This disjunction creates a false consciousness among the less powerful, taking the pressure off the society for change and sowing self-condemnation and blame among the losers while bestowing prestige and honor upon the privileged.

Third, power order is corrupted in the interest structures of society when sharp disparities of power provide the privileged with victims to exploit in the pursuit of their own interests. Then to be powerless is to be without adequate access to and control of social institutions and organizations which offer full shares in society's goods and services, to lack transactional and intersanctional power and thus to be the victim in the vertical constraints of the power order and loser in such vertical conflicts as occur. To be powerless is to be empty-handed in the adjudication of competing and conflicting interests, and to suffer injustice, exploitation, and — for the poor — suffocating oppression. Dominating power violates the powerless, depriving people of dignity and hope, distorting identity and contributing to the denigration of self and a sense of worthlessness. It presses people into a sloth of the most inhuman kind, wherein one gives oneself to apathy and despair because one is worn out by oppression and barricaded life chances.

To be powerful at the expense of others is to hold benefits and privileges one only partially deserves and to have inordinate access to and control of institutions and organizations. Inordinate power is social cannibalism, feasting in luxury on the fruits of society which others need for survival. Inordinate power leads to an exalted view of one's worth and accomplishments. It violates God's intentions for community. Even its "charity" is paternalistic and degrading.

REDEEMED POWER

History is where we find the realities of corrupted power, but it is also where we find God's activity. He is the Lord of history at work throughout his creation seeking to redeem it from the bondage of sin and death. This is not to identify God with everything that happens in history; to be history's Lord does not mean to be its dictator. It does mean that God moves in the affairs of men and that history draws its meaning from Him. His work is not confined to "spiritual" enclaves or colonies or atomistic individuals. Rather, God works also in the hard, angular junctures of existence, the places where men are destroyed and made. No corner of life, no process of history, no expression of creation can shut Him out.

He is the out-of-bondage-bringing God. He works to emancipate people from the slaveries of alien principalities and powers. The One who created the world and became incarnate in Jesus Christ has through His Spirit become indwelling in history, and lands which oppress and deny men dignity are arenas of God's liberating activity. One such arena is that of power order. He comes to deliver his people from powerlessness to promised fulfillment. God has also called out a community of faith and this section of the paper will deal with the response of the church to God's activity in the redemption of power. Because of God's liberating activity and because he loved us we are enabled to love him and to express our gratitude in love for others. Let us then turn first to a discussion of faith expressing itself in love of neighbor and the relationship of this love to power.

Power, Responsible Society and Reconciliation. What is the response of the Church to God's activity in history? A faithful response is one that lives in trust of God, which seeks to ascertain God's liberating activity and join him in the work of the future — the fulfillment of God's intentions for his creation. We shall look at the response of faithfulness as it expresses itself in love in three aspects. The first is love in its personal dimension. What does it mean to love one's neighbor? From Jesus' Good Samaritan story we gather that human need lays a neighbor claim upon us, and faithfulness expresses itself in personal concern for our neighbor's welfare. From the perspective of the Christian church we understand that the person who loves humanity but cannot stand people is not faithful; Christian love must be intensely personal.

It must also be social. As difficult as loving the neighbor is in personal relations, it is even more difficult when considered in terms of the thousands and millions of persons with whom we share society and international destiny. In these complicated relationships neighbor needs bombard us constantly. To meet these needs in any sense requires that love of neighbor distribute itself into a concern for responsible society. "A responsible society is one where freedom is the freedom of men who acknowledge responsibility to justice and public order, and where those who hold political authority or economic power are responsible for its exercise to God and the people whose welfare is affected by it." Abstractly considered, the responsible society is a composite norm of freedom, justice, equality, and order which interpenetrate and work in polar tension with each other.[20] Thus the second expression of faith in love is through the actualization of the interpenetrating and tensional claims of responsible society.

The third expression is love as reconciliation. This is the ministry which seeks reunion of the separated, to bring back together those who have been alienated.[21] Ultimately this means reconciliation of people to each other and to God. In its full sense love as reconciliation is the fulfillment of love as responsible society.

Power complicates this picture. Love of neighbor and love as responsible society are frustrated by a demonic power order. The interpenetrating and tensional claims of responsible society are not sustained in the face of sharp inequities of power, whether conceived domestically or internationally. Responsible society cannot be built around a demonic power order. To put it positively, *a power order characterized by transactional and intersanctional power is a neces-*

sary but not sufficient condition for responsible society. It is necessary because the adjudication of the claims of persons and groups to the rights, privileges, goods, and services of society is not carried out responsibly in the face of institutionalized power disparities. This is partly a result of man's egotism, of course, but by no means wholly so. A demonic order by the very fact that it is *order* has crushing effects upon powerless persons.

However, while necessary, a relatively equitable power order is not sufficient for responsible society. When seen as love distributed, as the institutionalization of social justice, responsible society cannot be reduced to reciprocal prudence between groups capable of helping or damaging each other. Social justice involves ingredients of its own beyond prudential calculations. The integral justice of responsible society requires that human groups and nations go beyond power stand-offs; it requires vision and planning beyond begrudged concessions. Integral justice requires: (1) a fair ordering of society with equal opportunities institutionalized into the life chances of all; (2) political, legal, social and economic systems which nourish freedom and articulate together in behalf of persons; (3) the absence of overt and covert violence, and so on. To be sure, social justice in history is relative and partial, but to reduce it to the prudential reciprocity of a balance of power constitutes an inadequate faithfulness to the power of God in history and reduces Christian love to spectatorship since it has no special contribution to make to the calculated, mutual brokerage of greed.

The ministry of reconciliation, as we have seen, is a response of the Church to God's activity. As the fulfillment of love is social justice, reconciliation between human groups does not occur in the absence of social justice. There is no reconciliation between the oppressor and the oppressed until the oppression is ended, between the exploiter and the exploited until the exploitation is stopped. Put positively, *responsible society or social justice is a necessary but not sufficient condition for reconciliation*. Reconciliation is an event of oneness between people and groups when the dividing walls of hostility have been broken down. In one sense this has already occurred in the completed act of Christ's atoning death. (Ephesians 2:12–17). Yet, its benefits await appropriation by the coming generations of men. (II Corinthians 5:14–21, esp. vs. 20.) Reconciliation is a gift received and a vision of hope, and the church is called to be the ambassador of Christ and agent of reconciliation among men.

In sum, a sequential relationship exists between power order, responsible society, and reconciliation. A relatively equitable power order is a necessary but not sufficient condition for responsible society and the latter is a necessary but not sufficient condition for reconciliation. Let it also be clear that there is nothing automatic about the sequence. An equitable power order does not guarantee social justice. For example, it often occurs that two groups are relatively equal in power, but the relationship is one of deadlock rather than social justice. Also with social justice and reconciliation, two groups may be characterized by the former in their relationships but not by the latter.

Strategic Implications. On the basis then of what we have said about power, responsible society, and reconciliation, what are the strategic implications for the church? I shall discuss these from the perspective of the societal dilemma posed above. For our purposes a strategy of attack against a demonic power order and the social reconstruction of a new one must make three challenges. And while we distinguish them here, they are, of course, not separable in practice. Moreover, these guidelines will have to be adapted to a given context.

The first challenge is to the established constraint system. The constraint system of a responsible society should be characterized by a pluralism of legitimate interests with the claims of all represented in the power order. Where powerless groups have been pressed down, a sharp consciousness of their material interests and mobilization around them is necessary to counter other interest structures. When latent interests become manifest and people are mobilized around them, power is created through organization. Moreover, as people become more equally represented in the constraint system, covert violence against the formerly powerless sharply diminishes and overt violence, whether of an expressive or instrumental sort, wanes because those with newly found power now have something to lose, and those who formerly dominated them find it in their interest to deal with them in a different way. Ralf Dahrendorf has argued that vertically antagonistic conflicts of this type decrease in violence when (a) political and social conditions exist which allow for organization around structural interests; (b) when the "absolute deprivation of rewards and facilities on the part of a subjected class gives way to relative deprivation"; and (c) the conflict is effectively regulated (I would say politicized). What this means is that challenges to the constraint system do not have to be violent. However, continued deprivation of the material interests of the powerless is covert violence, and the unwillingness of the established constraint system to be open to politicized change in the face of an awakened powerless people encourages the eruption of overt violence.[22]

The second challenge comes at the point of the congruity of the constraint and consensus systems. In terms of our geometric conception, a demonic power order can be challenged by reducing the overlap of material interests and cultural values. By calling into question unjust distributions of the society's goods and by providing new definitions and perspectives of legitimacy, strain between the consensus and constraint systems can be generated.

We must mention in this connection the enormous influence of "servant weakness" in affecting power order. There are times when empowerment has no chance against the iron heel of totalitarian power. Then the blood of martyrs must corrode the foundations of dictatorial coercion and bring it down. In terms of our analysis, martyrdom reveals the blatant inhumanity of institutionalized cruelty and withdraws its legitimation. Moreover, it often sharpens the sensitivities of different oppressed people to their structurally shared interests and to the antagonism of those interests with those of an exploitative system—important first steps in the development of rebellion. This is not to suggest that martyrdom is always strategic but that God's emancipation can work through weakness.

The third challenge is to the consensus system. The ways in which men define their conditions and situations have far-reaching effects on their lives. Man's capacity to define, to name, was given to him by God (according to Scripture), and this capacity is one of his most distinguishing characteristics. It makes him capable of bearing and passing on culture. It makes of man a maker of culture and history; it also makes him a victim of them. In the face of a demonic power order, new cultural values must be constructed and some old ones redefined or destroyed. Constructively, the innovations of charismatic leaders and the support of social movements which give expression to new values and concretize them in experimental institutions and alternate life-styles are characteristic of some ways cultural change has taken place in the past. To detonate established values, it may be necessary to alienate people from cherished cultural myths. If United States citizens see the entirety of their history as one in which our forefathers' "stern impassioned stress a thoroughfare for freedom beat across the wilderness," then it needs to be made clear that some of the very men who signed the Declaration of Independence—affirming that all men were created equal—were at that very time slave masters and continued a conscious, willful participation in the system of chattel slavery; and that at the time of the signing one American in five was a slave. If people believe pioneers were nothing but courageous, goodly people, then the record of our nation's treatment of the Indian should be simply and dispassionately, but accurately, made known. That women were among the last to be given the right to vote, and that every immigrant group from Southern Europe, not to mention Asia, has had to force its way to the rights and privileges of our society are counter facts for cherished myths. The destruction of established perceptions is painful but it may be necessary. Nonetheless, let the basic note be positive. The task is construction, and the responsibility of the Church to pour its message into the ethos of society is more basic to its responsibilities than simply calling the beast by its name — as important as that is.

Finally, theologians and strategists of cultural change should keep in mind at least two problems. The first is that a cultural ethos is populated with unintended consequences. If one accepts even the broad outlines of Weber's thesis regarding the Protestant ethic and the spirit of capitalism, it suggests the kind of distortion which was perpetrated on Calvin's teaching. The "works righteousness" of later generations was hardly consonant with the vision he projected. We cannot control the effects of all we do, especially in attempts to shape ethos. Purveyors of simplistic notions of cultural change would do well to take this caveat into account. While this should throw cold water on any romantic utopianism, we should not cast out hope, for despair is as serious in faithlessness as idolatrous utopias. Worship of the "realism" of one's position is commensurate with the adoration of some human vision of achievement. We must respond to the activity of God with realism and vision; to sever either from that response is to answer as partial men.

The second problem is the incredible malleability of cultural values. Human collectivities are capable of legitimating the most wicked enterprises thinkable in the name of values such as freedom, justice, equality and public order. A prophetic ministry exposes the cardboard facades of morality covering man's inhumanity to man. In this the Church has a monitoring as well as a naming function to perform.

In summary, the redemption of power takes place when men respond to the emancipating activity of God in both the constraint and consensus systems of society. Liberation in the constraint system comes with the empowerment of the powerless so that people in human collectivities have transactional and intersanctional power to participate in decisions affecting their welfare and intrinsic to their fulfillment. Liberation in the consensus system comes through strengthening and infusing cultural ethos with values which enhance human life and permeate the power order so that constraints exist for people, not people for constraints.

CONCLUSION

This view of a Christian understanding of power attempts to relate a confessional statement about God's activity to a view of the nature of man which includes socio-cultural dimensions. Several conclusions may be derived from the paper. First, power is good. It is good in God's intentionality and as his gift. God made men to find fulfillment with Him as a community of co-creators making history. Secondly, power is corrupt. As abuses of freedom, arrogant power and slothful irresponsibility are forms of its corruption. Corrupt power also victimizes people against their wills especially when institutionalized at the level of societal order and/or when organized around dehumanizing cultural values. It violates men and constricts opportunities for selfhood, growth, and community. Finally, power is redeemed in the emancipating activity of God. He is breaking down the captivity structures of man. The response of the Church to God involves a ministry of empowerment and the humanization of cultural ethos.

NOTES

1. Peter Blau, *Exchange and Power in Social Life* (New York: John Wiley and Sons, 1964), p. 118.

2. Dennis H. Wrong, "Some Problems in Defining Power," *American Journal of Sociology,* 73 (May 1968): 673–74.

3. E. Clinton Gardiner, *Biblical Faith and Social Ethics* (New York: Harper and Row, 1960), p. 111.

4. Dan Rhoades, "The Prophetic Insight and Theoretical-Analytical Inadequacy of Christian Realism," *Ethics* 70 (October 1964): 81.

5. Among Reinhold Niebuhr's works, see *Moral Man and Immoral Society* (New York: Charles Scribner's Sons, 1949); *Faith and History* (New York: Charles Scribner's Sons, 1949); *Christian Realism and Political Problems* (New York: Charles Scribner's Sons, 1954); *The Children of Light and the Children of Darkness* (New York: Charles Scribner's sons, 1960); *The Nature and Destiny of Man,* 2 vols. (New York: Charles Scribner's Sons, 1941).

6. John C. Raines, "Sin as Pride and Sin as Sloth," *Christianity and Crisis* 29 (3 February 1969): 5.

7. Rhoades, "The Prophetic Insight," p. 11. I gladly acknowledge my use of Dr. Rhoades' paper in this section and encourage a reading of it for more extended discussion of many of these points.

8. Harvey Wheeler, *Democracy in a Revolutionary Era* (Santa Barbara, Calif.: Center for the Study of Democratic Institutions, 1970), pp. 186, 189.

9. Walter G. Muelder, *Power Structures, Ethical Concern, and the Church in the World* (Cincinnati, Ohio: Women's Division of Christian Service, 1962), p. 10; see also his *Religion and Economic Responsibility* (New York: Charles Scribner's Sons, 1953), pp. 18–22, 243–51; *Foundations of the Responsible Society* (New York: Abingdon, 1959), pp. 47–52, 86–90, 244–66; and *Methodism and Society in the Twentieth Century* (New York: Abingdon, 1961), pp. 26–28.

10. Muelder, *Power Structures,* p. 20.

11. I gladly acknowledge that the keen insight and comprehensive breadth of Muelder's mind have outrun the inadequacies of a consensus model of society. Moreover, his work within Boston University, the United Methodist Church, the ecumenical movement, and secular life bears witness to his intimate acquaintance with both the consensus and constraint dimensions of social order.

12. Gerhard E. Lenski, *Power and Privilege* (New York: McGraw-Hill Book Co., 1966), p. 20. Lenski's italics.

13. Ibid.

14. This model is open to considerable differentiation, even geometrically. Concentric circles, overlapping circles, and multiple circles within each system can serve to illustrate the multidimensional, intra- and intersystem congruities and conflicts. I would also like to

acknowledge my indebtedness to Eugene L. Lowry and Penn Morgan in the construction of this model.

15. Alvin Gouldner, *The Coming Crisis of Western Sociology* (New York: Basic Books, 1970), p. 330. Gouldner's italics.

16. Arnold Rose, *The Power Structure* (New York: Oxford University Press, 1967), p. 53.

17. See David M. Potter, *People of Plenty* (Chicago: University of Chicago Press, 1954), p. 92.

18. Alexis de Tocqueville, *Democracy in America*, 2 vols. (New York: Vintage Press, 1962), 2:11; John B. Kirby, "Violence and American Values," in *The Human Arena,* Gilbert Abcarian and Monte Palmer, eds. (New York: Holt, Rinehart and Winston, 1971), pp. 298–307. I am indebted to Kirby for the line of thought in this paragraph.

19. "In late 1946, the U.S. Department of Labor said that an income of $9,191 would enable a city family of four to maintain 'a moderate standard of living.' Only about one-third of *all* American families reach that now dated standard." Brendan Sexton, " 'Middle-Class' Workers and the New Politics," *Dissent* 16 (May–June 1969): 232.

20. Amsterdam Assembly of the World Council of Churches, *The Church and the Disorder of Society* (New York: Harper and Bros., 1948), p. 192; Muelder, *Foundations of the Responsible Society,* pp. 20, 33.

21. Paul Tillich, *Love, Power and Justice* (New York: Oxford University Press, 1960), pp. 18–34.

22. Ralf Dahrendorf, *Class and Class Conflict in Industrial Society* (Stanford, Calif.: Stanford University Press, 1959), pp. 239, 206–38; cf. Henry Bienen, *Violence and Social Change* (Chicago: University of Chicago Press, 1968), p. 83. We need very much the development of a theology of material interest in the church. A lot of practical work has been done by churchmen in community organization, especially in the Alinsky style, but I have seen very little explicit attention given to it in a comprehensive way.

6 The Disciplines of Power: The Necessity and Limits of Coercion   *Joseph D. Stamey*

T H E present paper is an attempt to understand the necessity and means for the control of violence, both within the nation and in international affairs. Or, to extend the context, it is an attempt to explore some essential aspects — the necessity and limits — of coercion (a term more inclusive than *violence*) in contemporary society. The topic is particularly appropriate for a volume of essays honoring Walter G. Muelder. In the view of the present writer, Dean Muelder has contributed significantly to our understanding of the issues that anyone must confront in trying to think seriously about the problem of coercion. He has also insisted on the principle that "Christian social ethics is an interdisciplinary field" in whose methods "science, philosophy and theology interpenetrate and converge." He has rigorously applied that principle in his analyses of law, government, community, power, authority, and responsibility. Thus he has contributed significantly to the solution of the difficult problems — theoretical and existential — that we must each decide if we are to continue, or to begin, to live as responsible men in a revolutionary world.[1] The present paper attempts to use the method that Dean Muelder recom-

mends. It also makes use of some of the major themes that character-
ize his reflections as a Christian social ethicist.

COERCION AND ITS LIMITS

Hannah Arendt in a recent, valuable study has emphasized that a
number of terms, related to each other but different in meaning, must
be distinguished before we can understand the relation of violence to
power and authority. Specifically, she attempts to clarify the terms
power, strength, force, authority and *violence.* Power, she says,
"springs up wherever people get together and act in concert. Violence, on the other hand, is instrumental; it is an instrument of coercion where the power to act (in the sense defined above) is lacking.
Violence does not depend on shared beliefs or common values; it
depends on the effectiveness of the means of coercion. Power, which
is the essence of all government, does not need justification. Violence
needs justification; it must be justified by the end pursued, and "its
justification loses in plausibility the farther its intended end recedes
into the future." [2]

Perhaps the main point of Arendt's argument is that, far from
being identical, power and violence are opposites. Except in patho-
logical cases, a collectivity — a group or a government — resorts to
violence only when it lacks power; when it does not have — or feels
itself losing — the ability to govern, to order its life on the basis of
power arising from those who will be affected by its action (those
whose consent, cooperation, and commitment will be necessary if its
ends are to be realized).

Thus, the problem of coercion must be seen against the background
of the larger question of governmental power and its legitimation.
The terms *force* and *violence* need to be distinguished if we are to
make sense of the role of coercion in the contemporary world. J.
Glenn Gray cites the Oxford Universal Dictionary's definition of
violence as "the exercise of physical force so as to inflict injury on or
damage to persons or property." At least one dictionary almost gives
as one meaning of *force* the following: "Power or [strength] considered as exerting constraint or compulsion; coercion." [3] If we allow

for the condition that force as constraint does not have to be coercive — it may aim at physical destruction, rather than at coercion, as in a war of annihilation or as in Hitler's attempt to destroy the Jewish population of Europe — then we can use this definition (and the earlier definition of violence) to clarify the relation between coercion and violence and between both and power. Coercion involves the use of force, but coercion need not always use violence. Coercion may rely on psychological or cultural factors — e.g., appeals to feelings of guilt, the force of public opinion, threats of ostracism — as well as on physical force (violence). Violence may be an instrument of coercion, in the sense that Arendt describes, but it need not be, it can be an instrument of destruction or extermination pure and simple. Violence as an instrument of simple destruction will receive only passing mention in this study, as I find it hardly credible that such use of violence needs moral evaluation. Coercive violence is another matter.

Naturally, not all influence is coercive. As Walter Muelder has written, "Political power rests on obedience by free rational beings." Obedience in this sense — related to the notions of consent, cooperation, and commitment (passive or active) — can be related to Hannah Arendt's discussion of power. Muelder further noted: "Such power may be either moral persuasion or coercion." [4] It seems that here is the true crux. Although Arendt's discussion of power and its legitimation is illuminating, her model of the basis and function of government, really a social contract model, gives too static an image of the dynamic process of government, which always involves emergent leadership and changing patterns or response. As Muelder has often pointed out, man is not an isolated entity who gets together with other isolated entities to form a society. Men are by nature interdependent, communitarian. And all society involves government; not necessarily a state, but processes and institutions by means of which ordering takes place and in terms of which there are efforts to influence — either by persuasion or by coercion — other social participants. Government is an active, dynamic process first rather than the result of the process. It both creates and is created by, depends on and organizes, a system — the system of relationships inclusive of all those affected by the exercise of power or by attempts to create power. Thus coercion, whether violent or nonviolent, may be seen as an instrument used in the attempt to create power — to establish order or unity necessary for government — where power (in the sense of consent, cooperation, and commitment) is lacking.

Coercion entails either the threat or the use of force. Threatening to use force is itself one use of force, at least in a psychological sense. Generally, in coercive violence, the use of violence comes only if its threatened use has failed to achieve the desired ends; psychological and physical force thus are inextricably bound to each other. Kenneth Boulding has distinguished three kinds of threats that function in international conflict: threats of punishment, threats of conquest, and threats of annihilation.[5] Even when annihilation is threatened, the function is coercive, as annihilation of the enemy is not seen as desirable for its own sake; it is rather involved in the effort to influence him, to constrain him to behave in ways held to be desirable by the threatening party. In war, where physical force *is* used, it is usually not merely the destructive effects of actual violence that are counted on to overcome the enemy; psychological pressures are mixed with the physical means of war — propaganda, exhaustion, terror, harder conditions of life — to wear down the enemy. The late B. H. Liddell-Hart, a brilliant strategist and student of military history, described military strategy as "the art of distributing and applying military means to fulfill the ends of policy."[6] The purpose of military strategy is to diminish the enemy's power of resistance. Ideally, it produces a favorable decision without serious fighting — without the *use* of physical violence. The aim of dislocation, a dislocation of the enemy that will cause the dissolution of his ability to resist.

It has sometimes been argued that the essence of political authority rests in the power to exercise coercive force. This point will be discussed in a later section of the essay. At this point, it will do to suggest that there are limits to the ability to coerce, no matter how much force may be applied. These practical limits are not unrelated to moral limits that should be recognized as applying to the intention to use coercion.

To take an example from the area of moral or psychological coercion: it has often been argued that one of the reasons it is desirable to grade students is to encourage them to work hard enough to receive a passing or better than passing mark. Thus, there is a promise of ego gratification coupled with a threat of loss of ego gratification, depending on whether the student performs satisfactorily or not. But a student may not care whether he passes the course or may be unable to learn the materials or acquire the skills required by the particular course; or if he has lost hope about his ability to do so, or is subject to attitudes — apathy, boredom, frustration, rage (whatever their cause) — that prevents him from concentrating on the course, then the threat of failure can scarcely be expected to have much effect in achieving the intended results. Some observers have argued that one of the reasons for what has often appeared as irrational political behavior on the part of leaders of the underdeveloped nations during the past two decades has been their perception of the increasing gap between standards of living in the "Northern," rich nations of the world and those in the "Southern," poor areas, a gap that they see no present possibility of closing.

COERCION AS A FUNCTION OF GOVERNMENT

We have argued that coercion is resorted to in the attempt to govern when the power that comes from free consent is lacking. This was recognized in the traditional theory of justified war as developed by Christian theologians from Ambrose and Augustine to the sixteenth century Spaniards Vitoria and Suárez.[7] For the traditional just-war theorists, the right of a political society — a nation-state — to wage war did not derive from an unconditional right of self-preservation or self-defense. The problem that just-war theorists saw themselves as confronting was to determine whether and under what conditions war — the use of violence in the relations of independent political units — could be justified from the point of view of Christian ethics.

The problem was seen as having two aspects. The first was whether the use of violence could ever be reconciled with the basic commitments and values of the Christian life. It was regularly discussed under the heading: "Whether making war is always a sin." [8] The answer to this part of the problem was that war could be exercised justly if it could be made to fit under the general Christian solution to the problem of legitimate violence—namely, the theory of the legitimate coercive role of government (or the sovereign) to preserve order in society by restraining wrongdoers (with the sword if necessary) (Romans 13:1–7). The second aspect of the problem, as the just-war theorists saw it, was how, specifically, the exercise of violence against one independent political unit by another could be made to fit as one of the proper functions of government under the theory of legitimate coercion. The theory held that the sovereign could, as an impersonal and disinterested third party standing above conflicts within society, render objective judgment and justly enforce that judgment; but it was asked how the sovereign as an interested party in a conflict with another soverign could function as disinterested dispenser of justice. The criteria of the traditional just-war theory were developed largely to provide an objective structure for prospective and retrospective decisions in such cases. (They were widely used in connection with confession and penance.) The right to resort to war was seen as an emergency action, an exercise of punitive justice by a state in the international area—that is, in an area where it did not normally possess legal jurisdiction. Thus, according to the theory, there must be more stringent moral limitations on the sovereign in the (abnormal) exercise of war than in the (normal) exercise of punitive justice within his own political society.

The three primary criteria of the just-war theory, present in Augustine's writing and repeated in the medieval collections of canon law and by Aquinas, provide the basic structure intended to limit the exercise of war: (1) war can be exercised only under the authority of the legitimate sovereign of a political community acting as an impersonal minister of justice; (2) war can be resorted to only in circumstances where it is made necessary by a grave violation of right, inflicting great harm, by the government or citizens of another state; (3) war must be waged with right intention, with the intention of creating a condition in which the injustice that occasioned the war will be corrected and a better peace established. Ideally, the third criterion specifies that the motive of war must be Christian love, concern for the welfare of all who will be affected—the citizens of the enemy state as well as the citizens of one's own society — and that the goal must be a condition in which the welfare of those affected will be better than it would have been if the war had not been fought. Additional criteria were added to the original three over a period of time, largely in the attempt to make the structure more specific and objective and less subject to interested interpretation. These included conditions that war must be waged only (1) with right means; (2) when there is a reasonable hope of success; (3) as a last resort, when all other means of securing a just settlement have been exhausted; and (4) when the harm or evil done by the war will not exceed the evil of not waging it (i.e., of tolerating the situation that the war intends to correct).

The point is not whether the rules of justified war were strictly adhered to during the medieval period — at times, as in the Spanish conquest of the New World, they were used cynically to justify brutal conquest; although, surprisingly to us perhaps, in many instances and in the confessional they were taken with an awful seriousness.[9] The point is that the just-war theorists saw the exercise of war as an attempt at government (of a limited kind) where the normal and accepted criterion of legitimacy (sovereign authority) did not apply. Their attempt to deal with the paradox that they saw in this situation allowed them to perceive the real analogy between the exercise of coercion by a government within its society and the exercise of coercion against another government.

Perhaps the greatest weakness of the traditional just-war theory is that it leaves unanalyzed the notion of sovereignty — a crucial notion, as it provides the basis for objective legitimation in the form of the official declaration of war. By and large, the just-war theorists accepted a normative conception of sovereignty derived from the Platonic/Aristotelian tradition: it is the function of political authority in the state to secure the common good; thus the essence of legitimate political authority is that it is directed to the common good, not to the good of any particular group.[10]

Augustine provided a descriptive concept of the basis of political community, which might have been developed into a descriptive conception of the basis of sovereignty that would be coherent with

Hannah Arendt's discussion of power: "a people is an assemblage of reasonable beings bound together by a common agreement as to the objects of their love . . . whatever it loves.[11] The interesting problem would have been to explore the possibilities of bringing into closer relation to each other the normative theory of sovereignty and the descriptive conception of the basis of political community. Augustine himself suggested a solution: "whatever it loves, if only it is an assemblage of reasonable beings and not of beasts, and is bound together by an agreement as to the objects of love, it is reasonably called a people. [Nevertheless] it will be a superior people in proportion as it is bound together by higher interests, inferior in proportion as it is bound together by lower."[12] Walter Muelder has formulated the issue of the interrelation of the descriptive and the normative clearly enough: "There is always a dynamic interrelation between man and his environment, i.e., between person-and-community when an ethical judgment or moral decision is made. We may formulate this interrelationship as a question of *responsiveness*. The social sciences study [of] man's *responsiveness* . . . as a social and psychological fact underlies *responsibility* as an ethical reality."[13]

What is being suggested in the present discussion is that though there is a necessary methodological distinction between normative and descriptive components in ethical theory, no absolute separation of the two is possible. "The behavioral sciences . . . are themselves replete with value judgments for the simple reason that they deal with man, who is a goal seeking and a valuing creature."[14]

One of the major themes in Walter Muelder's work has been the necessity of bringing the normative and descriptive dimensions closer together in the analysis of the nature of political community, power, and authority. We have argued that the problem of coercion must be understood in the context of this problem. The just-war theorists, even as Plato and Aristotle, rejected on fundamental philosophical grounds a "positivist" or "command" theory of the basis of political obligation and legitimacy. In modern times the command theory has been associated with the names of the nineteenth-century British theorist John Austin and the seventeenth-century philosopher Hobbes. In the Greek world, the theory was advocated by some of the Sophists. As

Austin states it, the theory specifies that law is command, and that it is binding by reason of superior power — the power of the superior to enforce penalties for noncompliance. Thus, for the command theory, political authority derives from the ability to exercise coercive force.

Muelder has contested this view not only on normative philosophical grounds but from the standpoint of the behavioral and historical study of man. In distinguishing between *institutional* and *operational* motifs in ethical thought, Edward LeRoy Long, Jr. has written: "In one, law, order, and due process are acknowledged and cherished; in the other emphasis is placed upon the power configurations of society and the political maneuverings by which laws are enacted and decisions made. In the one, law enforcement is the function of an 'office' and the policeman's role is one of authority; in the other law enforcement is seen as a matter of dominion and the policeman is deemed effective because he possesses superior power." [15]

If Walter Muelder is correctly called an institutionalist, it is not merely because he has cherished "law, order, and due process" rather than placing an emphasis upon power; it is because he has seen power as deriving not primarily from the means and use of coercion and manipulation, but from (to use the present writer's terminology again) consent, cooperation, and commitment. To make this point, he has sometimes quoted Lewis Mumford's aphorism: "Any fool can solve the problems of political power by martial law; but only a fool would mistake that process for government." Even more frequently, he has quoted R. M. MacIver: "The notion that force is the creator of government is one of those part truths that begets total error. . . . To say that in the struggle of groups the more powerful wins is to say nothing, for the power of a group is no simple function of the force it disposes; it depends no less on its solidarity, its organizing ability, its leadership, its resources and its resourcefulness, its tenacity of purpose, and other things." [16]

The Spanish philosopher Ortega y Gasset, making the same point, has cited a remark that Talleyrand is supposed to have made to Napoleon: "You can do everything with bayonets, Sire, except sit on them." The same point, as a piece of hard data derived from the behavioral study of man, is given concreteness in a recent study by

Michael Barkun, who cites as definite evidence against the command theory of law the following considerations:[17]

1. The use of coercive force, or sanctions, as a response to disobedience of laws rests on the assumption that only a *small* minority will be involved in lawbreaking.

2. The use of sanctions rests on the assumption that disobedience will be scattered, or staggered, over time.

3. The supposed deterrent effect of sanctions is meant to apply only to a minority of potential lawbreakers, not to the majority who are well-socialized citizens.

4. Since politico-legal systems are problem-solving systems, one can argue that social support for the law is primarily a function of satisfaction on the part of citizens.

5. The available evidence from comparative study of societies indicates that norms "precede rather than follow the means for their enforcement, suggesting that enforcement is a later refinement and is not essential for the existence of a legal system."

6. Totalitarian regimes have depended, for their continued existence, not on the ability to coerce their subjects so much as on enthusiastic support of a large part of the population (as in Nazi Germany) or on the apathy of the great majority (as in contemporary Haiti).

Barkun's analysis here supports the fundamental argument of this paper, and the contention of Dean Muelder that "Behind force in all constituted government lies authority of some sort and authority is responsive to the underlying social structure, both economic and non-economic. Government is but an instrument of authority, and authority when it endures depends on the basic attitudes and loyalties of those over whom it is exercised."[18]

COERCION IN CONTEMPORARY NATIONAL AND INTERNATIONAL LIFE

For the just-war theorists, coercion could be exercised in human affairs only as an exercise of legitimate authority to govern. The criterion of legitimacy was that governmental power be exercised for the common good; but the title to legitimate authority was God-given, and for the most part, God was to be relied on to redress any abuses that the sovereign might commit. The trouble with the just-war understanding of sovereign authority, we have suggested, is that it did not relate the descriptive to the normative — the relation of the sources of power to the concept of legitimate authority. The theorists saw the problem of authority as much harder to deal with when one considered international conflict than when one considered the conflicts within a particular society. One of the marks of the present age is that the very notion of legitimate authority has become problematic and that the right of the governing power to exercise coercion within society is being radically challenged. At the same time, the exercise of coercion — war — in the international system, given the destructive capacity of modern weapons and the ideological divisions in the world community, has become a distressing, difficult problem.

Many observers have pointed to a breakdown of governmental structures and institutions in the most advanced, industrialized communities. André Philip was writing specifically of the Western European countries, but his observations apply equally to the United States and the U.S.S.R., when he described a crisis in traditional political institutions — governmental and party — caused by their inability to respond effectively to social, economic, and technological change. The growth of huge economic interests, transnational in scope, is just one of the factors involved. Hannah Arendt has pointed to "disintegration processes which have become so manifest in recent years — the decay of public services . . . the pollution of air and water — [which] are . . . automatic results of mass societies that have become unmanageable." This disintegration is, she believes, accompanied and accelerated by a decay of political institutions, affecting both Western institutions designed to make representative self-government possible and Eastern institutions designed to make "absolute rule over vast territories . . . effective." A recent study by historian John Lukacs has given a penetrating if melancholy analysis of these processes.[19] Many have argued that the most advanced industrial societies are suffering not only from unwillingness on the part of those with governmental authority to respond to the need and wishes of people in their society, but also from the structural incapacity of basic political institutions to allow effective response.

If this is so, then one can understand the widely dispersed sense of alienation on the part of many in contemporary society. Specific events and issues, such as the war in Viet Nam and continued discrimination against racial groups and the poor, have contributed to widespread movements of protest and disaffiliation from American society. But, beyond the protest and alienation resulting from specific causes, there seems to be a general feeling of powerlessness and normlessness on the part of many — the young, members of minority groups, many among the opinion elites in the universities, the churches, and in the intellectual community. One of the results of the present sense of alienation has been a fundamental contesting of the legitimacy of institutions and established processes of government. Thus, the use of coercion to establish or preserve order — whether directed against members of the Black Panthers or against demonstrators at the Democratic National Party Convention in 1968 — has been challenged not only or even primarily because such exercise of coercion was held to violate criteria of lawfulness, but because the established governmental processes and institutions were held to be fundamentally illegitimate. Sometimes the challenge has been made in terms of Marxist theory of the economic class function of the state, sometimes in terms of anarchist theory that repudiates all exercise of coercive power, sometimes merely as an emotional repudiation of "the Establishment." What is evident in contemporary society is a genuine decline in the power (and authority) of the state, a decline in its ability to govern on the basis of consent, cooperation, and commitment. One of the lessons of this loss of power is the limited utility of coercion in instances where the true sources of power have decayed. It is possible, although I do not judge it to be likely, that we are about to pass through a period in which, as John Lukacs suggests, conflicts within our social system will resemble those in the international system, in which semi-autonomous, illegal armed groups will provide whatever order exists for limited geographical areas.

In this connection, recent studies of the international system reveal some of the paradoxes of the present situation. Michael Barkun, in the study cited earlier, argued that traditional European conceptions of sovereignty fail to account for the existence of law in stateless, horizontally ordered systems — such as the segmentary lineage system of the Nuer in the Sudan. According to the positivist or command theory of the basis of law, law could not exist in such societies. Its existence would also be problematic, although less so, for thinkers such as Augustine who were in the institutionalist tradition. Barkun's study of horizontally ordered societies, however, discloses at least two significant bases of law in their social structure.

First, he has shown that in stateless, horizontally ordered societies there is an operative system of law that binds the jural community together. There is even something analogous to the legitimate authority of vertically ordered societies — the impersonal disinterested third party that functions as judge and enforcer in the just-war theory's understanding of the sovereign's function. What plays the role of legitimate authority — the sovereign — in horizontally ordered societies is a mediator of some sort. In some cases, the mediator is a qualified expert (e.g., "the leopard-skin chief" among the Nuer) whose findings ordinarily are supposed to be factual rather than normative and are not binding on the parties to the dispute. Even more basically (when there is no third party called in to mediate) Barkun has found that there is an "invisible mediator" present in conflict bargaining situations, effecting transition from two-party to three-party interaction. In such cases the implied but invisible third party turns out to be the shared perceptions of the participants, the values that bind the parties into a system — in short, a shared perception that the system itself is valuable and that any solution to conflict must be a system-preserving one. The invisible third party tends to moderate the demands of the parties to the conflict. Thus order and law may exist and may endure without a structure of political authority and without independent legal institutions.

The second lesson to be learned from Barkun's study at this point is the obverse of this: order may exist without political institutions and without a structure of legal authority; but without them, significant and sustained change toward a more just social order becomes practically impossible. This is a significant insight not only for specific societies whose political institutions are under attack and perhaps in need of transformation; but also because the international system — as the just-war theorists recognized, and as Barkun argues — is a horizontally ordered system.

Traditionally, the conception of sovereignty — defined at least since the beginning of the modern era in terms of control over a geographical area — has defined the units in the international system. But, as Barkun shows, the geographical control definition of sovereignty, because of technological and political developments, has become problematic. (Do nations have the right to absolute control of air space over their territories? In the age of space exploration?) Also, the fundamental difficulty that any horizontally ordered society confronts in conditions of increasing complexity is raised for the present international system in a particularly grave form: "Implicit mediation . . . is a self-help system par excellence; the disputing parties function not only as the police but as judge and jury as well. In such a system the legal concepts are the lenses through which the particular world is seen and the resultant perceptions dictate the alternatives. But it [is] a precondition for successful operation of implicit mediation that the world be an intrinsically simple world, and the more involved reality becomes the more will uncertainty becloud the decision-making picture." [20]

There can be no question that both functions that we think law should serve are at stake in the contemporary international system. Order without satisfaction of demands for justice produces normlessness and anarchy.

Since the end of the World War II, a relative order, based on the nuclear deterrent capacities of the United States and the U.S.S.R., has emerged. But certainly the order that exists is constantly being eroded in various contested areas of the world. This erosion occurs not only where the two superpowers or their clients confront each other; it is also occurring within the two alliance systems. Further, although each of the superpowers has resorted to military intervention within its recognized sphere of interest — the U.S.S.R. in Hungary and in Czechoslovakia and the United States in the Dominican Republic and in Cuba — to some extent successful, disaffection with the status quo (as in Poland or in almost all of Latin America) indicates an increasing erosion of power of the superpowers to dominate their blocs. Further, American intervention in Viet Nam has revealed some of the practical limits to the ability to coerce as discussed in the first section of this essay. Certainly the United States and the U.S.S.R. will continue to exercise a massive influence on the configuration of the international system for the foreseeable future. But it would seem that the traditional concept of spheres of influence — however defined — must be seriously revised in accordance with the preceding discussion of power and authority. Further, the development of genuine autonomy (including economic well-being and political power) among nations of the third world would seem to be a condition for stability.

Michael Barkun has drawn attention to three aspects of the present international context that necessitate a redefinition of the traditional conception of sovereignty and that might fundamentally alter the structure of the international system. These are: (1) the non-sovereign character of various kinds of technological development, such as space exploration (and, one can add, of technologically produced problems, such as pollution, affecting the whole world); (2) the equivocal status of international organizations; and (3) growing international recognition of the rights of the individual.[21] Taken together, (2) and (3) suggest that transnational political structures and institutions are developing in the international system. International organizations — such as the United Nations and the European Common Market — that do not fit the traditional definition of participating agents or units in the international system, are nevertheless accorded this status in international law. As to (3), for the first time in the modern period — largely as a result of the refugee problem and revulsion at the crimes against humanity committed during World War II — individuals have been recognized as having rights as human beings, rather than merely as citizens of a nation-state. Thus, to some extent individual persons are coming to have status within the international system. It seems to me that these developments are the most hopeful of our time and that one of the overarching imperatives for anyone living now is the development and sustenance of political structures and institutions legitimately based on consent, cooperation, and commitment of those affected by them. Factors limiting the effectiveness of existing transnational and international agencies are obvious. As long as the present world power configuration remains mostly in force, the effectiveness of these agencies will be limited by the degree of willing cooperation given them by the superpowers. With the loosening of a bipolar power-structure, however, the delegation of power to international agencies is becoming even more imperative. And it is surely in the long-term interest of the superpowers to promote wider cooperation and a greater degree of hope and satisfaction by encouraging third-world peoples' meaningful participation in the determination of their own destinies. Existing structures — those within particular societies and embryonic ones in the international community — should be given support. Thoroughgoing transformation of some existing structures may be necessary. Nevertheless, as Walter Muelder has written: "The church has the resources to show appreciation for the protest against alienation in today's world and it can involve the dissidents in an open strategy of social action. . . . Their methods of 'participatory democracy' do not work and will not work when applied over a long period of time. Sooner or later one has to learn the hard lessons of institutional continuity as well as the ephemeral joys of discontinuity." [22]

If one wants justice in society and in the world — and not the ephemeral and immediate joys of negation — then one must support at least some existing institutions (even while working to transform them) and strive to bring into being others that will be responsive and responsible — that will respond to our needs as persons-in-community.

THE ETHICAL DIMENSIONS OF COERCION

The legitimate exercise of coercion is rightly defined by the relation to power. At best the exercise of coercion must be justified, legitimated, prospectively and retrospectively, by intention and accomplishment. We can agree with Hannah Arendt that power and violence are not the same; in the sense that she specifies, they are opposites.

In an earlier study, I argued that the traditional just-war conception of legitimate sovereign authority could be better expressed by the concept of "force seeking legitimacy."[23] This phrase expresses more of the dynamic dimensions of political authority as discussed above and focuses attention on the ethical problems involved in the use of coercion in the international field. I would like to extend the recommendation to the field of domestic interaction as well; for however great the technological resources or the numerical strength a government commands, it receives its legitimacy, and ultimately its power, from the "consent, cooperation, and commitment" of the governed. It must be responsive to them and it must be responsible to them.

The exercise of violence, whether open or clandestine, is *one* form of coercion for which governments must seek legitimacy; but it is only one. It may be as questionable for a rich country to attempt to topple the government of a poor country by economic pressure as by means of a military invasion. In many ways, the problem of seeking legitimacy for the exercise of coercion by one government against another is similar to the problem of creating safeguards for people (employees, consumers, etc.) against the enormous economic power — a virtual form of government — exerted by the gigantic corporations.

There should be objective requirements that a government must meet to justify the use of force, either against certain segments of its own population or in the international field. It is extremely difficult at any given moment to justify the use of force; but certainly over a period of time any force that is used should be justifiable in terms of these requirements. Nor should justification be merely, or primarily, retrospective; here the criteria of reasonable expectation of success and greater good are relevant. It must be remembered that the greater-good criterion specifies that it is the good of *all* affected that must be considered. Sir Robert Thompson, the British expert on counterinsurgency wars, listed among the requirements a "just" counterinsurgency war must meet, that the government have as a clear political aim the establishment of a "free, independent and united country, which is politically and economically stable and viable"[24] and that the government function in accordance with legal norms of justice and due process. On the basis of these criteria, Thompson criticized both the policies and conduct of the Diem regime in South Viet Nam

—although he was fundamentally in sympathy with the aim of defeating the insurgency—and the tactics and strategy adopted by the American military—specifically "search and destroy tactics" and the massive, indiscriminate use of artillery and air power which occurred after American intervention.

At this point in time it is very easy to scoff at Sir Robert's scruples, as the idea of just counterinsurgency war has fallen into almost total discredit. I think that his point is nevertheless sound, and it applies across the board, to revolutionary as well as to counter-revolutionary struggles. If, over a reasonable period of time, a force proposing itself as a legitimate government, whether established or revolutionary, cannot—within the context of adherence to norms of justice and due process—win popular consent, then it forfeits all moral right to continue to try to function as a governing power.

Essentially, legitimate authority means responsible authority and depends on responsible exercise of power as defined by the First Assembly of the World Council of Churches: "A responsible society is one where freedom is the freedom of men who acknowledge responsibility to justice and public order, and where those who hold political authority or economic power are responsible for its exercise to God and the people whose welfare is affected by it." [25] Responsible government involves responsible procedures for gathering information and for establishing and criticizing policies in accordance with recognized moral norms, authentic descriptions of fact, and possibilities for mobilizing and maintaining resources of whatever kind may be needed to succeed in carrying out policy decisions.

It would seem that it is neither possible nor desirable to rule out the possibility of justifiable war or even of justifiable nuclear war, given the configuration of military force in the world at the present time. One may be able to conceive of situations in which the threat of nuclear war, even against cities, might be justified as an attempt to deter some wholly unacceptable action—some action that would threaten the viability of the international system. But this is a judgment made at a high level of abstraction. It does not mean that an abstractly conceived possibility, such as some circumstance that might justify the threat of nuclear war, would in fact justify concrete long-term policies that see the nuclear deterrent capacity as the continuing basis for world order within the international system.

If ethical reflection is not to fall into the trap of serving as ideological license to justify existing policy—that of a particular nation or group—it must focus on the relation of policy to the realities that such policy seeks to interpret and transform. The traditional just-war theorists in attempting to define the just-cause criterion focused on the element of necessity. They attempted to limit the right to wage war to cases in which war would be clearly analogous to the exercise of punitive justice within society. One can argue that this was unfortunate, as the notion of punitive justice as a function of the "third party" makes little sense in a horizontally ordered society. We have already seen that this was the point at which the theorists of justified war felt most uneasy. In the international system at present, war must be seen as the outcome of long-term conflict processes rather than as a response to particular, isolated acts. In one sense, conflict is endemic and in this sense the just-cause criterion is nonoperational. One goes to war as a result or as a part of policy. Nevertheless, one can argue that, if pressed, the analogy that the just-war theorists used might help transform the notion of punitive or penal justice in vertically ordered societies. For the real cause of social deviance, like the real cause of disorder in the present international system, may well be alienation—the powerlessness of many who are expected to identify with the system and to play constructive roles in it—and the normlessness of the system itself.

The real solution to the problem of disorder both within society and in the international context is not *punitive* justice or threats of the exercise of military force but *justice*—the granting of power in accordance with recognition of basic human worth and rights to participation and autonomy. War may be, at best, as Kenneth Boulding has suggested, a characteristic of a system of deterrence under urban, "civilized," conditions. That is, it may be suited to a world system where there is conflict between rich and poor nations, developed and underdeveloped nations, and where there is competition among developed nations for control of the underdeveloped areas of the earth.[26]

War has been tolerable in the past — *if* it has been tolerable in the past — because man did not possess the technological capacity either to create weapons of ultimate destructive capacity or to bring an end to conditions of life dominated by scarcity and competition between haves and have-nots.

Many students of political decision-making have argued that in the contribution to policy formation, decision-makers at the highest level of governmental hierarchies are as much influenced by their general picture of the world as by classified or technical information that is available to them and not to the general public. It would seem that any ethic that continues to hold that coercion — the threat or exercise of war — may still be justified on the grounds of moral necessity in the present world context must give high priority to protecting policy and decision-making against inadequate images of the world. If a responsibly formulated policy provides for the possibility of using coercive force to secure any of its goals, then the use of force must be justified by the goals it seeks (as well as by the means it uses and its effectiveness in securing consent of those affected by its actions). It is doubtful whether force alone can secure the goals. Necessary coercion, where it is really necessary as an instrument, must be justified within the context and implementation of policy that seeks the common good. Here then, Augustine's suggestion that the superiority of a community must be determined by the quality of its interests is highly relevant. The values that policy promotes must be inclusive and open, and ultimately universal in scope.

THE RELEVANCE OF THE PACIFIST WAY

One of the major themes of Walter Muelder's ethics — and it seems to me it is another theme that has emerged from bringing the descriptive and the normative components of ethical reflection in closer relation to each other — has been an insistence on the interpenetration of means and ends. Some commentators have found tension between Muelder's institutionalism and the pacifist faith he has espoused. I must confess that I find tension between these aspects of his intellectual commitment; but it is the kind of tension I believe to be increasingly relevant in modern society. As an institutionalist, Muelder has focused on the processes and structures by means of which personal values and meanings are actualized in human society. He clearly admits that we are stuck with certain systems, structures, and processes that we may not approve of and that we must learn to work with and transform. This limited acceptance would, I think, include even the nuclear deterrence system on the systemic level: you don't reverse the direction of a jet plane or of a battleship immediately; you have to change its course. But along with this theme has been his commitment to pacifism as a way of life and his recommendation of the pacifist way as an alternative to the war system.[27] I think that the key is to be found in the fact that his fundamental vision of the world—that tentative but emergingly coherent view of reality informed by scientific, philosophical, and theological sources—is one of religious actualism. I use the term in the sense in which it has been used by Erik Erikson in his study of Gandhi: "Gandhi's actualism . . . first of all consisted in his knowledge of, and his ability to gain strength from, the fact that nothing is more powerful in the world than conscious nothingness if it is paired with the gift of giving and accepting actuality."[28]

Those who have been Walter Muelder's students will recall his profound insight into the social functions and significance for personal life of the disciplines of religious devotion and of religious mysticism. It is the capacity to transcend the given definitions—of reality, criteria of success, power, or achievement—that religious experience provides in the preeminent sense. Thus Muelder has written: "The death of Jesus is universally extolled as part of his way of salvation. But the crucifixion of Jesus is insufficiently accepted as an essential portion of the demand which the law of love makes upon every individual at every moment of ethical decision in every social situation. The cross, therefore, is coherently involved in the essential content of love. Faith in God's creative and redemptive power despite personal death is the ultimate rootage of the pacifist way of life. The pacifist lives as he does because Jesus lived and died as he did."[29]

Walter Muelder—like a host of others, from Marx to Marshall McLuhan—has discerned that we live in a world in which "Mankind has become the unit of cooperation."[30] It is only against this background—the normlessness and powerlessness that many feel in this "global village"—that we can fully understand the strength of what appear to be extremely nationalistic or separatist movements. Here it seems that the religious actualism of Walter Muelder is most relevant to our present situation. John Lukacs has suggested that we live in a time of "internalization, . . . of the deepening—often painful and confusing—of human consciousness, through which people become more introspective, trying to come to terms with their personal characteristics, among which their national origin is a most important one." [31] And, as Lukacs suggests, what people think and how they feel have become increasingly important determinants of their behavior, hence increasingly important determinants of the future. In this context—where it has been fashionable to speak of violence and of killing as therapeutic (Fanon, Sartre) — the religious actualism of Walter Muelder, based on the contemporary encounter with one who died on the cross, is highly relevant.

It has already been suggested that the exercise of force in the present age is both actually and morally limited by its potential effectiveness. What would have seemed unrealistic two decades or a decade ago— that a powerful nation like the United States should take into account as an integral part of the national policy the needs and aspirations of the powerless of the world—may now have become an imperative of policy as a large segment of its own population now consciously identifies with "the wretched of the earth." If this analysis is correct, then true power in the present international context will be gained to the extent that governments are willing to surrender some of the prerogatives of power of an earlier period.

We are in an era of transition. As in all such times, a number of alternative life-styles are presented to individuals who are concerned about achieving a coherent life pattern. Again, for one who would call himself, even if only to himself, a Christian, the religious actualism based on contemporary encounter with one who died on the cross, is relevant, and not just relevant, but normative. This can perhaps be expressed by inverting the title of a recent book by Paul Ramsey: "For Whom Does the Church Speak?" [32] One answer would seem to be that the Church has always understood itself as, by vocation, being under the necessity to speak for God. This does not mean that even if the Church is correct in its vocational interpretation, its statements are self-validating. Nevertheless, there is theological precedent of the strongest kind for saying that in understanding itself as required to speak for God, the Church must see itself as spokesman for man. At least, one dominant theological image that the Church has invoked historically to interpret the significance of the concrete events that are its central symbols — the life, death, and resurrection of Jesus — has been expressed by saying that in these events God was standing and speaking for man and acting on his behalf. Since the Church calls itself the Church of Jesus Christ — through whom God has acted for man, in behalf of all men — when the Church claims to speak and act for God, it claims to speak and act for all men, on their behalf and in their interest. If the Church does understand itself as required to think of itself in this way, then the society represented by the Church, the society with whose interest it identifies its interests, must be wider than any national, racial, cultural, or existing social group.

Thus, the significance of Walter Mueller's pacifism; for in an age in which mankind has become the unit of cooperation, the Christian must take his place in the universal community of confessors of the Name and must identify himself with the needs of the universal community.

I would find it difficult to argue for the pacifist position as an absolute moral position. Nevertheless, as a symbolic expression of solidarity with all men, the pacifist commitment does seem to me highly relevant as a Christian vocation. The pacifist way has also led to the exploration of strategies for bringing about social change nonviolently. I think we have been too prone to notice its limitations here and to forget its successes. Certainly there might be situations where the use of violence is morally preferable to the attempt to use nonviolence. One gain of taking the example of men like Martin Luther King, Jr. seriously is that we have come to meet conflict situations with the presumption that nonviolent avenues of conflict must be tried in good faith and exhausted before violence can be justified. This presumption, although one of the traditional just-war criteria, has not been an operational norm for most governments, nor have citizens insisted that their governments recognize and abide by it in international relations. But both the symbolic and the practical possibilities of the pacifist way, in spite of the tremendously impressive examples of Gandhi and King, have barely begun to be explored.

We must see, then, as Erikson shows us what Gandhi saw, that "in all parts of the world, the struggle now is for the anticipatory development of more inclusive identities," for an end to the "pseudo-speciation" of man. But this position will not divorce us from existing structures — from the particular institutions of church and society — even if our commitment to them must be critical. "Gandhi was never too proud to find universal meaning in petty circumstances, for he knew that one must build on the values of one's childhood, as long as they are revalidated by experience, until one perceives a wider truth which may make them relative or obsolete." [33]

Such a position may not strike us as providing the excitement provided by the rhetoric of conflict, violence, and immediacy that one has heard from many contemporary protestors. But rooted in the religious experience that both frees us from bondage to existing reality and commits us to its transformation, it offers us the chance of a world in which coercion — duress — may be increasingly replaced by autonomy, persuasion, cooperation, and freedom.

NOTES

1. Walter G. Muelder, *Moral Law in Christian Social Ethics* (Richmond: John Knox Press, 1966), p. 20; idem, *Foundations of the Responsible Society* (New York: Abingdon Press, 1959), chaps. 5, 6, 14; and idem, "Christian Bases of Morality and Ethics," paper presented to the Council of Bishops of the United Methodist Church, 9 April 1969, p. 2.

2. Hannah Arendt, *On Violence* (New York: Harcourt, Brace & World, Inc., 1969–1970), pp. 44–46, 52.

3. J. Glenn Gray, *On Understanding Violence Philosophically* (New York: Harper & Row, 1970), p. 12; Fung & Wagnalls, *Standard Dictionary International Edition*, 2 vols. (New York: Funk & Wagnalls, 1961), 1:493. I have said "almost" because Funk & Wagnalls uses *energy* where I have used *strength*.

4. Walter G. Muelder, "Concerning Power in the State," *Philosophical Forum* 5 (Spring 1947): 6.

5. Kenneth E. Boulding, *Conflict and Defense: A General Theory* (New York: Harper & Row, 1963), p. 256.

6. B. H. Liddell-Hart, *Strategy* (New York: Frederick A. Praeger, 1965), pp. 335–38.

7. The development of the just-war tradition and its limitations are dealt with in my doctoral dissertation, "Christian Ethics and Violent Conflict: The 'Just War' as an Ethical Model" (Boston University, 1968).

8. Gratian, *Decretum Magistri Gratiani* causa xxiii, q. 1.

9. One has only to read Frederick G. Heymann's *John Ziska and the Hussite Revolution*

(Princeton, N.J.: Princeton University Press, 1955) to see that both the decision to wage war and the manner of waging war were much influenced by the rules of the just-war theory. Even more impressive, perhaps, is the evidence of lifelong acts of penance imposed on participants in battles where particularly savage methods were used, as in the Battle of Hastings.

10. Aristotle, *Politics* III 1279A–1279B.

11. Augustine, *City of God* 19. 24.

12. Ibid.

13. Walter G. Muelder, "Christian Bases of Morality and Ethics," pp. 13–14.

14. Ibid. And, one can add, because they are creations of men. This is entailed by one of the fundamental principles of Boston Personalism as developed by Dean Muelder and others — the Kantian notion of the primacy or priority of practical reason. In these days when many students of the behavioral sciences are beginning to insist that there is no value-free science (see Alvin W. Gouldner, *The Coming Crisis of Western Sociology* [New York: Basic Books, Inc., 1970]), it is perhaps useful to suggest that this recognition did not mean, either for Kant or for the Personalists, that one is at liberty to disregard the necessity for developing and adhering to rigorous criteria of objectivity. One should be all the more careful of them, since one understands the tentative and problematic nature of claims to having reached objective truth—Nor should one conclude that he is at liberty to substitute invective for analysis provided that the cause is just.

15. Edward LeRoy Long, Jr., *A Survey of Christian Ethics* (New York: Oxford University Press, 1967), p. 268.

16. Mumford quoted in Walter G. Muelder, "A Personalist Critique of Marxism," unpublished paper, p. 9; R. M. MacIver, *The Web of Government* (New York: The Free Press, 1965), pp. 15–16.

17. Jose Ortega y Gasset, *The Revolt of the Masses* (New York: W. W. Norton & Company, Inc., 1932), p. 127; Michael Barkun, *Law without Sanctions* (New Haven: Yale University Press, 1968), pp. 61–65.

18. Muelder, "A Personalist Critique of Marxism," p. 10.

19. André Philip, "The Revolutionary Change in the Structure of European Political Life," in *Responsible Government in a Revolutionary Age*, Z. K. Matthews, ed. (New York: Association Press, 1966), p. 121; Arendt, *On Violence*, p. 84; John Lukacs, *The Passing of the Modern Age* (New York: Harper & Row, Publishers, 1970), chaps. 4–5.

20. Barkun, *Law Without Sanctions*, p. 117.

21. Ibid., p. 134 ff.

22. Muelder, "Christian Bases of Morality and Ethics," p. 14.

23. Stamey, "Christian Ethics and Violent Conflict."

24. Sir Robert Thompson, *No Exit from Vietnam* (New York: David McKay Company, Inc., 1969), p. 163.

25. Amsterdam Assembly, *The Church and the Disorder of Society*, p. 192, quoted in Muelder, *Foundations of the Responsible Society*, p. 19.

26. Kenneth E. Boulding, *The Meaning of the 20th Century* (New York: Harper & Row, Publishers, 1965), p. 82.

27. Walter G. Muelder, "Why I Believe in Pacifism," a paper presented at the Conference on Church and War, Detroit (Spring 1950), pp. 5, 11.

28. Erik H. Erikson, *Gandhi's Truth* (New York: W. W. Norton & Company, Inc., 1969), p. 397.

29. Muelder, "Why I Believe in Pacifism," pp. 3–4.

30. Muelder, *Foundations of the Responsible Society*, chap. 2.

31. Lukacs, *The Passing of the Modern Age*, p. 69.

32. Paul Ramsey, *Who Speaks for the Church?* (Nashville: Abingdon Press, 1967); see Muelder, *In Every Place a Voice* (Cincinnati, Ohio: Woman's Division of Christian Service, Board of Missions, the Methodist Church, 1957).

33. Erikson, *Gandhi's Truth*, pp. 398, 433.

7 The Dilemma of Christian Social Strategy   *J. Philip Wogaman*

CHRISTIAN social strategy is the attempt by Christians to organize most effectively their capacity to achieve social objectives consequent to their faith as Christians. It is the attempt to seek such objectives intelligently and can be contrasted either with visceral, uncoordinated, unplanned activism or with abandonment of the effort to achieve social objectives at all.

For a generation or so prior to the 1960s, the mood of much Christian thought was unreceptive to social strategy. This was partly because of disillusionment with the results of Prohibition and other causes. It was largely because theology in some quarters appeared to call into question the moral claims made for particular values and objectives. During the 1960s the mood of Christian leadership shifted rapidly toward active concern for the realization of social goals. The legitimacy of social goals and action, as such, is now less frequently questioned.[1] Indeed, social activism is much more frequently regarded as a necessary part of Christian life. The newer activism has, to some extent, been strategic; but it has more often been ad hoc or even romantic. The temptation has often been to engage in social action on behalf of what seem to be good causes without subjecting either means or ends to the disciplines implied by Christian social strategy. The meaning of those disciplines has been suggested in a formula proposed by Paul Deats, Jr. and Herbert E. Stotts: "The clarification of ethical norms, the appraisal of social needs, the assessment of costs and resources, and the deployment of energies to establish and accomplish institutional goals."[2] In this formula, social strategy is seen to involve Christians in both intensive theological and ethical analysis and in careful sociological analysis and factual research. On the one hand, Christians must face in great depth the question of what objectives are implied by Christian faith. On the other hand, they cannot avoid the hard practical questions of what can, in fact, be done. It is doing these two things together that is so unusual and yet always necessary.

This paper will deal with a persistent dilemma in Christian social strategy: the question of to what extent those desiring social change should work in and through "the system" and to what extent they should work outside it to achieve their goals.

The question has both ethical and practical ramifications: ethically, it involves the question of the legitimacy of the system involved; practically, it is a question of what, in fact, can be accomplished through the system. The dilemma occurs as the Christian strategist faces the possibility that the apparently effective forms of strategy may not be moral or that the apparently moral forms of strategy may not be effective. The dilemma appears in its sharpest form as the Christian social strategist relates to social systems. The social system itself may appear to be moral; but it may also appear that important moral goals can only be gained by pursuing methods *outside* a system. For example, formal political democracy (a morally approvable procedural system) may in given circumstances have to be bypassed for the sake of such important moral goals as peace or economic justice. On the other hand, an important goal sometimes can be gained only by seeking it *through* the normal channels of an immoral system. Then the question is whether one should engage in actions which, while promising success vis-à-vis a particular goal, will at the same time strengthen an immoral system. The dilemma is particularly frustrating because, for the Christian, effectiveness itself must be defined in moral terms.

The whole problem is much more complex than many social activists and publicists suppose as social systems are almost infinitely complex phenomena. They exist on many different levels, organizing different aspects of life which are sometimes parallel, sometimes hierarchical in relation to each other. Despite the great diversity of social systems, there is a sense in which all known social systems are interrelated — illustrating Walter Muelder's dictum that "mankind is the unit of cooperation." [3]

Our understanding of *system* must therefore be broader than that implied by most rhetoric in defense of or in opposition to "the system." We may understand the term to mean all regular patterns of social interaction in which the expectancy is widely shared that certain forms of action will evoke predictable results. Social systems, according to Wilbert E. Moore, minimally consist of "role-players or actors in interaction governed by rules of conduct that entail rewards for compliance and penalties for noncompliance. . . . Such systems," he continues, "may vary in size from a pair of friends to the large national state, in duration from the barely more than transitory encounter to a nominally eternal administrative organization, in range of common interests from the collector's club to the family or community, and in a multitude of other ways. No simple and universal explanation, such as sociability, will account for this variety, and dealing with variety has been one of the main preoccupations of social science. Descriptive generalizations about particular types of systems and explaining the types in their settings constitute the bulk of our very incomplete knowledge of 'social systems.'" [4] We can speak meaningfully of political systems, economic systems, familial systems, etc., on the basis of the principal objectives of the system and the nature of distributed rewards. We all participate simultaneously in a complex web of social systems.

Defined in this broad way, it is evident that social strategy has to operate in and from social systems of some sort. A totally revolutionary strategy — in the sense of absolute discontinuity with all present social systems — is inconceivable. The practicalities of strategy cannot simply be determined, therefore, by a decision for or against social systems. It is rather a question of determining which kinds of goals can and ought to be sought as the objects of a Christian social strategy and what kinds of strategic methods, either from within or outside a defined social system, are relevant to the desired changes.[5]

The first requisite of Christian social strategy is a clear understanding of its objectives: What social changes or stabilities are to be sought, and why, precisely, should Christians work for such goals? Social strategy may be peculiarly complex for Christians because the identification of the good in concrete social form involves both tangible and intangible realities. It is much easier to organize strategy around clearly tangible goals. But in a Christian perspective, tangible ends are subordinated to intangible ones. The intangible goals are the ultimate, intrinsic objectives; the tangible objectives are instrumental. For instance, the immediate goal of much Christian social action during the 1960s was racial desegregation—a goal which could be spelled out in terms of the destruction of certain quite tangible barriers to authentic human interaction among persons of different racial backgrounds. But the more ultimate goal was integration—a transformed spiritual and relational reality. In effect, tangible goals such as desegregation are means rather than ends. To speak of the ultimate goals of the Christian as intangible is not to say that they are unreal, but rather that they are immeasurable and, in the last analysis, dependent upon factors over which strategy and action can gain no final control. Fulfillment of the community of love and justice which Christians understand by faith to be the kingdom of God necessarily involves the attitudes of free human beings; and both the freedom of persons and the theological point of reference transcend the manipulable objects of experience. Moreover, human freedom implies the perpetual opportunity of humans to sin and thus, also, the continuing vulnerabilty of every human accomplishment. Even Walter Rauschenbusch, who is sometimes falsely associated with the view that the Kingdom of God can be built by man, had a more realistic view: "Imperfect moral insight will work hurt in the best conceivable social order. The strong will always have the impulse to exert their strength, and no system can be devised which can keep them from crowding and jostling the weaker. . . . At best there is always but an approximation to a perfect social order. The Kingdom of God is always but coming." But, he continues, "every approximation to it is worth while." [6]

Of what might an approximation to the Kingdom of God consist? To speak of approximations or of proximate ends may seem to suggest that, while the transcendent reality of God's Kingdom cannot be realized fully by human agency, some proportion of it can. It suggests that we can come more or less close to the goal while never expecting finally to achieve it. But the problem with this way of viewing our proximate goals is that no matter how close we come to devising the best external arrangements and institutions, the gap between such objective factors and the intrinsic realities of loving community remains yawning before us in the absence of an affirmative response from other (partly) free human beings. Man may continue to be estranged from fellow man in spite of favorable external arrangements. Notwithstanding improvements in the objective situation, we find ourselves, as Christian strategists, further away from God's intended community of love because of a deepening human selfishness. Thus, progress toward the ultimate, intrinsic goals cannot be measured only in terms of objective improvements in the human situation.

How, then, are we to speak meaningfully of concrete, attainable strategic objectives whose status is derived from the transcendent reference points of Christian faith?

A more promising approach to this problem treats proximate ends quite frankly as instrumental goals. Certain concrete goals are sought because they serve the more ultimate, transcendent realities. Some worldly conditions aid, while others impede, the realization of transcendent ends in the actual world of experience. As Dietrich Bonhoeffer put it, "if . . . a human life is deprived of the conditions which are proper to it, then the justification of such a life by grace and faith, if it is not rendered impossible, is at least seriously impeded. . . . The hungry man needs bread and the homeless man needs a roof; the dispossessed need justice and the lonely need fellowship; the undisciplined need order and the slave needs freedom."[7] Such needs are not identical with the transcendent need, but their provision serves the transcendent all the same. Hence, while instrumental goals (the proximate ends) cannot be regarded as intrinsic or ultimate, they are invested with moral seriousness all the same. Food for the hungry man is not itself ultimate; but since in the world of existence man needs food in order to survive, and since man's survival without dehumanizing degrees of suffering is a precondition of his participation in God's intended human family of love on earth, it follows that food for the hungry man belongs to God's intention and is therefore properly to be regarded as a "Christian" goal. We may speak similarly of other economic, social, political, and legal conditions and relationships. Programs to erase famine or illiteracy or racial discrimination gain ethical status from the fact that such conditions make it more difficult for people to live a human life in community — as that life is most profoundly disclosed to Christian understanding. The creation of better governmental institutions, housing, educational institutions, social security, guaranteed income, etc., can represent efforts to improve the conditions necessary to man's life in community.[8]

Is Christian social strategy in this sense restricted to the pursuit of objective conditions on the instrumental level? While the ultimate, intrinsic realities which are the final goal of Christian action cannot be reduced to objective conditions, there is, nevertheless, a sense in which the Christian strategist can act more directly in pursuit of the ultimate itself. That is by his attempt to communicate to others (the alienated and unjust alike) his own full acceptance of them as children of God, brothers, and fellow heirs of the promise. Social strategy can have a certain symbolic character which is distinct from actions to change objective conditions. A given line of social strategy may be useful on either or both levels, or its utility on one level can be negated by its inutility on the other. Both levels of strategy have their risks. Communication or symbolic action may lead to neglect of objective conditions and serve as a mask (or ideology) for the maintenance of evil conditions. Action dealing with objective conditions alone may, on the other hand, neglect the deeper human realities those conditions are intended to serve. Those who are serious about either of these levels will be serious about the other as well. A good illustration of both is afforded by the 1963 March on Washington sponsored by civil rights organizations. On the more obvious level, the march was designed to get Congress to enact legislation to establish objective conditions considered necessary for the restoration of black people to full participation in the life of community. But a very important aspect of the churches' participation in the march was the desire to communicate a reconciling acceptance of and identification with the disinherited.[9]

Both types of social strategy are important and both gain their ethical legitimation from the quality of the goodness which they serve. They suggest that the key strategic questions, which locate the goals for Christian strategy, are these: (1) What, in our age and understanding, are the objective conditions necessary or desirable to the life of persons and communities in the Kingdom of God; and (2) How can we best communicate the reconciling reality of that kingdom to persons estranged from it?

The Church itself is a characteristic embodiment of these twin aspects of Christian social strategy. It cannot be viewed simply as an agent of change, for it also has its own corporate embodiment, its own objective structure and dynamics. It can be studied empirically as a social phenomenon, and often it must itself be the object of the social strategy of Christians. But neither is the Church purely temporal for, as the Church, it is also a fellowship of faith. As such it can bear witness to the transcendent realities of its faith, while seeking in its own institutional life to embody those realities and acting to secure conditions appropriate to those realities in the world. Muelder's little book, *In Every Place a Voice*,[10] captures this sense of the Church as manifestation, witness, and agent of the Kingdom in a perceptive commentary on the line from the Message of the First Assembly of the World Council of Churches: "We have to make of the Church in every place a voice for those who have no voice, and a home where every man will be at home." With this understanding of the objectives in mind, we may return to the problem of Christian social strategy in relation to given social systems.

"THE SYSTEM" AS A PROBLEM IN STRATEGIC PRACTICALITY

It has already been observed that social strategy must operate in and from social systems of some sort and that the practicalities of strategy cannot simply be determined by a decision for or against working within the system. But it now must be observed that any social system involving leadership (as most certainly do) has a hierarchical power structure which can either be confirmed or challenged by the strategy employed by the social-change agent. Should the attempt be made to work through this existing power structure, or should the change agent try to organize a new power base from which to gain control of the entire system?

The problem can be illustrated in the social science literature on racial desegregation in which the role of the "gatekeeper" has been emphasized.[11] The gatekeeper in any social institution is understood to be the person who, more than others, ultimately determines whether minority group persons are to be admitted. An industrialist might be the gatekeeper so far as job opportunity is concerned, a realtor or apartment house manager could be the gatekeeper in housing, a minister the gatekeeper with respect to church membership. To effect desegregation one tries to persuade the gatekeeper, either through rational or moral appeal or through pressure tactics. The legitimacy of the gatekeeper's position in the social system is not generally questioned in the social science literature on this subject published in the 1950s.

The basic concept is readily applicable to other problems of social strategy: the gatekeeper can be understood as the point where the power of any social system, as a system, is focused.[12] Thus, in legislative politics, a committee chairman may exercise a gatekeeper role in the operative system; or, in a local school system, the superintendent or key board members may play the role. In many cities of middle size, a rather small elite may exercise gatekeeper power for most key local decisions in business and politics.

A fundamental decision confronts the social change agent as he contemplates the system: will he attempt to work through the gatekeeper, thus in effect supporting existing power relationships, or will he attempt to challenge the gatekeeper by constructing a new series of power relationships? Recent attempts by the Senate Foreign Relations Committee to share powers in foreign relations now exercised predominantly by the president can be understood as a modified attempt to construct new power relationships. On the other hand, efforts to influence the president's policies (via telegrams, visits by delegations, etc.) can be understood as working through the gatekeeper and thus confirming existing power relationships. If the change agent does decide to work through the existing power structure an inevitable consequence of his decision is to confirm and probably strengthen that structure — even if he is successful thereby in gaining his own immediate objectives. From a purely practical standpoint he ought therefore to weigh any negative effects in strengthening an existing power system against the positive effects in gaining his original objectives.

One social scientist, James B. McKee, raised precisely this question in relation to what he considered the over-reliance of social scientists upon existing gatekeepers in their race relations strategies in the 1950s. Working primarily with existing power elites, he argued, gives them "effective control over the scope and direction of the program, keeps the issue out of the hands of a more militant leadership, offsets the chance of the rise of new leadership, and thus lessens the threat to the status quo in power, and offers a fresh and important situation to be exploited for validation of its moral and civic leadership."[13] Considerations of this kind led the Office of Economic Opportunity, in devising its local community-action programs, to prescribe the "maximum feasible participation" of poor people themselves. Community Action Councils were purposely structured so as to keep as much power as possible over the designation and funding of local projects in the hands of poor people. Existing community leadership, including public officials, was not given a dominant role. The effect (eventually perceived by most local political leadership) was to begin to create a new power base.

The inability to arrive at clear decisions between working with existing elites or attempting to replace them can seriously weaken social strategy, although some combination of the two approaches is not unthinkable. One of the weaknesses of the McCarthy campaign of 1968 was the confused interaction of two major goals: peace in Viet Nam (and reordering of national priorities) on the one hand, and reform of the Democratic Party on the other. The second objective, while it was consonant with the drives for nominating convention delegates in New Hampshire, Wisconsin, California and a handful of other states, precluded effective bargaining with the important kingmakers, such as Mayor Daley of Chicago. Prior to his assassination, the genius of Robert F. Kennedy's campaign was its apparent ability to attract reformers (whose most important substantive case was peace in Viet Nam) without necessarily alienating the bosses. But the key to this strategy was its emphasis upon peace in Viet Nam and its relative lack of emphasis upon reform of the party's procedures.[14]

Broadly speaking, the basic strategic decision we are considering involves a choice between a *reformist* or a *revolutionary* orientation, as these terms have been understood especially in classical socialist circles. But it needs to be remembered that even these terms are relative. This relativity can also be illustrated in relation to the McCarthy campaign of 1968. In comparison with the approach of militants who viewed all electoral politics with contempt, the McCarthy campaign was reformist. But from the standpoint of the White House and Democratic Party loyalists, that same campaign might properly have been called revolutionary because it sought structural change in the de facto power system. The campaign was reformist in the sense that it sought reforms without challenging the underlying system of Constitution and law; but it was revolutionary in the sense that it challenged the nominating system in the Democratic Party.

We need to be clear that the choice between violent and nonviolent tactics does not correspond to the decision to work through or against a power elite. Violence can be directed toward the overthrow of a power system, either by removing it directly or by making it impossible for the system to govern. But violence can also be employed to wring concessions out of a power system; that is, it can be used to influence a particular decision without challenging the power system fundamentally. Likewise, nonviolent tactics are not necessarily reformist. Gandhi's campaigns for Indian independence illustrate how nonviolent tactics can be used for the revolutionary purpose of destroying a whole system of power and replacing it with another.

Moreover, the choice between strategies of *education* and *direct action* does not correspond to the decision to try to influence elites or to work against them. Education can be directed toward the enlightenment of an elite, or it can be directed toward the masses in order to begin the formation of a new, revolutionary power base. Similarly, direct action can merely refer to the actions of a power elite in the social process (such as President Truman's executive order desegregating the armed forces), or it can mean direct action to replace a power elite. Somewhere in between, direct action can be used as a means of persuading or influencing a power elite. Education and direct action are both significant aspects of all social strategy. Education is properly understood as preparation for action, whether in the context of a predominantly revolutionary or of a reformist strategic perspective. In either case, the choice between reliance upon education rather than action will hinge upon one's assessment of the degree of readiness to take action. In a strategic context the two belong together.

STRATEGIC ANALYSIS OF SOCIAL SYSTEMS

Ethical questions involved in the decision whether to work with or against a power elite will be considered below. Before dealing with those issues we should, in a preliminary way, consider certain practical problems. The strategist must balance the undesirable consequences against the desirable. But what are the resources available to him, and what are the foreseeable obstacles should he desire to circumvent or to replace a power elite?

We return to the observation that social systems are complex webs of interdependence. Systems are more or less functional with respect to end and needs. Robert Merton has pointed out that social phenomena may serve both "manifest" and "latent" functions. The former represent the publicly recognized purposes, the latter refer to less obvious forms of need-gratification.[15] One must expect great resistance in attempting to dislodge the leadership of a social system if that leadership is viewed as highly functional by a large proportion of the participants in the system. Attempts to replace the seniority system of congressional committee leadership have usually failed despite the fact that many intelligent observers outside Congress as well as within regard the system as a major frustration. It has survived most attacks upon it because it continues to serve the (primarily latent) political and personal functions viewed as necessary by a large-enough majority of members of Congress. Even the House Rules Committee, which was notoriously obstructive for a period of years under the leadership of Congressman Howard Smith, performed latent functions which were apparently appreciated even by many congressmen who publicly called for reform. It buried bills which congressmen had introduced only under political duress, and in other ways it saved them the embarrassment of having to vote on politically divisive measures. Similarly, big-city political machines, in spite of their notorious corruption, often performed services that were valued highly by recent immigrants.

Revolutionary change in leadership generally presupposes existing widespread discontent or the capacity to create such discontent within the system. Accurate analysis of the manifest and latent functions performed by a social system, including analysis of the participants' perceptions of those functions, should therefore precede any judgment as to the practicality of challenging the system's power elite. In some cases, it may be evident that the elite is imposed or exploitative or simply inadequate and that discontent either exists or can be aroused. In other cases, where there is no prospect of developing a new power base, it may be more practical to work through an existing elite.

A new power base can sometimes be established by involving outside forces or forces derived from a more inclusive system. For example, the revolution in voting rights for black people in the South could hardly have been accomplished through persuasion of existing southern power elites; nor could the white majority, particularly for the sake of that objective, have been used as a power base to replace those elites. But it did prove possible to involve the wider federal system of the United States to accomplish that objective, and thereby also to begin to reconstitute the power structure of the South itself. The 1968 Soviet invasion of Czechoslovakia is a comparable illustration (practically, if not morally). Those in Czechoslovakia wishing to re-establish an authoritarian Stalinist regime during the Dubcek reform period (1967–1968) found themselves quite powerless within Czechoslovakia itself. The overwhelming majority of the Czech people and most Czech institutions eagerly supported the reforms and were determined to resist a return to authoritarianism. The actual destruction of the reform movement could be effected by power imposed from the wider Warsaw Pact system — in particular the Soviet Union. This outside power was able to return the tiny authoritarian circle (probably a small fragment of the Communist Party itself) to rule.

The problem is thrown into sharp relief by the strategy and tactics of many New Left activists in the late 1960s. While, on the face of it, the tactics of disruption and confrontation (and in extreme cases, of bombings) have seemed to restrict rather than to enlarge the revolutionary power base, those who have employed such tactics have regarded them as contributing to ultimate control of the American system. In a perceptive study of protest movements of this period, a task force of the National Commission on the Causes and Prevention of Violence has summarized the case for confrontation tactics as argued in New Left documents and as stated by New Left leaders in interviews with commission staff:

1. *Confrontation and militancy are methods of arousing moderates to action.* The creation of turmoil and disorder can stimulate otherwise quiescent groups to take more forceful action in their own ways. Liberals may come to support radical demands while opposing their tactics; extreme tactics may shock moderates into self-reexamination. . . .

2. *Confrontation and militancy can educate the public.* Direct action is not intended to win particular reforms or to influence decision-makers, but rather to bring out a repressive response from authorities — a response rarely seen by most white Americans. When confrontation brings violent official response, uncommitted elements of the public can see for themselves the true nature of the "system." . . .

3. *Confrontation, militancy and resistance are ways to prepare young radicals for the possibility of greater repression.* . . .

4. *Combative behavior with respect to the police and other authorities, although possibly alienating "respectable" adults, has the opposite effect on the movement's relationships with nonstudent youth.* Educated, middle-class, nonviolent styles of protest are poorly understood by working-class youth, black youth, and other "dropouts." Contact with these sectors of the youth population is essential and depends upon the adoption of a tough and aggressive stance to win respect from such youth. . . .

5. *The experience of resistance and combat may have a liberating effect on young middle-class radicals.* Most middle-class students are shocked by aggressive or violent behavior. This cultural fear of violence is psychologically damaging and may be politically inhibiting. To be a serious revolutionary, one must reject middle-class values, particularly deference toward authority. Militant confrontation gives resisters the experience of physically opposing institutional power, and it may force students to choose between "respectable" intellectual radicalism and serious commitment to revolution, violent or otherwise.

6. *The political potency of "backlash" is usually exaggerated.* Those who point to the possibility of repression as a reaction to confrontation tactics wish to compromise demands and principles and dilute radicalism. Repression will come in any case, and to diminish one's efforts in anticipation is to give up the game before it starts.[16]

In this overall strategic perspective, even an increase in overt repression may be desired because it helps to heighten the contradictions within the system, creates wider public awareness, and increases the discontent from which a revolutionary power base can be formed. The defeat of liberal reformism may therefore even be considered desirable.[17] Sometimes "things have to get worse before they can get better."

This strategic perspective is not, on its face, unthinkable. But its practicality would seem to depend upon key assumptions concerning the degree to which American society, as a systemic whole, is functional. It may be worth remembering that in very few instances have genuinely revolutionary movements succeeded in industrial countries and that those few instances of success have almost invariably represented right-wing movements or coups—sometimes as reactions to ill-conceived left-wing revolutionary efforts. The reason for this may be that in industrialized societies too many people believe they have too great a present stake in the existing system—thus leading them to react personally to perceived threats to the existing order. Revolutionary strategies can thus create more power base, not for revolutionaries but for reactionary demagogues.[18] But, on the other hand, there are numerous illustrations of success by reform strategies which do not threaten the underlying system of order itself. Such strategies can be perceived as improving the functional character of the society. In recent history, revolutionary movements have enjoyed much greater success in nonindustrial societies where very substantial discontent already exists.

Strategic analysis must therefore encompass realistic study of the balancing of forces potentially oriented for or against change. Equilibrium theory, of the sort developed by Robert M. MacIver, seeks to develop a typology of possible balances of this kind.[19] A "tense equilibrium," for example, is a highly polarized situation accompanied by emotional stress. Overt conflict is likely to result in general deterioration of the situation rather than in either side gaining its objectives. An "indifferent equilibrium" is one in which there is little strong sentiment either for or against change—a situation in which vigorous leadership can be very effective. A "precarious equilibrium" is one in which change is very likely, but in one direction only—as in the case of a rock precariously perched on the side of a cliff. Here the question is whether or not the status quo will be maintained; if it is not, the direction of change is clearly predictable. A "moving equilibrium" is a dynamic situation in which there is no stable status quo to be defended or attacked but rather a flux of events presenting greater or lesser opportunities to all parties.

While few social situations are likely to illustrate any of these types perfectly, such a conceptualization may provide useful tools for analysis. For example, careful analysis may show that a situation is actually an indifferent equilibrium and that overwhelming support could be gotten for change—in spite of the initial fears of leaders that strong action might precipitate polarization. In some such situations, people are likely to follow the established leadership in almost any direction. For a number of years following World War II this may have been essentially true of the tendency to support American Presidential leadership on almost all foreign-policy questions. During the periods of major escalation of the Viet Nam War, from 1965–1968, when public opinion generally seemed to support all of President Johnson's moves, it is not unlikely that public opinion might just as readily have supported total disengagement or other alternatives. The public may have been interested in supporting the presidency as a fundamental national institution, but comparatively indifferent to particular policies regarding Viet Nam.

Or, to use another illustration, during the fragile career of the Weimar Republic, the democratic center was precariously balanced between a militant left and a militant right—both regarding the centrist regime with contempt. In retrospect, it is evident that this was a "precarious equilibrium." The situation was highly unstable; but change, if any, would be toward the right and, ultimately, fascism. Major movement toward the left, as envisaged by Communists and other radical socialists, was never a real option. Social-change agents on the left, therefore, really had only the options of helping to preserve a status quo (which might in the long run have proved most useful to them) or permitting power to move sharply to the right.[20] In the Russian revolutionary situation of 1917, precisely the opposite kind of precarious equilibrium existed. There, the military forces, workers, peasants, etc., would hardly have tolerated a swing rightward, back to the Czarist regime; but a fragile center proved vulnerable to pressure from the Bolsheviks on the left. Those interested in preventing a Communist victory could have acted relevantly in that situation only by strengthening the constitutional democratic regime. There was no possibility of a Czarist restoration.

Such assessments must be made with great care. Timid conservatism may too readily believe that any change will be for the worse, while immature radicalism may too quickly assume that any change will be for the better. Specific analysis of the situation is required.

STRATEGIC RELIANCE UPON GOVERNMENT

A very basic strategic question involves the choice of primary reliance upon government as over-against nongovernmental power systems for social change. For example, should churches deal with poverty, housing problems for the elderly, medical care needs, etc., directly (using their own resources), or should they seek to involve the government in such areas? Should the attempt be made to impose more serious governmental regulation or even to nationalize the corporations? [21]

In an analysis of this problem, George D. Beam has argued that in fact little is to be gained through the political arena: "With the expansion of the civil service to include more and more government employees, with the increasing wealth and consequent power of conglomerates, pension trusts, and insurance companies, and with the continuous demand for technically sophisticated and expensive defense equipment by the military, the *initiative and direction* of American policy has shifted out of the political arena to the areas of administration, economics and the military." He therefore contends for a strategy of "action geared toward taking over and making one's own the real factors of contemporary society—the administration, the economy, and the military." [22] Presumably this should be done directly, not through regular political channels.

It is indeed arguable that nongovernmental power centers and the major civil-service bureaucracies can be infiltrated or otherwise influenced. Creative efforts have been made in recent years to do just that.[23] The Project for Corporate Responsibility, which sought to muster voting strength at the General Motors stockholders meeting of 1970 in order to force that corporation to adopt more responsible policies was at least partially successful, even though only 2.73 percent of the vote was finally mustered. Church and educational groups have begun to make some small difference in the policies of corporations and banks through the manipulation of invested funds. Social-change movements have in recent years become much more effective in such maneuvers because of a growing understanding of actual power relationships. In particular, the potential economic power of such hitherto passive institutions as pension funds has been exposed to view.

Without denigrating the value of such nonpolitical strategic orientations, it needs to be remembered that only government brings to focus the power of the whole conglomerate of social systems making up a national society. Political power, as Talcott Parsons has observed, "is capacity to control the relational system as a system." [24] It can be contrasted with other forms of power, such as private economic wealth, which are quantitative and, in the last analysis, subordinate to the political. Political power is, in fact, "a mobilization of the total relational context as a facility relative to the goal in question." Political power is therefore the maximum point of strategic leverage upon everything else. Private measures can gain control over small segments of decision-making, but only government possesses ultimate power over the whole. For all the difficulties in the political system, it is probable that government is the most strategic point of access to the decisions that will affect most social issues. Redistribution of income, control of the environment, international policies, the definition and enforcement of civil rights, control of police policies, reform of prison, transportation, housing, and medical policies — these all can be affected more profoundly by government than by any other form of power.

This should be particularly obvious in relation to economic matters. The funds available from private groups for welfare projects are nothing compared with the funds available through the taxing powers of the government. Even with very sacrificial giving, all the churches in America would be hardpressed to mount a welfare program equal even to present inadequate public welfare programs. The demand of James Foreman's "Black Manifesto" in 1969 for $2 billion in reparations from American churches was and seemed utterly beyond possible expectation; but that amount is still less than one percent of the federal budget. Moreover, as the Synagogue Council of America noted in a statement responding to the manifesto, "it is clear that even if these demands were met in full, these inequities and injustices would not be rectified." The council urged that "a far more reliable guide for priorities is to be found in the Kerner Commission Report, the 'Freedom Budget' of the A. Philip Randolph Institute and in the National Urban League's 'Domestic Marshall Plan,'" each of which, it may be noted, places primary reliance upon governmental action. It may be that the net effect of the manifesto was to become — for both its advocates and opponents — a diversion at a time when there was need for increased church efforts to involve government in the problems of black economic empowerment.[25]

This is not to suggest that all social strategy to be effective must be oriented toward governmental action. Some objectives doubtless cannot be reached in this way, and sometimes the political climate is so utterly unfavorable as to present the strategist with the choice between actions through private channels or no action at all. Moreover, nongovernmental groups can sometimes stimulate social change through small-scale demonstrations of new possibilities or through action to create conditions to which government must then respond. Action in nongovernmental groups can also establish power bases relevant to governmental action. Significant power in any non-governmental system is likely in various ways to translate into power in the governmental system itself.

"THE SYSTEM" AND DILEMMAS OF STRATEGIC MORALITY

Christian social strategy is committed to ethical criteria of effectiveness. For present purposes, we have already defined its objectives as (1) the objective conditions necessary or desirable to the life of persons and communities in the Kingdom of God, and (2) the communication of the reconciling reality of that kingdom to persons estranged from it. These proximate goals are understood as serving the fullest possible realization of God's intended loving community of mankind on earth. How does such an understanding of strategic objectives affect our approach to social systems? In a very immediate sense, it precludes our ever treating persons simply as functions of systems or as enemies to be disposed of or disregarded. But it also confronts us with deeper moral dilemmas.

The basic dilemma can be put for us by Walter Rauschenbusch's discussion of the difference between Christian and unchristian social orders. "An unchristian social order can be known by the fact that it makes good men do bad things, [whereas] a Christian social order makes bad men do good things." [26] It is plainly evident in this that Christian social strategy must declare war upon all systemizations of violence or racism or economic injustice in which even good men are, in effect, compelled to perpetuate social evil by participating in ordinary institutional life. But, if effective strategy requires use of systems of power, it may involve the change agent in evils ancillary to the system — whether intended by him or not. Making use of the power systems and structures of society, whether or not these are governmental, almost inevitably involves the Christian in sanctioning coercion or appeal to sub-Christian motivations or confirmation of stratification systems in which "inferiors" are alienated from "superiors."

One necessary answer to this dilemma is that the Christian social strategist, in his choice of methods, places every means under the transcendent criterion of God's ultimate intentions and not merely under the criterion of effectiveness in reaching a proximate objective. Every measurable goal is still only a proximate or penultimate end. Thus, the Christian cannot chart his social strategy on the basis of simple pragmatic calculations. In the more ultimate perspective, some apparently effective approaches are not understood to be effective at all.

But to leave the problem at this point is probably to become irrelevant to most human experience. To be human is to be involved in systems which perpetuate evil; it is even to contribute to their effectiveness in perpetuating evil. Many, even, of those who protest most vehemently against the involvement of Christians and churches in immoral social systems urge cooperation with revolutionary movements whose violent methods present prima facie contradictions of the community of love envisaged by Christian ethics. Similarly,

Christians who have recoiled at the participation by some of their radical brethren in revolutionary movements have often been blind to their own personal and corporate involvements in vast systems of institutionalized racism and violence. The ultimate criterion of the Kingdom of God remains above all Christian strategy and action; but the tension between that criterion and human systems cannot be represented as simple negation.[27]

A more relevant form of this tension may be expressed in a Christian methodological presumption: a methodology of judgment which is based upon an initial presumption in favor of methods and movements believed to be directly consonant with God's intended kingdom of love and justice — and an initial presumption against all that seems to alienate or repress or coerce man. Such a Christian methodological presumption needs to be open, however, to the possibility that that which is presumed to be the better or the worse may, in specific circumstances, not prove to be so. What the presumption does is to locate the burden of proof. A strategic method which is initially presumed to be wrong will not be employed unless it can be shown to be necessary for the sake, not of a purely proximate end, but of the ultimate end. Would worse evil ultimately befall man if the problematic means were not used than would if it were? Just-war doctrine illustrates the method. According to that doctrine, social violence is presumed to be off limits for Christian approval or participation unless in a given case war is able to meet several criteria. In cases of continuing doubt, one should *not* engage in social violence.

Lest this approach be dismissed too quickly as temporizing with evil, we should remember that the alternative is nothing short of anarchism. Anything other than social anarchism is at least open to the use of some social coercion, some reliance upon other than purely voluntary observance of social norms; and thus to limit the moral freedom of others. If we are to sanction and make use of social systems which "*make* bad men do good things" (emphasis supplied), then we are already involved in the use of methods which are problematical under the transcendent criterion of God's kingdom of love. The worse of it is, we may also have to make use of systems which at least tempt good men to do bad things. We may have to rely upon economic or other incentives which foster selfishness, since the functioning of any social system is likely to depend upon motivations which are extraneous to the purposes to which we intend to put it. We may have to make use of stratification systems which deepen man's alienation from fellow man. We may feel that we have to appeal to the unadulterated sense of self-interest of exploited people in order to organize them into an effective new power base for change.[28] In situations where new power bases are manifestly impossible to organize, we may have to cooperate with selfish power elites and thus provide them with further legitimation. But genuinely Christian social strategy does not merely try to weigh the negative against the positive in some sort of cost-benefit analysis. It seeks to maintain the tension by placing an initial burden of proof against the negative. When in doubt, the benefit of the doubt is accorded to the positive.

That the burden of proof can so often be borne results from the universality of human sin. We are required, as Luther saw, to erect dykes against sinfulness. But, as Luther also saw, the human strategy of the Gospel must operate in two realms simultaneously: the level of dealing in and through human institutions and the level of proclamation of the gospel. Luther's method of correlating the two tracks was inadequate; but his approach is a useful reminder that it is never enough merely to deal with tangible goals. There must be a parallel strategy of witness.

The social strategies of Martin Luther King, Jr. illustrate a more creative way of relating the two. King was ready when necessary to bargain with corrupt power structures for the sake of tangible improvements in the situation of black people. But the concrete actions of his movements were interpreted as, directed toward, and consistent with human reconciliation. His campaigns were based upon the correct ethical assumption that, if anything, repression more seriously damages the soul of the oppressor than that of the oppressed. The strategic formula thus included (1) maximum arousal of a sense of injustice and discontent among the oppressed (thus heightening and making more visible the conflict between oppressor and oppressed); combined with (2) strong motivation within the new

base of power thus formed for reconciliation with the oppressor —
but on the basis of justice rather than subservience. The strategy was
effective politically in that its commitment to nonviolence tended
to shift the onus for violent counterreactions onto the opponent —
thus extending its own base of political power to include many of
those who abhor violence and disorder. The strategy had revolutionary impact upon American society, but it was not revolutionary
with respect to the basic constitutional system; its victories, by and
large, needed to be registered *within* the political system in the form
of new definitions of rights and responsibilities.

Subsequent spokesmen for the New Left have questioned not only
whether strategic objectives can be gained effectively through democratic political processes, but even whether it is moral to try. George
D. Beam, for instance, cites the tendency in "usual politics" to confuse "the values of democracy with the means used to attain them."
He argues that the procedures of majority rule and compromise can
result in gross evils. Compromise is to be rejected "when the procedure does not result in the implementation of democratic values." [29]

This viewpoint, which cannot be considered in detail here, raises
the broader question of what stake a Christian social strategy may
have in the maintenance of procedural systems. To be committed to
a procedural system, as Beam rightly notes, is to be willing to accept
a distasteful outcome. But the whole history of civilized human life
suggests the preferability of procedural systems to raw power struggles. Compromises resulting from commitment to what is regarded on
the whole as being a good procedural system have to be evaluated
not simply in terms of the immediate issue at stake but also in terms
of the wider social results of breaking down the procedural system
itself.[30] The *nature* of the procedural system is thus itself of concern
to Christian social strategy. A procedural system based solely upon
majority rule, without provision for the guarantee of certain basic
rights, could not be accepted as ideal by Christians. One of the best
brief formulations of ethical criteria of procedural systems is that
contained in the World Council of Churches' definition of a "responsible society." That formulation emphasizes the accountability
of all political and economic power to those affected by its exercise

in a context providing for freedom, justice, and public order. Modern society should be such "that the people have freedom to control, to criticize and to change their governments, that power be made responsible by law and tradition, and be distributed as widely as possible through the whole community." Nor is this limited to purely political processes: "It is required that economic justice and provision of equality of opportunity be established for all the members of society."[31]

THE SYSTEMATIC CONSOLIDATION OF STRATEGY

Much social strategy fails, ultimately, not because it is defeated but because its victories are not consolidated and preserved. Even revolutionary strategies may not be prepared for consolidation on a moral plane. It may simply be assumed that the new power elite will govern for the people whereas the old governed against the people. But Christian social strategy is concerned, not simply with the attainment of conditions more conducive to God's intended community of love and justice, but also with the permanence and future improvement of those conditions and with the way in which people respond to each other in the new situation. In part, the institutionalization of new conditions into social systems may require some new reliance upon social violence or social coercion — as when laws establish penalties for the violation of the civil rights of others or when new cultural attitudes make it less profitable for businessmen to pollute the water and air. But effective consolidation in a Christian perspective seeks to incorporate opponents into the acceptance of new definitions of justice and decency. Moral consolidation is incomplete without reconciliation, and the prospect of reconciliation should, as we have emphasized in other words, be an ultimate criterion of Christian strategy.

NOTES

1. Concern for Christian social strategy has been a striking point of continuity in the thought of Walter G. Muelder. While resisting the tendency to treat human institutional goals as ultimate, Muelder likewise avoided the opposite mistake of treating human institutional goals as irrelevant to the ultimate objectives of faith. Social goals could be advanced

provisionally, but nevertheless normatively. His insistence upon correlating the insights of normative disciplines with those of the social sciences has, moreover, helped to protect his work from both unthinking activism and intellectual aloofness from the world of action.

2. Herbert E. Stotts and Paul Deats, Jr., *Methodism and Society: Guidelines for Strategy* (Nashville: Abingdon Press, 1962), p. 112.

3. Walter G. Muelder, *Foundations of the Responsible Society* (Nashville: Abingdon Press, 1959), pp. 39 ff.

4. Wilbert E. Moore, *Social Change* (Englewood Cliffs, N.J.: Prentice-Hall, Foundations of Modern Sociology Series, 1963), p. 24; cf. Talcott Parsons and Edward A. Shils, eds., *Toward a General Theory of Action* (New York: Harper and Row, 1951), a discussion of the theory of social systems by leading social scientists.

5. It is beyond the scope of this paper to consider in detail the contemporary sociological discussions of the processes of social change, including the question whether change basically arises within social systems (endogenously) or from without (exogenously). One can, in fact, speak of a variety of "causes of change," including the effects of major physical or environmental changes, increased contact with other cultures and technologies, assertions of social power from without, and social invention occurring within a society. The present paper assumes that man possesses sufficient transcendent freedom to be a purposive innovator of social change and that social behavior is sufficiently predictable to make social strategy possible. For an unusually good discussion of the relationship between personal freedom and social determination in social science, see Gibson Winter, *Elements for a Social Ethic* (New York: Macmillan, 1966). See Amitai and Eva Etzioni, eds., *Social Change: Sources, Patterns, and Consequences* (New York: Basic Books, 1964); Warren G. Bennis, Kenneth D. Benne, and Robert Chin, eds., *The Planning of Change* (New York: Holt, Rinehart and Winston, 1961); and S. N. Eisenstadt, ed., *Readings in Social Evolution and Development* (Oxford: Pergamon Press, 1970) for leading viewpoints on the sociology of social change.

6. Walter Rauschenbusch, *Christianity and the Social Crisis* (New York: Macmillan, 1907), pp. 420–21; cf. Walter G. Muelder, *Moral Law in Christian Social Ethics* (Richmond, Va.: John Knox Press, 1966), pp. 163–64: "God's relation to man is of a moral and spiritual order and therefore man's response cannot be coerced. The future must always, therefore, be a fresh victory for the forces of redemption. Though cosmic and historical resources are available, they must constantly be sought after in new struggles with evil."

7. Dietrich Bonhoeffer, *Ethics* (New York: Macmillan, 1965 [1949]), pp. 134, 137.

8. In his *Foundations of the Responsible Society,* Muelder helpfully analyzes the significance of various structures of human experience.

9. A very real objective of this and similar events was the attempt to forge a new movement. A movement, as such, can be understood in both instrumental and intrinsic terms. It is instrumental in the sense that it serves the goals of the cause to which it is directed (in this case, civil rights). It is intrinsic in the sense that the quality of fellowship and restoration of personal dignity within the movement already transcend the tangible, instrumental conditions of human existence. But as a movement directed toward transcendent ends, it knows that these intrinsic qualities must be undergirded by appropriate new social, economic, and political conditions.

10. Walter G. Muelder, *In Every Place a Voice* (Cincinnati: Woman's Division of Christian Service, Board of Missions, The Methodist Church, 1957).

11. See, for example, John P. Dean and Alex Rosen, *A Manual of Intergroup Relations* (Chicago: University of Chicago Press, 1955).

12. The reader will note certain variations in the way the key term *power* is defined and used in the different essays in this volume. Thorough analysis of the concept is beyond the scope of the present paper, but a comment or two of clarification may be useful. I am using the term power in the general sense of the capacity to accomplish a desired objective. It is important to remember that power has two main forms: control over nature and influence in the decisions of other persons. See Franz Neumann, *The Democratic and the Authoritarian State* (New York: The Free Press, 1957), pp. 3–19 for an excellent discussion of this

distinction. The distinction is lost when we think of *coercion* as though it were a purely mechanical way of making people do what we want them to do. Both the carrot and the stick are actually incentives — more or less effective means of making people want to do what we want them to do more than they want the consequences of not doing what we want them to do. Social power is represented in concentrations of those things which are most persuasive to people in determining their decision-making. I agree with those who insist that power in a community reflects more a merging of wills than an imposition of will, although people have often accepted (and therefore undergirded) tyrannies only because alternatives seemed even less acceptable. In the present context, the gatekeeper is in a position to make decisions for an entire community or institution only because, for good or bad reasons, others have accorded or surrendered that right to him.

13. James B. McKee, "Community Power and Strategies in Race Relations: Some Critical Observations," *Social Problems* 6 (Winter): 202.

14. No value judgment is intended here. It is arguable, as a value proposition, that since both peace in Viet Nam and party reform were of very great importance, it was morally preferable to lose while emphasizing both rather than to win while sacrificing one to the other. But there is not much evidence that the McCarthy campaign was clear about all this strategically.

15. Robert Merton, *Social Theory and Social Structure,* rev. ed. (Glencoe, Ill.: The Free Press, 1957).

16. Task Force on Violent Aspects of Protest and Confrontation of the National Commission on the Cause and Prevention of Violence, Jerome H. Skolnick, Director, *The Politics of Protest* (New York: Simon and Schuster, 1969), pp. 107–08.

17. See various articles in Priscilla Long, ed., *The New Left: A Collection of Essays* (Boston: Porter Sargent Publisher, 1969).

18. A striking illustration of how strategies can either enlarge or constrict a potential base of power is afforded by the contrast between the Viet Nam Moratorium of October 15, 1969 and the New Mobilization of November 15, 1969. The former, under the leadership of young people committed to a reformist perspective, snowballed dramatically into a major national event, with large numbers of public officials and leading private citizens participating. The event substantially increased public pressure against the Administration's Viet Nam policies. The New Mobilization, under the leadership of a coalition of organizations, some of which consciously sought greater polarization, succeeded in massing an immense crowd of protesters in Washington; but these were mostly young people, and the net effect of the event and its rhetoric was to constrict, rather than enlarge, the movement's base of power. These observations are based upon close personal contact with both events.

19. Robert M. MacIver, *The More Perfect Union* (New York: Macmillan, 1948), pp. 52–61.

20. See Walter Laqueur, "A Look Back at the Weimar Republic — The Cry Was 'Down with Das System,' " *The New York Times Magazine,* 23 August 1970, pp. 12 ff., for interesting reflections on the period.

21. See Phillip I. Blumberg, "Introduction to The Politicalization of the Corporation," *The Record* of the Association of the Bar of the City of New York, Vol. 26, No. 5 (May, 1971) for an informed discussion of the recent attempt to involve corporations more directly in solving social problems.

22. George D. Beam, *Usual Politics: A Critique and Some Suggestions for an Alternative* (New York: Holt, Rinehart, and Winston, 1970), pp. 191, 192.

23. See Blumberg, "Introduction to the Politicalization of the Corporation."

24. I use the term nonpolitical in the narrower sense of nongovernmental, although recognizing that it is quite legitimate to refer more broadly to the *politics* of any institution or group. In the narrower sense we have reference to the actions and institutions of the state in contrast to other kinds of groups and institutions. Talcott Parsons, *The Social System* (Glencoe, Ill.: The Free Press, 1951), p. 126.

25. Robert S. Lecky and H. Elliott Wright, eds., *Black Manifesto: Religion, Racism and Reparations* (New York: Sheed and Ward, 1969), p. 141. Another illustration of a tendency

to avoid strategies oriented toward government was provided in the late 1960s by a special committee at the U.S. Conference on Church and Society in 1967. The committee was created by the conference to formulate, for the churches, a strategy of response to the urban crisis. The strategic suggestions offered by the group had mainly to do with the churches' own education and action programs, investment of church money, etc. Only as an after-thought, and at the insistence of one or two members, was it added that Christians should "demand and mobilize support for legislation that will attack the problem of redistribution of power and income." *Report of the U.S. Conference on Church and Society* (New York: National Council of Churches, 1968), pp. 89–90. This document can be compared with the report of the Kerner Commission, in preparation at the same time, which emphasized greater governmental involvement in dealing with the problems of the cities.

26. Walter Rauschenbusch, *Christianizing the Social Order* (New York: Macmillan, 1912), p. 127.

27. See Jacques Ellul, *Violence* (New York: Seabury Press, 1969). See esp. chap. 2; cf. Walter Muelder's comment: "in order to save the world the church must to a degree identify itself with the world and is therefore to a degree compromised. The social order takes no apocalyptic leaps from injustice into the perfection of the kingdom of God. . . . The church to be effective must live in the tension between the social order as it is and the kingdom of God." *Methodism and Society in the Twentieth Century* (Nashville: Abingdon Press, 1961), pp. 388–89.

28. Cf. Saul D. Alinsky, *Reveille for Radicals* (Chicago: University of Chicago Press, 1964).

29. Beam, *Usual Politics*, pp. 115–16.

30. John Rawls has made a useful ethical distinction between "justifying a practice and justifying a particular action falling under it," in his article "Two Concepts of Rules," *Philosophical Review*, vol. 44 (1955). Paul Ramsey has explored this distinction in relation to Christian ethics in his *Deeds and Rules in Christian Ethics* (New York: Scribner's, 1967), pp. 123–44.

31. First Assembly, The World Council of Churches, *The Church and the Disorder of Society* (New York: Harper, 1948), p. 192.

8 The Demand for Economic Justice: Southern Africa and the Portuguese Colonies

François Houtart

In *Religion and Economic Responsibility,* Walter G. Muelder has a chapter on "Toward a Responsible World Economy," which includes a section on imperialism: "The upsurge of peoples from below, especially in colonial areas, against the long suffering of the plundered poor, is a major aspect of post-war economic life. . . . Imperialism is bound to be an important factor in world affairs so long as the national powers retain sovereign prerogatives, engage in a power struggle, and use military sanctions to conserve them."[1] It is in this perspective that we want to treat our subject. Of course, it is a complex one and only a broad picture of it can be offered in a few pages. What seems to be most important is to indicate precisely the relationship between the various aspects — historical and present, economic and political, local and international.

In 1455 the Portuguese discovered the islands of Cape Verde. During their southerly course of exploration around Africa, they made contact with the Congo in 1482 and with Mozambique in 1490 before continuing their expeditions toward Asia. It was much later that white colonists first reached South Africa, and not until the seventeenth century were the Dutch really settled there.

The first Portuguese establishments in the fifteenth century took the form of commercial settlements along the coast, where there were also small military garrisons. In Guinea, relations were established with a population of fishermen, whereas in the Congo and Angola the contacts were more organized because of the existence of major kingdoms in these areas.

In the sixteenth century, especially in Angola after 1576, the situation changed. The problem of manpower in the Americas had become acute, as the Indians were decimated, and it was necessary to recruit manpower elsewhere. It was the blacks of Africa who paid the price. Between 1576 and the end of the slave era (1836), more than three million people were deported from Angola. In Mozambique, slavery began to wreak havoc later, at the end of the eighteenth century when the population of Angola had already been diminished to a degree that made the colonizers feel very anxious. Although it was abolished earlier by most colonial nations, slavery continued in Mozambique through the nineteenth century. It is estimated that, between 1800 and 1850, approximately one million people were deported.[2] The slave trade provoked many clashes with the indigenous populations which were to continue until the beginning of the twentieth century.

In South Africa and Rhodesia the problem had a different dimension. White colonists began settling in South Africa in the seventeenth century, and in Southern Rhodesia at the end of the nineteenth century. These white populations were established by the expulsion of the African tribes occupying the best land; and Africans were gradually pushed back to the less fertile and healthful zones. This expulsion and resettling did not happen without numerous bloody incidents. South-West Africa was occupied at the end of the nineteenth century by the Germans, but only certain parts were really inhabited— the entire territory having a very sparse population.

Only *after* the Berlin Conference — i.e., between 1885 and 1890 — were the Portuguese territories truly settled. It was necessary to do so to avoid the risk of having her colonies taken over by other powers, especially Great Britain. It is noteworthy that the system of forced labor in the Portuguese colonies established during this period was one of the most inhuman used in the colonized countries. Even today, about 50 percent of the labor force of Angola is made up of laborers recruited by force in the villages.

The nature of the Portuguese colonization was very different from that of the British and Dutch. There is no racial segregation of the South African type in the Portuguese colonies. (Rhodesia, on the other hand, follows the South African course.) In the Portuguese colonies, alongside an extremely rigid legal system, to which we shall return, there exists what is called *fraternidade* ("brotherhood"). In truth, it is probably possible to have this relationship between the races because the Portuguese people brought to the colonies are from a socio-cultural level rather similar to that of the Africans. Colonists are often peasants from very poor regions, having simple needs and living in a manner similar to the African peoples. To be exact, however, aspects of this relationship of *fraternidade* are closer to that between a father and his children than that between brothers. It should be noted that this paternalistic aspect is typical of the relationship between master and slave, as it has been described by many North American or Brazilian writers.

One finds in this social relationship, already noted by Livingstone in the mid-nineteenth century, a transposition of the myth of the Portuguese ruling class that is perpetuated by a feudal system. One also discovers in *fraternidade* the ideological basis for the continuation of colonial exploitation.

THE BASIC COMPONENTS OF PORTUGUESE COLONIZATION UNTIL 1960

The motives given by the Portuguese political power for maintaining its presence in Africa are generally of a humanitarian and civilizing nature, which, of course, include religious motives, particularly the Christianization of the African peoples. Let us therefore look at the realities.[3]

Christianization. Starting from a medieval concept of identity of political and religious aims,[4] Portugal maintains that its secular goals are directed at evangelization and that the establishment of the Church should help make the inhabitants into Portuguese. But let us look at the facts at the beginning of the 1960s. In Portuguese Guinea, only 1 percent of the people are Christians, and even now there are no African priests. In Mozambique the percentage of Christians is about 5 percent. Only Angola has a higher figure: 40 percent (of which 15 percent are Protestants.) In none of the Portuguese colonies is there a native African bishop, for the concordat makes it mandatory for all to be Portuguese.

Education. In Portuguese Guinea, in 1960, only 1 percent of the African population of school age was actually in primary schools. In Angola it was 3 percent. There were five-hundred pupils in the technical elementary schools in 1960 and three-hundred in the teachers training schools. In the same year the Belgian Congo, on the eve of its independence, had 1.5 million children in primary school, thirty times as many as Angola (adjusted to consider their relative populations, the figure is ten times as many). In Mozambique only one secondary school is open to Africans.

Health. In 1960, Angola had 250 doctors, or one for every 18,000 people. In 1962, the number fell to 210. In 1959 there was an average of one doctor for every 34,000 people in Mozambique, while neighboring countries had the following figures per doctor: Malawi, 15,400 (1959); Zambia, 7,900 (1959); Tanzania, 18,000 (1959); Kenya, 11,000 (1958); and Uganda, 16,800 (1958).[5] In 1965, there were 4,645 hospital beds in Angola, whereas in 1956 the Belgian Congo had 71,800. In Mozambique, in the 1960s, the infant mortality rate has been estimated at 40 percent. During the same period in Tanzania, the figures are 13 to 20 percent, depending on the region.

Economy. The traditional economy is the most developed and borders on being a monoculture. The crop is coffee in Angola and cotton in Mozambique. In the latter country, which depends on Portugal for 40 percent of its exports, the law forbids the development of a textile industry; cotton must be sent to the mother country for processing and repurchased as textiles by the colony.

Angola is also rich in mineral products: diamonds, iron, and, since 1960, petroleum. In the exploitation of these resources, Portugal plays the role of intermediary between the colonies and the industrial nations, retaining the profit for herself.

Political and Social Rights. The classic division within all colonial countries exists in the Portuguese colonies as well, in spite of *fraternidade*. A very small minority of Africans since 1954 have reached the status of being "assimilated." There are five conditions for this status: a person must be eighteen years old, speak Portuguese correctly, practice a profession or regular trade, have good behavior, and possess a clean military record. Is it any wonder that in Angola fewer than forty thousand people out of approximately five million inhabitants have been able to obtain this status — less than 1 percent? In addition, this status is granted purely on an individual basis and cannot be passed on to one's children; and it can be lost through a simple administrative decision. In any case, the small number of schools means that few Africans can learn to speak Portuguese sufficiently well to qualify for assimilation.

At the beginning of the 1960s the vast majority of the people had no rights; political rights are still virtually nonexistent in Portugal itself, and there are even fewer in the colonies. Of course, the latter are represented in Lisbon solely by whites. As for workers' rights, there are none: no right of association and practically no legal defense against forced recruitments. Measures taken in 1961 are bringing a juridical change in the situation but have not effected much real transformation.

THE BASIC COMPONENTS OF THE WHITE SETTLEMENT
IN THE OTHER COUNTRIES OF SOUTHERN AFRICA

In South Africa, from the moment union was established in 1910 between Natal, Transvaal, the Orange Free State, and the Cape Colony, the legal separation of the races has been progressively established. A series of laws, of which the first was the Labour Bar in 1926, led up through 1946 to the official establishment of apartheid by the "ghetto act" of President Smuts. In 1950 the Population Registration Act Number 30 instituted the division of citizens into social categories. This law was amended in 1956 to add the presumption of belonging to the group of "natives," and in 1967 to set up genealogy tests.

In Southern Rhodesia after the constitution of 1961 the official policy of white domination was accentuated in anticipation of independence.[6] This constitution set forth the proportion of representation as fifty whites to fifteen Africans, but among Africans only twelve thousand had the right to vote. On November 11, 1964, the independence of Southern Rhodesia, under the name of Rhodesia, was proclaimed by Ian Smith. Economic sanctions have been directed against this political act by Great Britain and by the United Nations. All political negotiations failed. Internally the policy has progressively followed a line to complete apartheid through various new legal measures regarding landed property, displacement of population, and racial discrimination in schools.

THE BEGINNING OF THE STRUGGLE FOR INDEPENDENCE

The Portuguese colonies. The first organized resistance against Portuguese rule occurred outside the colonies. After World War II, a certain number of intellectuals met on various occasions and in 1959 in Paris founded the Anticolonial Movement, which set up headquarters in Algiers. In 1961 the Conference of National Organizations of the Portuguese Colonies (the C.O.N.C.P., which grouped together the Portuguese African colonies and Goa) was organized in Casablanca.[7]

Within the various countries, the struggle began about the same period. In Angola, the first political organization appeared in 1953. In 1956, as a result of fusing two movements, the M.P.L.A. (Popular Movement for the Liberation of Angola) emerged. In 1954, Roberto Holden founded what later became the U.P.A. (Union of the Peoples of Angola) which finally appeared in 1962 within the G.R.A.E. (Revolutionary Government of Angola in Exile), established at Kinshasa. The G.R.A.E. was recognized by the O.A.U. (Organization of African Unity), but in 1968 lost this recognition to the M.P.L.A. In 1966, the UNITA (National Union for the Total Independence of Angola) was created by Jonas Savimbi, the former foreign minister of the G.R.A.E.

Most of the nationalist leaders in Angola were imprisoned in 1959. In 1961, armed struggle was launched by the M.P.L.A. following the imprisonment of its leaders in the Luanda jail. The fighting increased and became a real guerilla war, which we shall consider later on. It caused much destruction and created a flood of refugees — from 1961 to 1965 three hundred sixty-two thousand people sought refuge in Kinshasa-Congo. The number of refugees presently living in countries bordering Angola is estimated at half a million.

In Mozambique, internal divisions, which were latent during the leadership of Eduardo Mondlane, have manifested themselves since his assassination, and various leaders have been expelled while some others even surrendered to the Portuguese. The armed struggle however continues in the two northern districts (Cabo Delgado and Niassa) and in the district of Tete. At the beginning of 1971 the Portuguese officially recognized that *guerilleros* were also active south of the Zambezi River.

In Portuguese Guinea, the P.A.I.G.C. (African Party for the Independence of Guinea and Cape Verde) was founded in 1956; in 1961 it also launched an armed struggle against Portuguese rule.

The Other Countries of Southern Africa. In South Africa two groupings met in 1955 to form the Congress Alliance: the African and Indian national movements on the one hand, and the worker movements on the other hand. The former groups had appeared at the end of the nineteenth century. The trade-union movements were founded after World War I, and, following a period of little activity due to brutal suppressive actions, reappeared in force after World War II. The two groups were severely repressed and in December 1956, 156 of their leaders — those who had participated in the adoption of the common platform of the Congress Alliance — were arrested and brought to trial. The armed struggle began in the Republic in 1961, but it did not develop as it did in the Portuguese territories because of tight police controls. The movement is led by the A.N.C. (African National Congress), but real guerilla activities have not been possible inside South Africa since 1964.

In South-West Africa, movements resisting the settling of white colonists appeared in 1957. But it was not until 1963 that armed fighting was launched by the SWAPO (South-West African People's Organization).

In Rhodesia, the first African movement, the City Youth League, was born in 1955. In 1962 the ZAPU (Zimbabwe African Peoples Union) was formed and began an armed struggle. An alliance was reached between the ZAPU of Rhodesia and the A.N.C. of South Africa.

The reasons for the birth of these movements, which were at first simple movements of revolt, is certainly obvious. At stake was the independence of the greater part of the African nations still under non-African rule. At this point, in 1961, Portugal declared that its colonies would henceforth form an integral part of the national territory as provinces. Of course, to test the truth of that statement, one need only look at the racial composition of the Parliament or the Portuguese government. If Portugal in fact is as it is legally defined, it is comprised of eight million Europeans and fourteen million Africans, and the majority within the government and in Parliament should reflect this fact.

In South Africa, Rhodesia and South-West Africa the reaction of the white minorities in power to the nationalist movements has been to reinforce segregation. And the nationalist movements, not being able to express opposition to policies without facing a violent reaction, have increasingly turned toward revolt.

TRANSFORMATION OF THE PORTUGUESE COLONIAL POLICY

From colonies for exploitation to colonies for settlement. There were several transformations in the colonies between 1960 and 1970. In 1900 there were nine thousand whites in Angola and fifteen-hundred in Mozambique. In 1950 the figures were seventy-eight thousand and forty-eight thousand respectively. Since this period, white settlement of the colonies has accelerated even more. In 1960 the figures were one hundred seventy-two thousand in Angola and eighty thousand in Mozambique, and in 1968, approximately three hundred fifty thousand and one hundred fifty thousand respectively.

This growth is linked to two factors. First, the Portuguese want to populate their colonies with whites in order to resist pressures for independence and to maintain them as an integral part of the national territory. Secondly, the demographic revolution in Portugal, in the absence of industrial development, forces significant numbers of people to emigrate. From 1951 to 1960 over six hundred thousand Portuguese left their homeland; in 1966, two hundred sixty thousand departed. In fact, Portugal can be classified as an underdeveloped country. There is little industry, and feudal structures still dominate in the rural regions (.4% of the land-owners possess 45 percent of the land). The social structure is built on a very large group of people who are kept subordinate and who are 40 percent illiterate. The per capita income is very low. In 1961 it was $250, equal to that of Colombia in South America. Political participation is virtually nonexistent.

From national agricultural colonies to international industrial colonies. Beginning in the 1960s, the exploitation of the natural wealth of the colonies for industrial purposes became a major necessity. Portugal was incapable of doing this unaided and was obliged to call upon foreign capital. From 1962 to 1966 the value of diamonds produced increased from 556,000 contos (1,000 escudos) to 1,163,000; iron, from 131,000 to 153,000; and petroleum, from 57,000 to 300,000. Between 1960 and 1967 the value of exports doubled. However, according to some calculations, barely 25 percent of this revenue is kept by the Africans. Economically speaking, Portugal too is progressively losing control of her investments, and her dependence on outside development becomes greater every day.

Collapse of the traditional system of legitimation. On the religious level, Portugal has attempted to legitimize its colonial enterprise through its work of evangelization, but the new situation places her in a paradoxical position. In Bissau, Portuguese Guinea, for example, the government favors the Muslims because certain of the nationalist leaders have been recruited from among the Christian minority. Some foreign missionaries have been expelled, and several Protestant schools have been liquidated. The episcopacy of Angola and Mozambique was absent from the pan-African meeting of bishops of Kampala, which was attended by Pope Paul.

Culturally speaking, an effort *has* been made to increase the number of schools. In Angola, between 1960 and 1966, the figures went from one hundred four thousand children in primary school to two hundred twenty-five thousand. In Mozambique the number in African primary school rose between 1959 and 1957 from seven thousand pupils to ninety-two thousand. It is true that, of these, a good number are children of the Portuguese colonists. However, in the long run under the pressure of circumstances, this increase, although very relative, can only be detrimental to the colonial regime itself.

And lastly, on the social level, *fraternidade,* which has been vaunted to such a degree by the Portuguese colonizer, is being destroyed because of a colonial war which often takes on dramatic aspects.

THE WARS OF LIBERATION

The wars are being carried out differently in the various territories. In Angola the M.P.L.A. claims to have liberated about one-fifth of the land, especially in the east.[8] The U.P.A. seems content with several forays out of Kinshasa-Congo. As for the UNITA, it appears to control a small part of the area occupied by the Ovimbundu (along the border with Zambia) — the home area of its founder, Jonas Savimbi.

In Mozambique in 1968 there were about ten thousand guerillas and fifty thousand men in the Portuguese forces. According to the FRELIMO (Mozambique National Liberation Front), two provinces have been almost completely liberated: Cabo Delgado and Niassa. However, sporadic fighting goes on in other regions, especially in the province of Tete, the location of the Cahora Bassa Dam.

In Bissau, Portuguese Guinea, at the end of 1969, about 70 percent of the territory was said to have been liberated by the guerillas. Since

1961, one observes an escalation in the number of Portuguese troops: three thousand in 1961, ten thousand in 1962, twenty thousand in 1963, thirty thousand in 1968, and around forty thousand in 1969. There are estimated to be about ten thousand guerillas. It is in Portuguese Guinea that the work of reorganizing the liberated territories is most advanced, especially in the areas of education, health, and even economics.

The situation is totally different in the other countries of southern Africa. In South Africa the A.N.C. have made only a few raids in the form of periodic sabotage. The same situation prevails in South-West Africa. As for Rhodesia, several groups there have been better organized since 1968.

In the Portuguese colonies, in contrast, a true colonial war is in progress. Almost two hundred thousand men are involved on the Portuguese side, of which one hundred fifty thousand are serving in Angola. In 1967, the war budget reached $51\frac{1}{2}$ percent of the national expenditures (or, according to certain economists, 59 per cent); this amounted to $400 million, to which one must add the approximately $25 million directly provided by Angola and $32 million from Mozambique. Military service in Portugal has just been extended to a possible seven years, which explains the number of deserters who go to other European countries, either as workers or as students.

Further, one is struck by a major change in the armed struggle in the colonies. At first a revolt with no other objectives save that of a protest against repression, it has become a real movement of national liberation. Organization has been vastly improved, not only on the military level, but also in the political field. Political platforms have been drawn up, and in Guinea and Angola, Portugal is faced with movements of deep political maturity.

Outside help to the liberation movements has come principally from the East. Some African countries also are helping, some through the Organization of African States and some directly (Algeria). Only since 1969 has Sweden begun to provide humanitarian assistance to the freed territories, followed by Denmark and Finland; in 1970, the Netherlands began to assist some activities of the FRELIMO in Tanzania. Recently, several private organizations, in particular those connected with Protestant or Catholic churches, have also started to provide health and medical assistance to the liberation movements.[9]

International solidarity has been established between the liberation movements of the Portuguese colonies, South Africa, South-West Africa, and Rhodesia and the revolutionary movements of Latin America, the N.L.F. of South Vietnam, and the Palestinian *fedayeen*. Increasingly, they believe they are fighting a common struggle, in which those who want to base their development on the autonomy of their peoples oppose those who simply want to exploit the wealth of the land.

The lack of unity between the movements is a dramatic aspect of their history. Some are divided between themselves — the ZANU and the ZAPU in Rhodesia (or Zimbabwe as the African nationalists name their country), and the MPLA, the UPA, and the UNITA in Angola — or even within where several movements have founded a front — as is the case of the FRELIMO in Mozambique. Similar divisions exist in Latin America among revolutionary movements, as they did in Europe among the liberation movements during World War II.

INTERNATIONAL ASPECTS OF THE CURRENT STRUGGLE

A two-fold solidarity is also being realized among the colonizers, as a result of the struggle just described. And for good reason, for the stakes are very high. Economically speaking, this region of the world possesses natural wealth in greater abundance than all of Europe or all of North America. It also has a sizable African population of over 25 million people, which can provide cheap labor. Hence, the need for threefold solidarity — economic, political, and military.

South Africa has major investments in Angola and Mozambique, particularly in the exploitation of mineral products: diamonds, iron, and petroleum. Three principal companies, the Anglo-American Corporation, the British South-Africa Company, and the Consolidated Mines Selection are heavily capitalized by South African business.

South Africa is also involved in financing public works, in particular the Kunene River and Matala Dams in Angola and the famous Cahora Bassa Dam in Mozambique. This latter, located on the Zambezi River, will be the largest in Africa. Its capacity will be twice that of the Aswan Dam, and according to the plans, should be in use by 1975. It is designed to provide 50 million kilowatts, of which South Africa will be the largest consumer.

Furthermore, south of this dam, in a region where the indigenous population is not high, the plan is to reclaim two hundred twenty thousand square kilometers of land, which will allow dense settlement of 1.5 million hectares and three hundred thousand non-irrigated hectares, thus permitting the settling of about a million colonists. In this region also are deposits of iron, copper, coal, manganese, beryl, graphite, nickel, butane, and aluminum. An international finance company, the Zamco-Zambeze, was organized to exploit this region. It is formed from German (Siemens and Telefunken), French, Italian, Portuguese, and South African capital. The secretariat is with the Anglo-American Company of South Africa. At the same time, a central power station has been constructed in Mozambique by the Escom (Electricity Supply Commission), a South African company, which is building fourteen-hundred kilometers of high tension lines to Johannesburg.

The ideological aspect of this project is very clear. Portugal's foreign minister, Dr. Joaquim da Silva Cunha, stated at an interview: "Thus we see once again the real conjunction of the interests of all countries of central Africa, the last bastion of Western civilization in a continent threatened by discord." [10] Following adverse international reaction to the project (especially from neighboring African states) the Swedes, who had also joined this economic venture, withdrew from the enterprise. Italian funds were also withdrawn. Other public works in Portuguese Africa financed by South Africa are the Luanda-Capetown road and the submarine telephone cable from Luanda to Lisbon.

Trade agreements have long been established between the Portuguese colonies and South Africa. An accord was reached between Mozambique and the Transvaal in 1928 (renewed in 1962) guaranteeing the delivery of a minimum of one hundred thousand workers per year to the South African mines. In fact, the annual figures between

1958 and 1962 averaged almost one hundred eighty thousand. In return, 47.5 percent of the exports from the Transvaal pass through the port of Lourenço-Marques. South Africa's need for petroleum is very great, for while the country's current rate of expansion is unequaled in the rest of the world, she depends entirely on petroleum purchases from abroad. The discovery of oil in the enclave of Cabinda in Angola was obviously a very important factor to the South African economy. Add to this the fact that 50 percent of the petroleum used currently by Rhodesia is supplied by the Lourenço-Marques refinery in Mozambique and you have a very profitable situation for Portugal.

Economic solidarity is obviously fundamental. It is complemented by political solidarity and cemented with a series of mutual official visits between South Africa and Portugal. But it is most apparent at the United Nations on votes relating to apartheid and colonialism. Finally, it should be noted that there is a Rhodesian diplomatic mission in Lisbon.

In military affairs too the alliance is in evidence. South Africa maintains military bases or forces in all of the Portuguese colonies. On the island of Sal in the Cape Verde Islands there is an air base, and another is located at Lutamba in the province of Tete, not far from the site of the Cahora Bassa Dam in Mozambique. Apparently, a secret air agreement was signed between Lisbon and Salisbury in 1962, for Rhodesian helicopters are helping Portuguese forces in their struggle against the FRELIMO. Moreover, it is clear that South Africa supplies arms to Portugal, for she has succeeded in equiping herself in this area as well. Missiles too are built on location with the help of West German advisors.

The Countries of the Atlantic Alliance. A second kind of solidarity exists between Portugal and the countries of the Atlantic alliance. It is evident in the same three areas of economics, politics, and military activities.

A rising investment of capital — mostly European but also North American — is made in the exploitation of natural resources in Angola and Mozambique. Between 1957 and 1967 the investment of foreign capital rose from 20 percent to 50 percent of the total investment.

In South Africa and Rhodesia, British capital is invested in large amounts; however, American investments are becoming more important with each passing day, for the rhythm of South African expansion is very rapid indeed.

The countries of the NATO pact have demonstrated, as the Portuguese foreign minister expressed it after the meeting of the Atlantic alliance at Brussels in 1969, a very good understanding of the difficulties faced by Portugal in Africa. This is particularly apparent each year at the United Nations, when the countries of the Atlantic pact abstain from voting and sometimes even vote *against* the independence of African nations under Portuguese domination. On other votes — for example, those pertaining to the treatment of prisoners of war — the NATO countries also show their solidarity with Portugal. Several governments, consulted on the subject of their foreign policy towards Portugal, replied that a wish to preserve the integrity of the Atlantic organization forces them to take such positions.

It is true that NATO has important bases in Portuguese territory. The most important American base in the Atlantic is on Terceira in the Azores. At Beja, 150 kilometers south of Lisbon, is the largest air base of the German Federal Republic. France has a ballistic missile base at Flores, and the British have a naval base at Montijo. Portugal thus plays a key role within the total Atlantic strategy. It is for this reason, moreover, that arms are supplied to her by these countries. Portugal receives airplanes from the United States, Italy, and Germany, tanks from Germany, helicopters from France, warships from Great Britain, and guns from Belgium.[11]

Portuguese troops are trained in part by German advisors, and pilots are trained at Luke Air Force Base in Arizona. Some of the most seriously wounded troops from the colonial wars are treated in German hospitals. Direct military aid is also provided by the United States, and this amounts to approximately $50 million a year, while German aid comes to about 10 million German marks.

On May 9, 1963, General Lemnitzer, Commander-in-Chief of the NATO forces, stated in reference to the war in Africa that "The Portuguese soldiers there are defending a territory, primary resources and bases which are not only indispensable to the defense of Europe, but to that of all the Western world." [12] Evidently a general, even a head of SHAPE, is not empowered to make political statements. NATO has no jurisdiction outside Europe, and Portugal has no right to use arms or funds from NATO for its colonial policy. However, the profound informal solidarity existing between Portugal and other NATO partners is a reality; and it is a fact that for years all the arms used by Portugal in its colonial war were furnished by the member countries of NATO. Some of them have stopped aiding Portugal in the last few years, but only the less important ones, such as the Netherlands and Belgium. Now, through industrial cooperation with these countries, Portugal is able to fabricate some of its own arms (namely the American G3 gun) and is buying more and more of her remaining needs from South Africa.

THE RELIGIOUS ASPECT

We have already indicated how the Portuguese use the Christian motive to maintain their presence in Africa. These same arguments are used by the leaders of South Africa and Rhodesia. The Portuguese church hierarchy has taken sides with the government policy. Numerous texts could be quoted to demonstrate this fact. It should suffice to cite the bishops' statement of January 13, 1961, commenting on the Portuguese decision to make her colonies an integral part of the national territory: "The expansion of the Portuguese nation in various parts of the world has been faithful to . . . the ideal within Christian civilization of a human brotherly communion. In this hour, when the West seems to have lost its self-awareness . . . Portugal is conscious of its evangelical and civilizing mission."

Nonetheless, within Portugal, a certain number of priests and laymen are in opposition to the African policy of the country. Several of them have been imprisoned, and clandestine newspapers circulate regularly. There have also been protests by Christians within the Portuguese colonies; and the majority of the African nationalist leaders are Christians or from Christian backgrounds. Several African priests have taken the side of the liberation movements, and some have paid with exile or prison for the position they took in favor of autonomy for their country. This was the case, for example, for Father Joaquim de Andrade, chancellor of the archdiocese of Luanda, exiled since 1960 to Portugal; he has undergone imprisonment six times in concentration camps and jails.[13]

The original protest of these churchmen was against the maintenance of a political regime not in keeping with the national independence of the Portuguese territories and the fundamental rights of the people. But the critics have since gone even further to denounce the entire Portuguese social and political system which permits such a colonial policy.

The World Council of Churches has taken very clear stands on the question on several occasions. It has generally linked the problem of apartheid in South Africa with that of the Portuguese colonies. The council decided in 1970, in its program to combat racism, to constitute a special fund of $500,000. An initial sum of $200,000 was allocated to organizations fighting racism in the Western countries and to liberation movements in Africa. Agreement was reached with representatives of the liberation movements about the utilization of the funds for education and health purposes. Some churches affiliated with the World Council of Churches reacted negatively to such a decision — particularly in South Africa, but also in Europe and North America. The main argument against the allocations was the use of violence by the movements. The World Council of Churches explained its decision by the responsibility of Christian churches in the present situation (some churches having investments in enterprises exploiting the Negro populations in southern Africa) and by the necessity of a transfer of power. The liberation movements do not have violence as their aim; violence has been imposed upon them. Their aim is the liberation of man, including education in the fullest sense of the word. In agreement with the movements, the funds are to be used for nonmilitary purposes; but other than the agreement, no controls will be exercised by the World Council of Churches, in order to respect the full responsibility of the movements themselves.

As for the Vatican, its attitude has been consistently ambiguous. Until now, no clear condemnation of the Portuguese policy has been made. In June 1970, Pope Paul VI received the three national leaders of the M.P.L.A., FRELIMO, and P.A.I.G.C. This was a remarkable gesture, but it was followed by a denial of a request for the diplomatic services of the Vatican, with the explanation that the audience had no political significance whatsoever. During his trip to Fatima, moreover, Pope Paul VI expressed his appreciation to Portugal for her civilizing work in Africa. Certain Catholic bishops in Africa, however, have taken a stand on the question, most notably the archbishops of Conakry in Guinea and Lusaka in Zambia. The pan-African conference at Kampala, however, has not broached the issue, at least officially.

Finally, at its national congress in 1969, the Belgian Justice and Peace Commission voted in favor of a motion for the independence of the Portuguese colonies.

In the other southern African countries, the Catholic hierarchy and the leaders of the Protestant churches have generally taken rather courageous stands. This is especially true in Rhodesia and in South Africa as well where, with the exception of the Nederduiste Gereformeerde Kerk (Dutch Reformed Church), the churches have made strong declarations against the policy of apartheid.

ETHICAL QUESTIONS

The problem raised in southern Africa and in the Portuguese colonies is fundamental. There are, in the first place, high economic, political, and military stakes, the importance of which should not be minimized in worldwide geopolitics. There is a real danger that this part of the world will be a future site for a serious international conflict. However, it is with some ethical issues that we would like to conclude.

Political Aspect. The moral aspect of political colonialism has been widely studied and this is not the place to go over its theoretical aspects again. It is commonly accepted in today's world that the first step for a nation in its way to development is political independence. This means the freedom to make autonomous political decisions related to the common good of the local population and not necessarily to the advantage of a metropolitan power. This has been recognized as a fundamental right by the Universal Declaration of Human Rights. Father Joaquim de Andrade expressed this principle well when in 1960 he declared to the police who arrested him: "Independence is to a people what liberty is to the individual."

Every principle, of course, must be tested with reality. It is quite possible that in particular circumstances the prolongation of a colonial system — adapted to the new situation and accepting some degree of internal autonomy — could be seen as a normal step toward later independence; at least such a prolongation would be better than a premature decision which would necessarily bring chaos. Also it must be recognized that in some circumstances the reality may be quite diverse. To keep to the question in Africa, we could ask whether Biafra or the southern Sudan has the right to independence?

In the situation we are examining, however, there is a clear issue. A European country, Portugal, refuses to recognize the right to independence of African territories and declares that they are provinces of the "Great" Portugal. Those territories are of course an artificial creation resulting from the division of Africa by the colonial powers. Nevertheless, the colonies have been political entities for at least two centuries; the other countries of Africa, which have gained independence in the last ten years, were in no better a position from this point of view. And we cannot judge the case of the Portuguese territories differently from that of the other political entities in Africa.

The official policy of Portugal is based on historical reasons (the long presence of Portugal in Africa, the assimilation of the local population into the Portuguese culture, the evangelization of Africans, etc.) which after analysis appear weak, if not illusory. Such reasons are used to legitimate the fact that independence is refused not only now but in the future as well. In order to maintain the policy against nationalist tendencies, force has to be used to keep law and order. The ethical question of colonialism is thus raised not only at the theoretical level of fundamental rights, but also at the practical level of the concrete situation. One could add that in view of the trends of contemporary international policy, the Portuguese option has almost no chance of success on the long range and that it can only prolong a situation of violence. The Portuguese are acting like the French in Algeria and Indochina and the Dutch in Indonesia.

Economic Aspect. The Portuguese motivation for staying in Africa is not primarily economic. Nonetheless, economic relations are playing an important if not central function in the colonial issue. It is quite astonishing to realize that Portugal has not used its African territories to foster economic growth. This can be explained by the fact that Portugal herself is still an economically underdeveloped and colonialized country; she has never reached the stage of an industrial economy but is still in a predominantly rural and mercantile one. The exploitation of the economic riches of the African territories has been given over to foreign interests helped by some Portuguese intermediaries. This began to change only after 1960. When the change of attitude began to occur, the investment capacity of Portugal was too small, and more and more she had to appeal to foreign capital. Thus, even with the transformation of perspective the economic relations remained fundamentally the same. However, the function of this foreign capital took new aspects. Taxes (even though relatively low) are increasingly important to finance the war, and the presence of foreign interests serves as a base for political support of tax measures.

The "neutrality" of economic interests is a myth, and we see that they are playing a role in the present situation. This role has to be understood, of course, within the general context of economic activities in the underdeveloped countries. Political colonialism was characterized by the absence of the power of decision within the country; the same lack of power is present in the economic field, and one can speak of economic colonialism — often spoken of as neocolonialism. Today this neocolonialism is evident in numerous African countries. In Portuguese Africa, for the moment, it plays a functional role on behalf of the metropolitan policy. That the sale of arms is one important aspect of the problem is clear when one knows how crucial it is for the balance of payments of some countries (France, Great Britain and the United States), for their economic prosperity (France and Belgium), or even for their industrial progress (United States).

International Aspect. Previously we have referred to some aspects of international involvement, namely the economic ones and the sale of arms. But the international links go even deeper, for the participation of Portugal in the Atlantic alliance is an element of the established solidarity between this country and the Western nations. Formally, of course, these nations are not engaged in the colonial policy of Portugal, either through NATO or through other institutions such as the European Council, or even through the economic institutions of the European Common Market. However, the multiplication of links— political, economic, and military — means that in fact Portugal could not continue its African policy without the implicit solidarity of the West.

This creates an ethical problem, for not only is the world human community today a reality implying new responsibilities, but the distinction between formal responsibility and indirect solidarity has also been shown to be no longer of any value.

Development and Liberation. If development is to mean more than growth and if it is related to the whole of man and to all men (*Populorum Progressio*), it must be defined in terms of liberation. We are indeed facing a reality in which the simple observation of the existence of poor and rich in the world provides no explanation of the process. It is only when we analyze the situation in terms of domination that we can come to an explanation, and consequently, to an adequate ethical judgment. In this sense development is a process of liberation from several types of domination (or alienation). Such alienations are not only economic, but also political and cultural. In this sense development is a continuing process, and is not limited to what we call the underdeveloped world. Such a process is also dialectical, because each time that man has solved one alienation by an act of liberation, he creates new types of alienations. This is the fundamental human condition, and one could wonder if this is not "original sin."

In this process, political independence is one step and, in a certain sense, the first step for a nation as a collectivity. It does not solve all the problems, as we know. New alienations, through appropriation of power by certain groups, may appear. But in the dynamism of human history, it is a central first step.

Violence. As in all collective conflicts, the problem of violence has to be raised. It is impossible to raise it *in abstracto*. Therefore let us examine some of its aspects in the case we have studied. It is very important to note that violence was used first by the forces of repression. Again and again, the liberation movements have said that they are not in favor of violence, but that violence has been imposed on them by the refusal of Portugal to take part in any negotiation which might lead to independence. In 1969 proposals were made by certain liberation movements to Portugal to bring the war to an end, but no answer was given.

Once the process has been put into motion it is very difficult to see when it will stop. Repression causes reactions in a vicious circle. We are clearly engaged in a war, and the only way of stopping violence is by negotiation. Meanwhile an ethical judgment on violence cannot be the same for the forces engaged in defending a colonial system and for those struggling for political liberation. However, this is not to say that the end justifies the means. Nonetheless, it is clear that the use of violence to defend injustice is surely not justified, and that in the case of a struggle against injustice, human beings may face a dilemma of conflicting values (the value of political liberation for a collectivity versus the value of human life) in which a choice cannot be indicated *a priori*.

Christianity as an Ideology. The final aspect which can be mentioned here as a point for reflection is the use made by the Portuguese political authorities of the Christian message as an ideological foundation. This means the identification between Christianity and a particular society. They speak about the defense of the "Christian civilization." The main question is: is there such a thing as a Christian civilization? If we consider human history as a continuing process of liberation and alienation, we must affirm that there is no such thing. Such a civilization will be accomplished only in the Kingdom of God through the new creation.

However, we do contribute to some aspects of this new creation by basing our concrete values on those Jesus Christ has described as the values of the Kingdom. The consequence is that there is a double Christian obligation: firstly, to show the meaning of the dialectical process — the total liberation, both personal and social, announced by Jesus Christ (we could speak of this as the terminal point of the dialectical process) — and, secondly, to be critical of any situation which pretends to be perfect. No one civilization and no one revolution may be confused with the Kingdom of God: all millenarianisms end in inhuman systems!

In the Portuguese case, the Catholic Church is linked with the legitimation system of the political power. As an institution it is liable to the same criticisms as the government. The same may be said for some other churches on an exclusively practical basis, for they too have the possibility of being present and acting in this society. But it is also an ideological link and demonstrates sacralization of the Western powers and a Manichaeistic attitude toward the colonial conflict. Such a position makes a real Christian thought impossible and reduces the Church to an instrument of the political power. An ethical judgment should be applied here too.

The case of the Portuguese colonies is more important for world peace than many people in the Western world believe. Information about the situation is scarce and not really systematic. It also raises many ethical problems for a Christian conscience; we have only indicated some of them, which require further development. However, they are not so different from the ones raised by the Viet Nam war, the exploitation of Latin America, or the Palestine question. In this sense, they are only one aspect of a worldwide reality which should be analyzed in terms of domination and liberation.

NOTES

1. Walter G. Muelder, *Religion and Economic Responsibility* (New York: Charles Scribners' Sons, 1953), pp. 234, 237.

2. James Duffy, *Portugal in Africa* (Cambridge: Harvard University Press, 1959), pp. 59, 96.

3. *Dossier sur les Colonies Portugaises* (Brussels: Vie Ouvrière, 1970), pp. 17–29.

4. See quotation from Portuguese Foreign Minister Da Silva Cunha below.

5. See *Bilan du Monde,* 2d ed., Publié par le Centre Eglise vivante (Louvain) et la

Fédération internationale des instituts de recherches sociales et socio-religieuses (Tournai: Casterman, 1964), T. II.

6. An observer with long experience in Africa suggests that the Africans had more rights in 1961 than they have had before or since. [Ed.]

7. Ronald H. Chilcote, *Portuguese Africa* (Englewood Cliffs, N.J.: Prentice-Hall, 1967), pp. 74–81, 98–104, 119–22.

8. The claimed one-fifth is mostly in Moxico, an area thought by some observers never to to have been as important to Portugal as the Cabinda region, where there is little M.P.L.A. military activity. Cabinda, separated from the rest of Angola by the Congo River and some of Congo-Kinshasa, is of strategic importance because of its oil. [Ed.]

9. This has been the case with the decisions of the World Council of Churches and with Entraide et Fraternité (The Catholic organization for development aid in Belgium), which have provoked quite a few reactions.

10. Quoted from an interview with Dr. Da Silva Cunha during an official visit to South Africa in 1969.

11. France is still a member of NATO, even though she has removed her military forces from the control of the alliance.

12. Neither author nor editor has been able to document this quotation. General L. L. Lemnitzer wrote on 7 June 1971: "My records are not at present available to me so I am unable at the present time to confirm or deny the accuracy of the statement."

13. Protestant missionaries have also spoken out, at the request of their African brothers, and were imprisoned and deported. They had, until the events of 1961 "assumed that it is better to be within the Portuguese territories, even though silent, than to be excluded as a result of having spoken out." The quotation is from Ralph E. Dodge, "Angola and Protestant Conscience," *The Christian Century* (22 November 1961).

BIBLIOGRAPHY

L'Angola. Information C.O.N.P. Algiers, 1968.

Bilchrist, Sid. *Angola Awake*. Toronto: The Tyenson Press, 1968.

Cabral, Amilcar. *Revolution in Guinea, Stage I*. London: Love & Malcomson, Ltd., 1969; New York: Monthly Review Press, 1970.

Chilcote, Ronald H. *Portuguese Africa*. Englewood Cliffs, N.J.: Prentice-Hall, 1967.

Davezies, Robert. *La guerre d'Angola*. Bordeaux: Duvos, 1968.

Dossier sur les Colonies Portugaises. Preface de F. Houtart. Brussels: Vie Ouvrière, 1970.

Duffy, James. *Portugal in Africa*. Cambridge: Harvard University Press, 1962.

Guinée et Cap Vert. Information C.O.N.P. Algiers, 1970.

Houtart, F. "La Conférence internationale de Khartoum et les mouvements révolutionaires en Afrique." *Cultures et Développement* 1, (1968): 619–48.

La lutte de liberation nationale dans les colonies Portugaises. La Conference de Dar es Salaam. C. O. N. P. Algiers, 1965.

Marcum, John. *The Angolan Revolution*, 2 vols. Cambridge, Mass.: M.I.T. Press, 1969–1970.

Mondlane, Eduardo. *The Struggle for Mozambique*. London: Penguin Books, 1969.

Le Mozambique. Information C. O. N. P. Algiers, 1968.

Nevinson, Henry W. *A Modern Slavery*. New York: Schocken Books, 1968.

Okuma, Thomas. *Angola in Ferment*. Boston: Beacon Press, 1962.

Shamuyarira, Nathan. *Crisis in Rhodesia*. Nairobi: East African Publishing House, 1967.

PART III

The Church and Social Responsibility

9 Political Participation –

A Christian View *George McGovern*

Human need cries out with unparalleled urgency in our time. The revolution in communications has brought the devastation of war, poverty, and natural disaster unrelentingly to our attention. Determined groups in our society will not let us overlook the new dangers of population and pollution. Along with other citizens, Christians have a responsibility to confront, understand, and attempt to solve these problems. The urgency of compassion has always been present for sensitive persons; but now the increased perils arising from the sheer increase in people and the revolution of rising expectations impress the importance of action upon all — if for no higher motive than preservation of self and the human species.

The tradition of concern and responsibility which calls Christians to work for a better world stretches back through the Social Gospel and St. Francis of Assisi to Jesus and the Hebrew prophets. Preoccupation with the hereafter on the part of some Christians has not prevented others from diligent endeavor in the here-and-now. A tendency toward the premature exploration of heaven has always been pulled back to earth by the focus on the quality of human life which dominates much of the Old Testament and the teachings of

Jesus. One of the more serious disagreements within the Christian community has been between those who emphasize *individual* achievement and charitable deeds and those who believe that love of God and neighbor requires dedicated action in and through *social* organizations—that is, through political participation. Without discounting the importance of individual relationships, this essay is directed toward developing a Christian perspective on participation in the political processes of American society.

PROBLEMS OF POLITICS FOR CHRISTIANS

In his perceptive book on church politics, Keith Bridston, himself the son of a North Dakota state senator, points out that "politics is considered intrinsically bad" by many if not most church members.[1] This pervasive attitude is only one of the problems confronting Christians as they seek to carry out their responsibilities in the political arena. Many of the problems are the same as those facing any citizen, regardless of his religious persuasion or moral convictions. Others, such as the argument that politics is "dirty," are especially likely to arise within the heritage of Christian experience and moral reflection.

For Christians in the United States, a basic consideration must be the context of religious pluralism and freedom which the principle of separation of church and state is designed to encourage and protect. Enshrined in the First Amendment to the Constitution, this principle has often been read as inhibiting participation by persons of religious conviction in political life, when in fact it has operated in just the opposite way to insure that no religious organization or orthodoxy will be established or given preference in the public arena. Freedom from persecution for religious beliefs and freedom to participate in the open marketplace of political action is thus guaranteed. Christians of differing views may act through the multiple channels available to carry out their responsibility for shaping a better future for mankind.

Given this freedom, the problems of understanding the political process and how best to participate in it remain. As the complex process for making decisions about social policy and the allocation of resources, politics is at best complex and at worst a jungle of competing interests and purposes. Ethical decision and action are difficult and fraught with perils even for those with good intentions. Moral ambiguities are the rule rather than the exception. No factions, parties, or programs are perfect; and, as has frequently been observed, those persons with high moral aims may do more harm than those with a less idealistic and more pragmatic outlook. Careful and responsible shaping of programs to realize specific human purposes requires a good information system and expert analysis. Even so, the uncertainties of political interaction make uncertain the results of the best-laid plans. Planning, therefore, is no substitute for experience in political strategy and tactics, which in itself constitutes another major area of problems for those who engage in politics — be they Christian or of some other faith.

Central to any discussion of political participation among Christians is the relation of love and power. Power and its exercise are at the core of politics, and power in the view of many contradicts the demands of love. But the other side of the dilemma is that love seems ineffectual unless it shapes and reshapes the political forces and works for greater justice in the laws of the land and in economic opportunities for all.

From consideration of these difficulties emerges the problem of setting priorities for political action and selecting specific issues on which to work. Providing food for the hungry of the world, alleviating poverty in an era of technological development, grappling with the deadly issues of environmental pollution, finding ways to control the population explosion that do not smack of racism, and building a world of peace with justice — these are urgent issues for all men today and must be placed high on any agenda informed by Christian faith.

Political participation may be carried on at various levels of involvement; but above all it means taking part in elections and party machinery, and perhaps running for office. Here the ethical problems and dilemmas suggested above are not academic but immediate and urgent and must be worked out at the hectic pace of a political contest. The name of the game is winning. Keeping ethical sensitivities from wearing thin and maintaining humanity in the heat of battle is perhaps the greatest difficulty for persons and groups involved in politics. For Christians, winning and losing must be kept in the larger perspective of God's purposes for his creation.

RELIGION IN A PLURALISTIC SOCIETY

The texture of social interaction in the United States has been conditioned decisively by the First Amendment, which reads: "Congress shall make no law respecting an establishment of religion, or prohibiting the free exercise thereof; or abridging the freedom of speech, or of the press; or of the right of the people peaceably to assemble, and to petition the government for a redress of grievances." [2] Not only is the reference to religion important, but its mention in connection with freedom of speech, press, and assembly is also crucial. The rights and freedoms belong together. The first article of the Bill of Rights guarantees to all citizens the right to participate in the political processes of our nation, as long as they do so by peaceful rather than violent means. The purpose of the action may be to secure correction of quite specific situations regarded as harmful (redress of grievances). Moreover, nothing in the language of the article or in its subsequent interpretation limits my action against what I believe is wrong to situations directly harmful to me. I may seek redress of wrongs against my neighbor. The Jew may seek to protect his own rights and the rights of blacks and other minorities. The Anti-Defamation League of B'nai B'rith has long been active in such causes. The Christian or the humanist, the follower of Richard Nixon or Robert Welch, Hubert Humphrey, Caesar Chavez, or Julian Bond, is guaranteed freedom to work for what he considers a better society. It is not a privilege but a right shared by every citizen.

This right is not limited to persons acting individually. It is also guaranteed to groups (the right of the people peaceably to assemble). Citizens may band together to work for causes in which they believe. Abolitionist societies worked to free the slaves in the decades before the Civil War. The Anti-Saloon League sought national prohibition and, once that purpose had been achieved with the passage of the Eighteenth Amendment in 1919, other groups worked against it and succeeded in having prohibition repealed with the Twenty-first Amendment in 1933. The right of women to vote was guaranteed by the Nineteenth Amendment. And so on. The complete list of political causes for which Americans have organized themselves would be very long and very diverse. There is nothing to prevent persons of Christian faith joining with one another or with persons of other religious and moral convictions to achieve any legal purpose or to change any law if it is regarded as wrong.

This freedom extends beyond assembly and group action. It includes also freedom to speak out and to publish the views held on public issues. This right to propagandize on behalf of a cause, to urge others to support whatever purposes and action a person or group believes in, makes for a lively and confusing political landscape in the United States. The mass media include not only entertainment and news but expressions of opinion and calls to act as well. The mail is filled with appeals to support the Save-the-Children Federation, Clergy and Laymen Concerned about Viet Nam, the Republican National Committee (receive a record of Spiro Agnew's speeches in exchange), the Sierra Club, various candidates for public office, the YMCA, et cetera, et cetera, et cetera!

In the light of these freedoms to participate, the guarantee of the free exercise of religion in the First Amendment takes on added meaning. No convictions are to be excluded from the political marketplace, whether held for short-range goals or out of the broadest moral and theological commitment. Christians, as well as persons of other persuasions, are guaranteed the right to act, to organize, to speak, and to use the communications media in order to carry out the responsibility which their faith and their heritage place upon them. The political participation which the Judeo-Christian community calls for is protected as a basic right by the United States Constitution.

What no person or group is protected from is opposing points of view. Indeed, the right of those with opposing convictions is protected equally. The opening clause of the First Amendment provides for the equal protection of all commitments: "Congress shall make no law respecting an establishment of religion." No religious group or convictions are to be given preference in the laws of the land. The Bill of Rights thus protects diverse levels of political participation — from individual action to organized action and propagandizing — and diverse purposes of involvement — from alleviation of specific grievances to the broadest of moral and religious convictions.

Freedom from persecution for one's views is guaranteed. But so also is the freedom to participate and act in the political arena for causes in which one believes. Many Christian groups in the era of the American Revolution joined with humanists, rationalists, deists, and others to secure these rights. Almost all Christian groups have come to support and to prize the broad pluralism which the Constitution provides. Pluralism in purpose, commitment, and program forms the exciting context of Christian political responsibility in the United States.

The separation of church and state to protect pluralism of conviction has been misread by some as prohibiting any relation between religious conviction and political process at all. "Don't mix religion and politics" is the battle cry of these militant but confused separationists. Both the legal interpretation and actual practice have been just the opposite. No organized religion is to be given preference, that is, established by the state, precisely to protect the freedom of citizens to bring *diverse* religious and moral convictions into the various channels of political participation. The president swears by his religious convictions, whatever they may be, to be faithful in his office. Congress opens with prayer, but a wide spectrum of faiths is represented and presumably any faith could be. The public addresses of political leaders in all eras contain expressions of their ultimate convictions which are presented for examination by the electorate along with the specific actions they propose. Separation of church and state protects rather than denies the mixing of religious convictions and political action. It is precisely the free exercise of diverse commitments in the public arena that the First Amendment guarantees. The political participation which the long heritage of Christian faith calls for is protected, for Christians and others alike, in the U.S. Constitution.

One of the most urgent issues of our time is the protection of that pluralism from various encroachments. Those who would limit public expression and action to a narrow political orthodoxy are attempting to subvert the guarantees in the Bill of Rights and destroy the American heritage of pluralism. They must be opposed.

A second issue of urgency today concerns access to the public media. Freedom of speech and publication is meaningless if only the wealthy can afford space and time in the mass media or broad distribution of printed materials. The cost of political participation has risen and endangers the constitutional guarantees of pluralism. Greater access to the public must be provided on some other basis than wealth. Christians have a great mandate growing out of a long heritage and a deep faith. And all Americans have a great heritage of pluralism in the public marketplace to be preserved and extended.

POLITICAL PROCESS AND MORAL DECISION

"Political problems," writes John Bennett, "have come to be the most fateful social problems." [3] Perhaps they have always been fateful, although many have regarded politics only as the reflection of economic conditions. Neither politics nor economics can be ignored in Christian social thought. Indeed it is the interplay of political and economic issues in the social sphere that provides the nexus of problems and the context of ambiguity with which social ethics must grapple.

The responsibility of Christians to feed the hungry, give drink to the thirsty, clothe the naked, aid the sick, and visit the imprisoned has never been without its social dimensions and ethical dilemmas. Moral problems such as paternalism are present even on the simplest level of one individual helping another individual. These difficulties are compounded, although the responsibility is not diminished, by the complexity of relations and purposes when the tasks of aiding those in need are delegated to a vast array of public and private agencies. The ethical issues are raised to a still higher level of complexity when the moral imperatives of the prophets, Jesus, and the Christian heritage are understood broadly as requiring responsibility for improving the entire human condition; in this view the injunctions to charity serve as symbols rather than as legalistic teachings to be interpreted in a narrowly literal fashion. And as the complexity increases so do the moral ambiguities surrounding the purposes, norms, and appropriateness of political decisions and action.

Despite ethical difficulties and social complexities, the mainstream of the Judaeo-Christian tradition — from the Old Testament prophets and the churches of the Middle Ages and Reformation to the Social Gospel and recent movements of political realism — has been committed to aiding the dispossessed, striving for justice, and improving the human condition through political channels. Jesus stood up in the synagogue in Nazareth where he had been brought up and initiated his ministry by reading these words from Isaiah: "The Spirit of the Lord is upon me, because he has anointed me to preach good news to the poor. He has sent me to proclaim release to the captives and recovering of sight to the blind, to set at liberty those who are oppressed, to proclaim the acceptable year of the Lord." This act has been interpreted as a charter and demand for social involvement of Christians. The response of love toward God and the neighbor, in the view of most leaders of the Christian movement, requires participation in the political process.

It is more accurate to speak of politics as a process than as a rigid structure. There can be no politics without formal and informal relationships characterized by diverse kinds of organization. Patterns of friendship and enmity, personal idiosyncrasies and preferences merge into social groupings and administrative units as these are set within the pressures of interests and the structure of government, law, and culture to make up the fascinating and variegated fabric of political process. But politics is not so much the strands and patterns as it is the weaving of them together. *Politics is the process within social organization by means of which social entities make decisions about policy and action.* The term politics is usually reserved for the processes of government of states and nations. But political process can also be discerned in all social units such as families, fraternal organizations, businesses, universities, pressure groups, political parties, etc. Writes Michael Curtis: "Traditionally, the student of politics has concentrated on the state, its organs, the functions exercised and the manner of procedure. More recently the central focus has been upon the manner in which decisions have been made and the factors, human and physical, that have influenced those decisions. The sphere of political interest has thereby widened immensely — it embraces not only formal political institutions, but also informal associations, parties and pressure groups, voting behavior, personality types, social behavior, the habits and conventions, the general culture and educational pattern of communities, the methods of communication and influence, the economic, technological and demographic conditions of the community."[4] All these may be observed in political perspective and each forms a part of the total political process in a society.

To speak of the process by which social entities make decisions requires speaking of power in its many forms. Political process is the interplay of power relations as these influence the making of social decisions. Power is not one thing but a spectrum ranging from physical force and legitimate authority through organizational capabilities, effectiveness of communication systems, prestige, and charisma to the loyalties and interests inhering in individuals and social groupings. Where there is no valuation there is no loyalty or interest and thus no political power. Political process always involves a conflict of values, and political decisions involve the ordering of values, the setting of priorities for action, and the allocation of resources. Interest is the core of political power, but it remains ineffectual if it does not participate in other forms of power. Because of the intimate relation between power, interest, and valuation, politics involves ethics as well as power and decision-making. Political participation requires the exercise of ethical judgment no less than the exercise of power.

When the conflict of values present in the power relations of political process becomes apparent, it is possible to clarify the moral ambiguity of political participation. The view holding that the moral issue is whether or not to involve oneself politically dissolves with the realization of the pervasiveness of the political. There is no escape. The real ambiguity of politics derives from two aspects of the prospects. First, the conflict of values acted out in political process provides no ground for absolute moral judgments. Politics is a darkling plain on which the hats of all contenders are gray. Only the morally insensitive or cynical can lay claim to purity. Yet participation requires deep commitment to causes and parties. Committed action in a context of imperfect motives and goals is a prime source of the morally ambiguous in politics. Second, there is the ambiguity of means and ends, of projection and result. What instruments will achieve a desired result? To what extent does a good end justify the use of dubious means? And how often will the results betray even the best projections or the consequential situation, even if achieved, prove no better or even worse than what preceded it? Can power be exercised on behalf of love? The future as it unfolds never fails to disclose the uncertainties both of action and inaction, and experience and knowledge of the past only serve to deepen the sense of moral ambiguity surrounding political participation.

In Christian perspective, the most serious threat to ethical sensitivity in politics is self-righteousness and the blindness it induces. The true believer is always a greater threat in politics than either the cynical realist or the naive idealist. Hopefully, there is space in the middle for the responsible agent who seeks realistically and without delusions of purity to achieve a world more fit for human habitation. Such responsible agency requires breaking through the constraints of narrow self-interest to humane goals, the willingness to seek and exercise power in areas of intense conflict, and a continuous realism about one's own motives and the limited possibilities of political action.

Beyond these ingredients of political participation that derive from awareness of the ambiguities of politics, there are further elements needed. One of these is careful analysis of information and judicious weighing of alternative courses of action. Moral judgment is never in isolation from knowledge and action but a pervasive dimension of them. Another need is a shrewd appreciation of political strategy and tactics. Moral realism and unlimited information are insufficient without the skills to act effectively. And a third is an understanding of the relation of power and love.

NOTES

1. Keith Bridston, *Church Politics* (New York: World Publishing Co., 1970), p. 15.

2. For treatment of hte disputed legal and historical issues surrounding the First Amendment, see Anson Phelps Stokes, *Church and State in the United States,* 3 vols. (New York: Harper and Row, 1950); Leo Pfeffer, *Church, State and Freedom* (Boston: Beacon Press, 1953); Anson Phelps Stokes and Leo Pfeffer, *Church and State in the United States,* rev. ed. (New York: Harper and Row, 1964); R. Freeman Butts, *The American Tradition in Religion and Education* (Boston: Beacon Press, 1950); and Mark DeWolfe Howe, "The Constitutional Question," in *Religion and the Free Society* (Santa Barbara, Calif.: Fund for the Republic, 1958).

3. John C. Bennett, *Christians and the State* (New York: Charles Scribner's Sons, 1958), p. xv; see also Thomas G. Sanders, *Protestant Concepts of Church and State* (New York: Holt, Rinehart and Winston, 1964).

4. Michael Curtis, in *The Nature of Politics,* ed. Michael Curtis (New York: Avon Discus Books, 1962), pp. xxvii–xxviii.

10 The Social Gospel and Race Relations:

A Case Study of a Social Movement

Preston N. Williams

Winthrop D. Jordan, in his already classical work *White Over Black,* has demonstrated to the satisfaction of all fair-minded and reasonable men that racial prejudice has been a major national sin of the American people, distorting their thought forms and social attitudes. A sin of such proportions could not but affect the normative understanding of the Christian faith and the life of the churches. The distortion that did occur provided legitimation for a racist interpretation of all the great documents of the new nation — the Declaration of Independence, the Constitution, and the Bill of Rights. Of all the ethnic groups to come to these American shores only the Black American was specifically excluded by the founding fathers from those liberties which they declared were the unalienable rights of all mankind. As early as 1638, Puritans enslaved Negroes, and by 1640 there is definite proof that slavery was also practiced in Maryland and Virginia. The complicity of Christians and the churches in slavery was evident by the fact that by 1700 it was generally recognized that the slave's religious condition had no relevance to his status as slave. By the end of that century one could say, "throughout the colonies the terms *Christian, free, English,* and *White* were for many years employed indiscriminately as metonyms."[1] Negroes had been set apart and Christian churchmen as well as churches were participants in that deed.

The decision of most churches and churchmen at the time of the Civil War to follow the views of the region in which they resided is but another indication of the churches' inability to transcend the limits of their cultural and national conditioning. The profound and pervasive nature of the racist interpretation of the understanding of the doctrine of creation and of the sovereignty of God is partly understood only when one realizes that men willing to fight and die to end slavery were unwilling to accept the Black American as an equal when freedom came. When the Supreme Court in 1883 declared the Civil Rights Act of 1875 unconstitutional, it was legally making provision for a pattern of discrimination practiced in the North and South by white persons of every religious or nonreligious persuasion. Washington Gladden, founder of the Social Gospel Movement, the first conscious attempt by the American churches to define the nature of their responsibility for justice in social institutions, was at this time in his prime, having been called in 1882 to the First Congregational Church in Columbus, Ohio. Walter Rauschenbusch, the most influential of the early Social Gospel prophets, was about to begin his career at the edge of Hell's Kitchen.[2] It is interesting that neither of these northern leaders of social and applied Christianity ever sought to attack vigorously the racism which was present and growing in their society. Why did they not conclude that "Christianizing the Social Order" required a Christianizing of white persons' views regarding the Negro? I will attempt to provide here the outline for a new understanding of the relation of these men and the Social Gospel to the Negro question. My thesis is that the Social Gospel not only spoke weakly to the question of race but that it helped to create a method of analysis that makes more difficult, even today, a solution to the racial problem. Since we are outlining an approach to the entire history of the Social Gospel we shall divide our analysis into periods.

1880–1920. Both Robert T. Handy and Max L. Stackhouse have in recent volumes attempted to defend Gladden and Rauschenbusch from criticism directed at their lack of attention to the question of race and especially to the plight of the Black American.[3] The defense of both authors is stated in a fashion that suggests the Negro question was quiescent while these men were seeking to make America and Christian churchmen sensitive to the social dimension of salvation and the evil present in social structures. It is necessary for all to know, therefore, that Gladden (1836–1918) and Rauschenbusch (1861–1918) both lived through the days of *The Betrayal of the Negro*.[4] In 1877 President Hayes inaugurated the betrayal by withdrawing Union forces from South Carolina and Louisiana and ushering in the era of good feeling between the North and the South. The new harmony of the whites was gained at the expense of the Black American. Tennessee began Jim Crow movements in 1881 and by 1907 thirteen other states had joined. In 1883 the Supreme Court nullified the Civil Rights Act of 1875, and by 1910 eight southern states had systematically excluded Negroes from political life. Further legitimation of these acts of injustice was provided by Booker T. Washington's "Atlanta Compromise" address of September 18, 1895, and the *Plessy* v. *Ferguson* decision upholding the doctrine of "separate but equal." Black dissatisfaction with the newfound white harmony was manifest by the activity of such men as W. E. B. DuBois, Monroe Trotter and black Social Gospel pastors such as Bishop Henry McNeil Turner, Francis Grimké, Dr. J. Milton Waldron, Reverdy C. Ransom, and R. R. Wright Jr. The new harmony produced as much violence as peace. Race riots occurred in 1898, 1900, 1906, 1908, and 1917. Blacks, adhering to legal remedies, established the Niagara Movement in 1905 and the NAACP in 1909. Certainly even this incomplete record of the period should cause one to dismiss the explanations of Handy and Stackhouse as too superficial. Gladden and Rauschenbusch simply did not speak out with consistency and force against the racial injustice of their day. What they failed to utter, as well as what they said, did, however, help to determine the response of American white Christians to the Negro question.

The failure of Gladden and Rauschenbusch is in part due to the fact that racism was so endemic to American life that it was a "ruling idea of all Americans and every age."[5] S. P. Fullinwider has asserted that it was an important element in the thinking of black intellectuals and clergy during this period; and Thomas F. Gossett has made the same assertion in respect to whites.[6] There seems to be little reason for excusing Gladden and Rauschenbusch from this general indictment. Racism during this period was so flagrant, few if any avoided it — certainly not the men of the Social Gospel. The question persists, why did these sensitive prophets not transcend the racism of their day? The place to begin a search for an answer is at the heart of the Social Gospel itself. It is a commonplace that this pattern of thought distorted some fundamental insights of the Christian faith about God, man, and sin; it is not as well-known that it also distorted what should have been common truths about Christian brotherhood.

The basic understanding of the social question that was utilized by the American activists was a European creation. It related to the growth of industrialization in the West, the fear that Western civilization would decay, and that class conflict would be exacerbated. Socialism and Marxism were the European secular answers to these problems just as *Rerum Novarum* was the answer of Catholicism. With the emigration of European thought and people to America, as well as the growth in America of industrialization, the so-called economic question became indigenous. Because Europe had no significant black population and America's blacks were on the farms (and were being educated to stay there) a simple capital–labor analysis was felt to be adequate for solving the problems of society. The Social Gospel spokesmen saw themselves at a new stage in the evolution of class relationships. That this had no reference to blacks was of little concern, for it was evident to all that blacks were a backward and primitive folk not yet suited for participation in the industrial revolution. Two very important considerations escaped the attention of these men; namely, that racial judgments derogatory of blacks were contained in socialist and marxist literature and that the American working class as well as organic communities were practitioners of racial injustice and violence.

Gladden and Rauschenbusch were, after the Civil War and Reconstruction, among the first to make the mistake of trying to analyze America in terms of class alone with no reference to race. This legacy they bequeathed to the social creeds of the churches, the Federal Council of Churches, and the Social Gospel movement in general. Because history was not taken seriously and understood in terms of America's past, as well as that of Jerusalem, Athens, Rome, and northern Europe, the Negro question was not adequately seen or attacked. This error, in the main, continues until today.

The astigmatism of the Social Gospel is not to be related only to its perception of the social question; it is present also in its reinterpretation of the Christian myth. The pattern for the new interpretation was set by Darwin's theory of evolution. In America, the Social Darwinist made use of the new science to supply a new foundation for the theories of white superiority present throughout the nation. While the social gospeler attempted in economic and political matters to separate himself from the views of the Social Darwinist, no attempt was made in the area of race. Yankee school marms, philanthropists, parsons, and social reformers were willing to accommodate themselves to the Southern conception of the Black American. They, of course, hoped — and the theory of evolution supported that hope — that progress, education and good will might in time bring some solutions; but in the present they accepted the status quo.[7] Nature had itself defined the place of the black man. Its laws had placed the white man first in knowledge and power and, while a hierarchy might exist among whites, there was between whites and blacks an unbridgeable gap. None needed to speak these words, although some like Lyman Abbott and Josiah Strong did.[8] Most, like Gladden and Rauschenbusch, had only to remain silent and seem at least to accept the assumptions on which the racial consensus rested. In a day when the South, with northern aid, was reenslaving the Negro and American scholars had adopted racist interpretations of culture, no one needed to say that social solidarity did not include the Negro.

The new science, so uncritically embraced by the Social Gospel, not only prepared the way for a new world-view congenial to doctrines of white superiority, it also made Christian doctrine more hospitable to racism. Evolutionary theory provided an explanation for the visible difference between blacks and whites and suggested a new understanding of God's creative act. The possibility of a multiple creation of mankind, a different growth pattern in racial maturation and in the development of civilizations meant a variant interpretation of equality and of brotherhood. Mankind's equality before God need not contradict segregation in America. Indeed it might confirm it. Moreover the understanding of God as Father tended to restrict God's sovereignty. The Lord God Almighty became a kindly Christian gentleman—even a white southern gentleman—using persuasion, love, and education to shepherd his well-intentioned children. Among whites, it led more frequently to paternalism and subordinate-superordinate relationships. The more optimistic doctrine of man tended, in addition, to increase the faith of the white man in other white men, but it did little to instill a new humaneness or equality in black-white relations. Finally the doctrines of the Kingdom of God and progress suggested that by personal conversions a time would come in some unspecified future when the majority of society would voluntarily agree to establish an intimate, organic set of social institutions. The ideal was fitted not only for middle-class programs of social reform but also for white-determined gradualism in race relations. The southern strategy for race relations could be accepted with a good conscience, for it fitted well with the new patterns of science, philosophy, religion, and social reform. The only difficulty was that the new accommodation permitted the carrying of the worst racial sins of the old order into the new order.

If Winthrop Jordan is correct in stating that by 1820 America had determined upon becoming a white country, one can from the perspective of the Social Gospel see abolition, the Civil War, and the early days of Reconstruction as only a short interlude in that program. The Social Gospel from its beginning until 1920 had done little to help the cause of the emancipation of the Black American. In 1920 free, white, and Christian were still employed indiscriminately as metonyms. Negroes had been set apart, and the most famous of the prophets, Gladden and Rauschenbusch, as well as lesser known white churchmen and churches, were participants in that deed.

1920–1940. Paul A. Carter in his analysis of this period defends the thesis that the Social Gospel was notably weakened during the first decade but was revived in the second decade. I think that conclusion cannot be seriously disputed, but that the decline of the Social Gospel in the twenties was more the result of prosperity than of either Prohibition or Fundamentalism. Carter is right when he states that "pragmatic 'materialism' was just as inescapable for the preacher of the Social Gospel as for the preacher of the *status quo;* therefore it tended to make any thoroughgoing pulpit attack upon that *status quo* seem a trifle academic." [9] Prosperity banished the "social question," that is the economic question. Under Harding's "normalcy," Coolidge's "prosperity," and Hoover's "years of grace," labor unions were dealt severe blows by the government and the courts; but the halt in immigration and the increase in industrial growth made most workers reasonably happy. If the Social Gospel was more alive in Detroit than elsewhere it was due to the intense class, race, and economic conflict in the automobile industry and not simply the genius of Reinhold Niebuhr.

A movement struggling to keep itself alive could be expected to contribute little to aid the advancement of Negroes. The Social Gospel did that little. During the twenties the Federal Council of Churches, whose Social Creed made no reference to the Negro question, issued pronouncements on racial matters, established a Commission on Church and Race Relations and began the custom of Race Relations Sunday and Brotherhood Week. All these activities as well as the educational enterprises of the churches were based on the assumption of separate and unequal status. Benjamin E. Mays — an admirer of Walter Rauschenbusch, a follower of the Social Gospel, and a participant in some of these courageous ventures of the twenties — confirms our judgment on the continued acceptance of racism. After recounting the stand taken by Will Alexander and the

Commission on Interracial Cooperation against the Klan he writes: "The Commission never sought to abolish segregation; it worked to improve conditions between the races *within the segregated system.*" Of the Y.M.C.A., for which he worked, he said: "The Y.M.C.A., like the church (and everything else) was rigidly segregated in the South — in the North, too, for that matter. Both complacently accepted the status quo of segregation."[10] The point Mr. Mays makes in his volume is that at this time no other option was available to these persons. I am concerned to stress another aspect of the situation: namely, that the world view, theological perspective, and way of work of the social gospeler tended to support melioristic solutions of racial ills. The Social Gospel never made a real case against segregation; it was content to seek improved race relations through evolutionary means.

The case of the Social Gospel against segregation could not be made without revising the Social Gospel itself. This became possible during the thirties when worldwide economic dislocation made the tragic dimension of life visible once more and the rise of Hitler made more clear the logic of genocide inherent in racism.

The person most responsible for a revision of the Social Gospel theology and as a consequence the church's teaching in respect to race relations was Reinhold Niebuhr. The new departure was set down in the provocative volume, *Moral Man and Immoral Society.*[11] The book was a new analysis of man and his relationship to his primary and secondary groups. Like much of the previous Social Gospel the major themes stressed capital-labor problems, the evils of capitalism, and the decay of Western civilization. A modified Marxian perspective rather than an optimistic evolutionary outlook provided the conceptual frame of reference. The shift provided a fresh insight into race relations. Race as a category of explanation for group and individual behavior was abandoned. Man's relation to social groups beyond the family was not determined primarily by organic ties but by egoism, self-interest, and impulse. The relationship among the groups thus formed was based upon power and coercion. Nationality, politics, economics, even race, were of importance as loci around which men gathered power and coercion for the self-interest of their own collectivity. Group relations were not, then, to be ordered according to some inevitable pattern of progress. They were instead the outcome of the interaction of political and coercive with ethical, moral, and rational factors. Nature was neither red in tooth and claw nor the peaceful harmony and beauty of the pastoral. Nature was the arena in which men capable of the highest good were tempted by their groups to embrace prejudice, passion, egoism, and self-interest.

In the light of this analysis, Anglo-Saxons as a race or a privileged class were humbled, for from either point of view they were the holders of power which tended to corrupt. The economic orientation caused the national- and class-ordering of society to be stressed more than the racial. No chapter in the book is devoted to an exclusive analysis of race although the thesis of the work includes race alongside the other social groups.[12] At the heart of the argument was the significance of disparities of power among groups in a society and the willingness of privileged groups to sacrifice social justice for social peace. In the American context, this type of analysis enabled the experience of the Black American to emerge as a whole, for the Negro was not treated by the society as an individual but as a social group. Niebuhr's analysis affirmed that the Negro's plight was the result of culture not race, that he was kept in his place by the actions of the privileged class, and that the improvement of his lot depended upon the exchange of passivity for aggressiveness and the adoption of militant, coercive nonviolence. Niebuhr's pessimism made class conflict more desperate and as a consequence the race problem more serious. Race was an important category for explaining the place of blacks in American society. One of the ironies of American society seemed to be the persistence of a race problem that demands attention as a race problem, no matter what other rubrics of understanding might be employed by the investigator. This lesson Niebuhr did not fully appropriate himself. Like others, he was to turn away from race to issues of "greater consequence" — war and international relations.

Although one cannot in the light of Niebuhr's writings and research defend the centrality of race as an issue, it is necessary nonetheless to acknowledge that his ethical insight provided a major reorientation in thought about race relations.[13] In this sense the Church or some churchmen were ahead, not behind, the rest of society in race-relations strategy. Niebuhr pointed out the fact that race relations were group relations not simply relations between individuals. This meant that they were political and not simply ethical. One could not, therefore, rely upon the good will of any group— southern or northern white—to voluntarily surrender their power over another group—the Black American. The concepts of the Fatherhood of God and the brotherhood of man were seen as not capable of easy transmutation into institutional norms of the worth and dignity of all persons or equality in historic social relations. Levels of evolutionary or cultural development did not necessarily insure any greater freedom from prejudice, passion, egoism, and self-interest. The distinction between violence and nonviolence was shown to be, at times, of no ethical significance. The oppressed, Niebuhr asserted, often had a more adequate view of justice and righteousness because they were the oppressed. Place in society, not genes, provided them with a purer vision of the good. One should not seek in history the Kingdom of God or the fully Christianized social order but higher levels of justice and equality for all persons. It was conceivable, therefore, that a revolution could take place in racial affairs; but this did not imply the removal of all hostility, hatred, and social injustice among the races. Nor did the revolution have to preclude coercion and the possibility of violence. By drawing a sharper distinction between the moral and social behavior of individuals and social groups, Niebuhr had made more clear the significance of race as a group category while removing from it racist overtones.

The new orientation of Niebuhr's did not stand alone. The theologically more liberal social gospelers continued employing the older approach to race relations, and they did much to soften the effects of segregation upon some Black Americans. Nowhere, however, were new patterns established which gave promise of a breakthrough. In time it was hoped that love and reason would bring about a gradual transformation of the society but none, not even the militant young Adam Clayton Powell, Jr., seemed to feel that segregation and discrimination could be declared unconstitutional or brought to a quick end.[14]

An additional factor of importance during this period was the growth of racism as an international problem. During the decade of the thirties, Hitler rose to power in Germany by awakening in Germans a new myth of racial superiority and inflicting upon Jews the most heinous crimes. The involvement of the European churches and the nature of the atrocities committed against the Jews made more urgent the question of race and called for a new response by Americans to the problem. That response was to be made in the next decade. The gap between the statement of the Oxford Conference on church and race and the nature of the merger consummated by the Methodist Church in 1939 illustrates well the contribution the ecumenical church was going to make to the American church's solution of the racial problem:

The sin of man asserts itself in racial pride, racial hatreds and persecutions, and in the exploitation of other races. Against this in all its forms the Church is called by God to set its face implacably and to utter its word unequivocally, both within and without its own borders.

Moreover, it is a first responsibility of the Church to demonstrate within its own fellowship the reality of community as God intends it. It is commissioned to call all men into the church, into a divine society that transcends all national and racial limitations and divisions. In the services of worship, in its more informal fellowship, in its organization, and in the hospitality of the Christian home, there can be no place for seclusion or segregation because of race or colour.[15]

When in 1939 the domestic reform called the New Deal was ending, the American religious community and the nation were on the eve of significant changes in race relations. This was because of the theological reformation of the Social Gospel, increased militancy among blacks, and the racism spreading across the map of Europe.

1940–1963. My remarks about the position taken by the Oxford Conference on race should not cause one to forget that during World

War II and the whole of this period the central concern of the Church, domestic and worldwide, has been totalitarianism, not race. Fear of nuclear war, communism, and revolution among the have-not nations have engaged more energy and money than has race. Neither Catholics nor Protestants have an enviable record on race. What progress was made came because race questions had a way of intruding themselves into matters of international relations, ecumenical affairs, and issues of the welfare state. The war was not then directly responsible for change in race relations. It did, like the depression, provide the occasion for change.

Perhaps two of the most direct results were the initiation of intervention by the federal government in matters related to equality of opportunity in employment and desegregation in the armed forces. The decisive act in the first instance was President Roosevelt's Executive Order 8802 in June of 1941 and, in the latter case, President Truman's Executive Order 9981 in July of 1948. The United States participation in the cold war as a defender of freedom no doubt also had some effect on the weakening of Jim Crow laws in Washington, D.C., the nation's capital.

Embarrassment before the nations of the world was not the only new force. Blacks themselves became more militant. A series of NAACP suits resulted in Negro admissions to institutions of higher learning, receipt of the franchise, and the outlawing of segregated public schools. Black militancy took an even more unexpected form when the Negro community of Montgomery, Alabama boycotted the city busses for more than a year, persevering until the Supreme Court upheld the ruling of the Federal District Court which had declared Alabama's city bus segregation laws unconstitutional. In 1960 in Greensboro, North Carolina, four Negro college students sat down, like Rosa Parks, in places restricted to whites, and the "sit-in" movements were added to the list of black originated protest. Finally in 1961 interracial Freedom Rides began and the black protest styles of this period were completed.

Now two branches of the United States government were involved, both stimulated by the action of black citizens. A. Philip Randolph's threatened March on Washington had triggered Executive Order

8802 and fair employment activities; the NAACP and the citizens of Montgomery had acted together with others to seek legal redress for wrongs committed by white persons. Black college students were involved, and whites too were beginning to expose themselves to the dangers of white brutality. In every action the executive or judicial branch of government had acted to sustain the protest. Only the legislative branch was absent.

From 1901 to 1929 there was no Negro congressman. During the period 1929 to 1943, one black sat in Congress. In the time span under study the lone congressman was joined by four others. Represented were the states of Illinois, New York, Michigan, Pennsylvania, and California. The states symbolized more than the men. The migration of blacks from the South to urban areas in the North as well as their reenfranchisement in the South gave them a new strength in Congress. Not until 1957, the same year in which Ghana became the first former African colony to join the United Nations, did the Congress pass a Civil Rights Law. Another was to be signed by President Eisenhower in 1960. Both laws suggest a new orientation on the part of the American populace to the civil rights of the Black American. Perhaps the zenith of this change of will took place on August 28, 1963 when two hundred thousand black and white men and women from every part of the nation marched down the streets of Washington in support of equality for the Negro. Between the year 1940 and 1963 the status of the Negro American improved. The improvements were not as great as were required for full citizenship. They were not given with joy but grudgingly. After they had been granted, violence, lawlessness, and dishonesty by public and private individuals frequently made impossible the black man's enjoyment of his constitutional rights. Nonetheless, blacks became more equal.

The age old maxim, "separate but equal," was replaced in law by the rule integrated and equal. There was a wide gap between practice and profession, and many refused to make the profession. Yet the change had come. Denominations hailed the new day with an increase in official statements. Characteristic of these statements was that of the Federal Council issued in 1946 in Columbus, Ohio: "The Federal Council of the Churches of Christ in America hereby renounces the pattern of segregation in race relations as unnecessary and undesirable and a violation of the Gospel of love and human brotherhood. Having taken this action, the Federal Council requests its constituent communions to do likewise. As proof of their sincerity in this renunciation they will work for a non-segregated church and a non-segregated society." [16]

In 1952 the council spoke again on this matter and in 1954 when the Second Assembly of the World Council of Churches met in Evanston, Illinois, it once again condemned segregation. The position of the Church was clear; still segregation of the races continued in the household of faith. Intellectually the case against segregation was best put by Dean Liston Pope of Yale University Divinity School in his small volume *The Kingdom Beyond Caste*. It was a social and theological analysis containing the best wisdom of the behavioral sciences, together with penetrating Christian insights. Included also was information about local black and white churches and racial practices in other church structures. The volume was written for a popular audience, and its appeal and impact were probably great. Other similar educational ventures were no doubt carried out in other areas of church life. Commitment to a "kingdom beyond caste" was now official policy even though as Pope noted: "Genuine integration requires much more, however, than a statement of policy, important as that is. It requires the authentic incorporation of minorities into the life and leadership of the churches." [17]

Whereas the contribution of the ecumenical movement and Liston Pope was to attempt the conversion of the Church, the militancy of the black community under the leadership of Martin Luther King, Jr. attempted the conversion of the society. King according to his statement in *Stride Toward Freedom* saw himself as the continuation of the liberal side of the Social Gospel. He claimed to have brought to the Negro community of Montgomery a philosophy which made their cohesion possible. That philosophy was nonviolence. It was shaped by Thoreau, Mordecai Johnson, Gandhi, Walter Muelder, L. Harold DeWolf and Allan Knight Chalmers. King's view of the processes of history and the evil in man had been toughened sufficiently by Reinhold Niebuhr to make King an admirer of but not a member of pacifist groups. He had accepted the view of both his Boston University teachers and Reinhold Niebuhr in respect to nonviolence in relation to black protest: "In 1954 I ended my formal training with all of these relatively divergent intellectual forces converging into a positive social philosophy. One of the main tenets of this philosophy was the conviction that nonviolent resistance was one of the most potent weapons available to oppressed people in their quest for social justice." [18] Previously Niebuhr had said: "Nonviolence is a particularly strategic instrument for an oppressed group which is hopelessly in the minority and has no possibility of developing sufficient power to set against its oppressors." Further, "any effort at violent revolution on the part of the Negro will accentuate the animosities and prejudices of his oppressors. Since they [white men] outnumber him hopelessly, any appeal to arms must inevitably result in a terrific social catastrophe. Social ignorance and economic interest are arrayed against him. If the social ignorance is challenged by ordinary coercive weapons it will bring forth the most violent passions of which ignorant men are capable." [19]

King was doing more, here, than balancing his mentors at Boston University against his knowledge of Niebuhr. He was reliving the pacifist controversy of the thirties and, despite his appreciation for Niebuhr, siding with the pacifist. Events were to strengthen his conviction because, unlike the labor unions in the thirties, the southern black would be supported by the courts; and the violence of the "red-necks," unlike that of the captains of industry, would create ill will toward the cause of southern whites. Moreover the passivity of the black man made him a better follower of nonviolence than the blue-collar immigrant from Europe. By analogy, even the notion of class struggle could be applied for in a true sense all the whites were the privileged class and all blacks the proletarian. In addition, the elements of paternalism potentially present in King's Personalism would be muted by his black skin and clergy status, while Personalism's concern for the worth and dignity of the individual would resonate well with the black man's desire to be somebody.

In the work of Martin L. King, Jr., the Social Gospel received new life. Conditions had so progressed that it could now act to bring radical change to blacks in the heart of the South. The direct-action technique which Negroes had used throughout their history was to become under King and others an adjunct to legal and court reform. Since this strategy had its roots more in the practice of Gandhi than in American Social Christianity, it too was to lead King further in the direction of nonviolence as a way of life. From the beginning, the philosophy King used to provide cohesion for the black community transcended the experience of the black masses he led. His love of opera, pride in northern institutions of learning, and reading of Western philosophy had no roots in the world of Rosa Parks or E. D. Nixon except as the exaggerated demonstration of learning which was expected of the black clergy. In the person of Martin L. King Jr., the Social Gospel brought its own world view. It was to lift as well as to make equal, and, like integration, it looked toward the destruction of much if not all black folk-culture. One needs to note especially the failure of King himself to attempt any transformation of the Negro church. Although a pastor, King worked outside the black church institution. He was at one with Reinhold Niebuhr —but not with his Boston University teachers—in dismissing the church as an effective instrument of social reform. The omission is a serious one in the light of the multi-cause involvement which characterized King's life and the constant appeal made to King by black clergyman who sought reforms in black religion. King, unlike other social gospelers, made race central and stressed more coercion and direct action within the context of nonviolence; but, like other social gospelers, he too possessed an optimistic conception of man and human progress, an idealistic conception of love, and a notion that a purified Western culture most resembled the Kingdom of God.

A third approach to problems of race was undertaken during this period by Waldo Beach. His was an attempt at a thoroughly theological-ethical analysis of the racial problem. He wanted to be considered loyal to no man, group, or nation. The theological motifs defined by a radical Christian monotheism were acknowledged as the source of insight and judgment. Beach's analysis found the sociologist's insights lacking only in depth:

in so far as racial tension is seen with Myrdal to be an internal problem, a problem in the conscience, the gap between creed and deed is expected by him and many like-minded sociologists to be in itself redemptive. In effect, man saves himself racially by the progressive approximation in practice to the ideals of equality and mutual respect which he has himself posited. Man initiates, pursues, and completes his own racial salvation. In terms of its whole world view, Christian theology finds this two-dimensional picture quite too moralistic and flat. A third dimension of the process must be seen. It is the Christian confession that we are redeemed racially, as in all other areas of life, by the grace of God, by an obedient and glad response to his forgiving and recovering work in human life.[20]

My recapitulation of some of the most salient events in the history of the Social Gospel is not complete. Much has been set aside that deserves to be included in this crucial period between 1940 and 1963. Nonetheless the historical outline is accurate. What one needs to conclude about the Social Gospel during this time can be ascertained from this account. In the light of our present task, three statements need to be made. During this period social gospelers began to set aside their racism and to affirm the necessity of "a non-segregated society." In addition, from a variety of perspectives they began to affirm integration as providing the only viable form for that church and society. Thus, Waldo Beach wrote: "the Christian theologian can certainly concur with the common assumption of most reputable social theorists: that integration presents among the viable options of racial relations, the morally normative form." [21]

Finally one must note that Martin L. King, Jr., who would do more than any other American to liberate his black brethren, was making nonviolence an absolute principle during this period. The method of social change, the form of the new society, as well as important aspects of the Black American's way of life was being determined, absolutely, before the black man had gained his freedom and the right to participate in the decision-making process.

1963–1968. Although it is difficult to imagine the civil rights legislation of 1964 without considering the death of President Kennedy in November of 1963, it is nonetheless true that two of the most significant pieces of legislation were the work of the Johnson administration. These were the Civil Rights Act of 1964 and the Voting Rights Act of 1965. President Johnson was also responsible for actions leading to the transformation of the Civil Rights Revolution into a Great Society Program. Class differences between rich and poor were seen to be more basic than racial problems. Finally actions by Johnson related to the Viet Nam war, together with the response of his critics, would lead to an abandonment of interest in the improvement of the condition of the Black American.

In addition to new legislation, an increasing series of disorders and turmoil characterized the period. The Selma drive took place in 1965 and the Meredith March from Memphis to Jackson in June of 1966. Violence also took place in Cleveland, St. Augustine, Philadelphia (Mississippi), Harlem, Bogalusa (Louisiana), Watts, Chicago, Newark, and Detroit. On April 5, 1968, Martin Luther King, Jr., the prophet of nonviolence, was struck down in Memphis, Tennessee. Again, it is important to remember that race, even during this period, did not receive among Social Gospel advocates the same consideration accorded the problems of the city, underdeveloped nations, situational ethics, medical ethics, and war and peace.

Without intending to do any damage to the supporting cast, I find it necessary to assert that Martin L. King, Jr. was most responsible both for sustaining an interest on the part of churchmen in race and for changing that interest into a concern for class and peace.

King's philosophy from the beginning had transcended that of the concerns of race. It was the old Social Gospel made applicable to matters of race by Reinhold Niebuhr and King's mentors at Morehouse College and Boston University. King was thrust into the role of race leader by the events of Montgomery. He had successfully carried the mantle and by 1964 had removed most of the practices of the South that were obviously demeaning to the Negro. The Black American could now be a somebody. He needed only to reach out and possess the prize. Two things alone were required: faithful performance by whites and initiative and industry by blacks. Assuming these to be the Gordian knot, the only question was how to undo the knot. The answer was ready at hand. The Social Gospel ideology said the problem should be approached through class legislation. A form of Christian socialism was needed that would make the proletarian class the bearer of justice in every aspect of society. Through one action, matters racial, economic, and international could be pushed through to a happy conclusion. In 1963 King proclaimed: "I have a dream that my four little children will one day live in a nation where they will not be judged by the color of their skin, but by the content of their character." His was the vision also of the Great Society. Despite the turmoil and chaos, nonviolence and love could outdistance ill will and achieve the good society and the promised land for all Americans. The anti-poverty campaign, whose outline appeared as early as 1965, could be utilized to reconcile poor whites and blacks. The new alliance would in turn reshape American society. To be sure there was yet the problem of race but because he "had also learned that the inseparable twin of racial injustice was economic injustice," he could hope to cure both ills at once.[22] Work on the poverty front would aid the Negro and America's other minorities. White lower-class violence and labor-union racism did not deter him. King was being driven by an idea and not the apparent facts of the situation. The logic of the Social Gospel was preparing the way for the transition from race to class action.

To decide for a class analysis was also to return to the violence-nonviolence issues of the thirties and to the ideal of the integrated society as the fruit of class harmony. In the previous period, the Social Gospel had come to these conclusions. With them King found no fault. The logic and morality were acceptable. Again the category of race receded because integration would assure the eventual recognition of race. A vignette from his last volume illustrates well his attitude. "Two years ago my oldest son and daughter entered an integrated school in Atlanta. A few months later my wife and I were invited to attend a program entitled 'music that has made America great.' As the evening unfolded, we listened to the folk songs and melodies of the various immigrant groups. We were certain that the program would end with the most original of all American music, the Negro spiritual. But we were mistaken. Instead, all the students including our children, ended the program by singing 'Dixie.'"[23]

If King protested even mildly he did not record it. He only states that he and his wife looked at each other with looks of indignation and amazement. He went home and wept: "I wept within that night. I wept for my children and all black children who have been denied a knowledge of their heritage; I wept for all white children who, through daily miseducation, were taught that the Negro is an irrelevant entity in American society." [24] King went on in the passage to deplore further this type of neglect but he did not suggest any cure other than self-assertion on the part of blacks. How this self-assertion went beyond placing one's children in an integrated school was not made clear. King seemed to be saying that integration is the solution because it will make possible interaction among the races. From there love, self-assertiveness, self-esteem will take over. No special program other than economic is needed for either blacks or whites.

When in 1966 King elected to involve himself in the issue of peace in Viet Nam, he was again electing to be faithful to the Social Gospel. Race was once more to be seen as but a small aspect of a more significant problem. The method of nonviolence was to become not only a domestic but an international strategy as well. King's commitment to the Social Gospel or, in this instance, nonviolence above race, is clearly stated by him in his writings. "Ultimately a genuine leader is not a searcher for consensus but a molder of consensus. I said on one occasion, 'If every Negro in the United States turns to violence, I will choose to be that one lone voice preaching that this is the wrong way.'" [25]

Our intent here is to show that King's program of social reform can be embraced by what is commonly termed the Social Gospel. In addition, we have suggested that the orientation of the Social Gospel is of such a nature as to lead King from a treatment of race as a special problem to considerations of class, international relations, peace, and the integrated society. Although we have failed to make judgments about King's social ethic, we do desire to suggest that the Social Gospel as presently conceived impedes the solution of the race problem. Our historical overview clearly indicates that the Social Gospel as originally conceived by Gladden and Rauschenbusch had little or nothing to say about race in spite of the fact that it came into existence during the days in which America gave birth to Jim Crow. This neglect we attributed to the too uncritical usage of the science of the age and the definition of the social problem in class and economic terms. In our view, change did not come until the thirties, when Reinhold Niebuhr was one of the persons responsible for this revision. Yet in spite of the greater attention given racial problems, no significant change took place in either church or society during this period. The new insights of the revised Social Gospel were still too much linked to class, and the social gospeler looked more to Europe than America for discovery of problems vital to Social Christianity.

Between 1940 and 1960 race came into its own as a problem for American Christians. This we suggested was due to its ability to ride piggyback on the West's concern with Hitler's racist policies and America's embarrassment in regard to its own record in race relations. Through historical accident, race became the major problem for Martin L. King and continued to be a predominant concern.[26] Before King's career ended in 1968, however, the logic of the Social Gospel was eroding the focus on race. Class, economic questions, and international relations were once again gaining prominence, not only in their own right as legitimate social concerns, but also as the avenue through which the problem of race must find its resolution. It is our conclusion that at every point—even at the time of greatest concern and gain in race relations—the Social Gospel has tended to make race a peripheral issue. In this, of course, the Social Gospel is not alone. The tragedy is that the Social Gospel is the churches' most liberal expression in race relations.

The failure of the Social Gospel is due, we have charged, to its bias toward a class analysis of American society which ignores the racist history of the nation and the fact that the black man is victimized by color not class. Color has determined his caste and class. In the final analysis, the burden he bears is not the product of the economic question, industrial society *qua* industrial society, or the fate of Western civilization. These, to be sure, have their effect; but the central problem is the white man's fear of black skin and kinky hair. Failure to recognize this means keeping black persons in a caste-like position in the society. Their lot is exacerbated not mitigated by seeking solutions along avenues only tangentially related to race problems. The possibility of mutuality between the races will be enhanced only when one can openly acknowledge race as a problem and seek solutions fitted peculiarly to it.

It also appears that, in the light of the gospel understanding of God's sovereignty, it would be desirable to consider integration and nonviolence as something less than absolute goods. There can be no doubt that Christians should seek a society where race counts for nought; but does that imply only integration? The negative phrasing — a "non-segregated" church and a "non-segregated" society — may be the most appropriate proximate goal for all Christians. The means to achieve this goal should not be defined only by nonviolence. On the one hand, the concept takes on too quickly the character of a faith; on the other hand it presupposes a strategy of mass confrontation. The strategy limits actions for social change too much; the faith overtones distort the proper conception of loyalty and commitment. What is required is a de-emphasis and a relativizing of both concepts. Integration needs to be differentiated so that we may speak precisely about what we desire in terms of social institutions, cultural symbols, and personality traits. Nonviolence needs to be replaced by specific references to mechanisms for both direct and indirect social action and social control. Race relations should never be confined arbitrarily to some church within the Church or some aggressive sects which have withdrawn from the Church and the world in order to conquer both at some future time.

The concern of the Social Gospel with the form of *society* rather than the Church needs correction. If the society is to be molded after the Kingdom, then the Church should be also. Indeed one should seek to make the Church a living model of what the society should be. The Church, therefore, cannot exclude the Negro from its neighbor-love and excuse itself on the basis of housing patterns, financial problems, or anything else. If the good people who sit in the pews cannot be converted, we should not expect whole societies to be constrained by Christian ideals and principles. We should quite frankly abandon the ideals and seek some other ways of reforming the Church and society. It would also seem unwise to expect the Black American, the victim of racial injustice, to be more Christian than the white American. One should note also that this expectation is present at every level of the Church's life, including the ecumenical.

More attention also needs to be paid to the black church. The recent civil rights revolution has exhibited the enormous potential of this institution, yet the Social Gospel's neglect of the white church has led to the neglect of the black church. The black church is used and abused by blacks and whites in the name of race relations; it is seldom given sufficient funds to enable it to do well its work in this area. One needs here to acknowledge the contribution of Dean Muelder in the training of black Ph.D.'s for the Church, even while one laments the irresponsibility of the Church and social gospelers as a whole.

Most especially must the Social Gospel movement be criticized for its failure to develop a tradition of scholarship and scholars. While we have not surveyed all the literature and have omitted the period since 1968, it can be said without fear of contradiction that those who have worked in the area of race relations have done so on the weekends. The church can boast of no Gordon Allport, George E. Simpson, J. Milton Yinger or Thomas Pettigrew. Is there any wonder then that racism has such a firm hold on the Church?

NOTES

1. Winthrop D. Jordan, *White Over Black* (Baltimore: Pelican Books, 1969), pp. 66, 74, 92–93, 97.

2. Robert T. Handy, ed., *The Social Gospel in America: 1870–1920* (New York: Oxford University Press, 1966), p. 24; Dores Robinson Sharpe, *Walter Rauschenbusch* (New York: Macmillan, 1942), p. 59.

3. Handy, *The Social Gospel;* Walter Rauschenbusch, *The Righteousness of the Kingdom,* ed. Max Stackhouse (Nashville: Abingdon, 1968).

4. Rayford Logan, *The Betrayal of the Negro: From Rutherford B. Hayes to Woodrow Wilson* (New York: Collier-Macmillan, 1965).

5. Gladden has a book of similar title in which he pays little attention to the Negro question: Washington Gladden, *The Ruling Ideas of the Present Age* (Boston: Houghton, 1895).

6. S. P. Fullinwider, *The Mind and Mood of Black America* (Homewood, Ill.: Dorsey Press, Inc., 1969); Thomas F. Gossett, *Race: The History of an Idea in America* (Dallas: Southern Methodist University Press, 1963).

7. A succinct account of the educational compromise is recorded in Henry Allen Bullock, *A History of Negro Education in the South from 1619 to the Present* (Cambridge: Harvard University Press, 1967), pp. 89–116.

8. Lyman Abbott after 1890 became publicly anti-Negro. Logan, *The Betrayal of the Negro*, pp. 274–75; see also Josiah Strong, *Our Country* (New York: Baker and Taylor Co., 1891).

9. Paul A. Carter, *The Decline and Revival of the Social Gospel* (Ithaca, N.Y.: Cornell University Press, 1956), p. 76.

10. Benjamin J. Mays, *Born to Rebel* (New York: Charles Scribner's Sons, 1971), pp. 72, 125.

11. Reinhold Niebuhr, *Moral Man and Immoral Society* (New York: Charles Scribner's Sons, 1932).

12. Ibid., p. xi.

13. Selections from the following pages of ibid. suggest in our view the whole strategy of Martin Luther King, Jr.: pp. 119, 121, 129, 252–54.

14. Adam Clayton Powell, Jr., *Marching Blacks* (New York: Dial Press, 1945).

15. Joseph H. Oldham, *The Churches Survey their Task* (London: George Allen & Unwin Ltd., 1937), pp. 72–73.

16. Quoted in H. Shelton Smith, Robert T. Handy, and Lefferts A. Loetscher, eds., *American Christianity: An Historical Interpretation with Representative Documents,* 2 vols. (New York: Charles Scribner's Sons, 1963), II:543.

17. Liston Pope, *The Kingdom Beyond Caste* (New York: Friendship Press. 1957), esp. pp. 117–18.

18. Martin Luther King, Jr., *Stride toward Freedom* (New York: Harper and Bros., 1958), pp. 90–107 and 24.

19. Niebuhr, *Moral Man and Immoral Society*, pp. 252–53.

20. Waldo Beach, "A Theological Analysis of Race Relations," in *Faith and Ethics*, Paul Ramsey, ed. (New York: Harper and Bros., 1957), pp. 221–22.

21. Ibid., p. 219.

22. Martin Luther King, Jr., "I Have a Dream," address at the Lincoln Memorial during the March on Washington 28 August 1963, printed in *Liberation* (June 1963); idem, *Stride toward Freedom*, p. 90.

23. Martin Luther King, Jr., *Where Do We Go from Here: Chaos or Community?* (New York: Harper and Row, 1967), p. 42.

24. Iibid., p. 43.

25. Ibid., p. 63.

26. King, *Stride toward Freedom*, p. 69.

11 Institutions, Unity, and Mission

James K. Mathews

T H E R E are those at present who would call into question all three of the above designations. Ours is a period of anti-institutionalism and the "Establishment" is challenged in every order of society.[1] After unity has enjoyed stage center in the life of the Church during recent decades, we are now informed that multitudes are "turned off" by the subject. With regard to mission, at the very point of their greatest missionary thrust, the churches have lost heart, a sense of goal and purpose; they have, in fact, lost their sense of *mission*. There is irony in the fact that just as it was concluded that "everything is mission," it became necessary to raise the question: "What *is* mission?"

THE QUEST FOR UNITY

We have no need, however, to be excessively disheartened. No doubt we must hear these voices but not really heed them, for they express half-truths, and to conclude that they speak wholly the truth would be to believe a lie. For it would be difficult or impossible to contemplate culture devoid of institutional forms. Moreover, it is notable that the most anti-establishment persons are sometimes during crises the very first to run for such cover as the much maligned institutions may offer. Again, while it could be observed a quarter of a century ago that the secular world had lost the experience of unity, it must be said today that it earnestly yearns for it, but at the same time reveals that it lacks the resources for its attainment. Meanwhile the Christian world has moved steadily and rapidly towards its recovery and may even yet be the chief vehicle for the realization of the unity of all mankind in fulfillment of God's purpose in Christ. Broadly speaking, this *is* the Church's mission.

Whereas institutionalism is rightly condemned, it would be a rarefied ecclesiology indeed which did not allow that the Church is in some sense an institution. It is instituted of God for the achievement of certain ends among men. The Gospel, the sacraments, the ministries all possess institutional dimensions. The Church organizes itself in some form to accomplish its witness before the world. The Church does somehow govern itself in a way which is visible to the world; it somehow plots its mission. The local church is in clearly observable ways an institution. The Church is one form, among numerous others, in which man relates himself to society. For the Christian, the Church is far more than institution, but it is no less. The classic marks of the Church: one, holy, catholic and apostolic, refer clearly to unity and mission; likewise, they imply the institutional. Walter Muelder, by his exploration and writing in this area and by his chairing of the World Council of Churches' Commission on Institutionalism, has placed the whole Church in his debt.[2]

It is not enough to acknowledge the validity of institutional expressions of the Church. One must go further and confess that present institutional forms tend to stifle fuller attainment of unity, or contrariwise they reinforce the tendency toward disunity. One need look no further than the organizational charts of any one of the great denominations. While acknowledged causes — education, evangelism, missions — are well entrenched, provided with extensive bureaucratic machinery and ample budgets, the concern for Christian unity is starved in terms of budget and administered on a part-time basis or as a "one-man show." This suggests that our structures are outmoded as regards ecumenicity and that new types of institutional expression are urgently needed. All this is widely sensed at present and restructuring is taking place at nearly every level. Here again there may be trouble, for structure for the sake of structure is not enough. It must be for fuller unity and fuller unity for Christian renewal, and renewal for more effective mission to the world. In any event increasing numbers of Christians are aware that the settled churches with which we are familiar are not entirely normative.

We are moving toward greater unity. Unity is of the essence of the Church. Its unity is spiritual but it is also corporeal. As yet we are not aware of what precisely its shape may be. Surely it will not be a case of one separated group of brethren going back to the position of some other separated group of brethren, but rather, it will be a going forward together to a goal, as yet hidden, but toward which the triune God is calling us. Dr. Nikos Nissiotis, Director of the Ecumenical Institute at Bossey, of the World Council of Churches, gives us a helpful reminder at this point:

> The division of the Church as a mystery hidden in the incomprehensible nature of God is not primarily either the result of hatred among the Churches, or of disagreement on fundamental views concerning Christian dogma. One is led by historical events to believe that at the root of the schisms in the Church there is one fundamental cause: the absence of *koinonia* between them, without which the vertical communion with God, though not broken, becomes a further power of alienation and isolation . . . Among the main reasons for the Church heresies, schisms and divisions is the lack of this inner power of mutual service, of mutual interdependent existence. The greatest sin of the people of God is that they have neglected to perceive the theological, vertical dimension of *diakonia* in the ecclesiological, horizontal one.[3]

THE ROAD TO ECUMENICITY

W. A. Visser t'Hooft has warned us that we should not be so consumed about the goal of unity that we neglect the road to unity. They belong together. What do we mean by the word *ecumenism?*

1. By ecumenism, we do not refer solely, and perhaps not even primarily, to the coming together of the churches. In the final analysis it has more to do with the relation of the Church to the world than of church to church. Its basic reference is, of course, to the whole inhabited world. It has to do therefore with a profound stirring in the depths of men — of all men — and a shaking of their orders to the foundation. It embraces also the whole sweep of history. Its reference is to what God intends among men, "namely, that the universe . . . might be brought into a unity in Christ," as Ephesians 1:10 has it.

Moreover, in this generation we are experiencing ourselves in a new way, a comprehensive way. By this we mean that we now know ourselves to be global persons. We are no longer confined to national or racial boundaries. Whatever concerns any man anywhere concerns us all. This means that provincialism and parochialism finally must be put aside. Our interest is now humanity itself, and we may comprehend the whole *oikoumene*. One runs into this perspective constantly. In one of his later writings we find Teilhard de Chardin speaking of the "planetization" of humanity which is stupendously accelerated today.

2. In a more specific sense, ecumenism connotes the whole Church throughout the inhabited world, particularly as it reaches toward a fuller and more visible expression of its unity. One recalls the expression attributed to Archbishop William Temple that he believed in one, holy, catholic and apostolic Church and regretted very much that it did not exist. This must have been voiced in a discouraging moment, for he was himself one of the great architects of ecumenism.

3. Ecumenism also refers to the whole task of the whole Church throughout the inhabited world. For the Church by its very nature is concerned about the whole *oikoumene*. It hardly need be stated that the modern ecumenical development has an essentially missionary origin. It is as if missionaries sent out by their various traditions found themselves at the same task, along the same road, in obedience to the same Lord. They said: "Why not walk together?" and they did. Sooner or later this raised the further question: "Why not *be* together?"

Arising in missionary obedience, ecumenism has a missionary task: in the most convincing terms to declare and demonstrate the love of God for every man and to invite their response to Jesus Christ as Lord. Sam Keen in his recent book, *Apology for Wonder*, suggests a highly imaginative and demythologized form in which to declare the Gospel:

> Look! Attend! Listen! A child is born, a new being, a new era, a new existential possibility has emerged. Novelty has entered history, and therefore you may be free of the binding illusion that your fate is written in the stars, that you are victims of an order that is determined with no regard for your freedom or care for your being. The fault lies not in your stars but in your own refusal to accept the gracious gift of human freedom. The ground out of which history springs is alive and gracious; therefore anything is possible. Live in openness, wonder, and gratitude, accepting the mysterious gift of the ability to create, act, and forgive![4]

This is the word of the cross, not conventional thinking nor sophisticated rubbish. It is God's offer and demand of life. Then this word of the Gospel is backed up and even provoked by the deed of the Gospel. To proclaim and embody this word is our common task.

Nowadays most churches have many ecumenical irons in the fire. For example, they are involved in the conciliar movement at every level: local, state, regional, national, world. Moreover they are engaged in cooperative endeavors of every conceivable type and again at every organizational level. Then, there are the world confessional families: Anglican, Lutheran, Reformed, Methodist, Baptist, and the rest. Once these were thought of as inimical to the ecumenical thrust. Now they are regarded more and more as legitimate and appropriate ecumenical manifestations, particularly when they exist not merely for the interest of their own confessional heritage but in behalf of the whole Church.[5] Another expression is the extension of dialogue between the various Protestant denominations and the Roman Catholic Church, or with the Orthodox family, or with conservative evangelicals. There are those who regard this as the most promising dimension of ecumenical engagement which looks toward fuller Christian reconciliation. Then, of course, there is that form of ecumenism which looks specifically toward church union. More than a score of these possibilities are currently under discussion in as many countries, and hardly a year passes without one or another of these explorations maturing into full organic union.

THREE ECUMENICAL MOVEMENTS

From this brief overview of ecumenism in general we turn more specifically to the ecumenical movement. By this movement we mean basically the fellowship of the churches directed toward common witness and action. As we have stated, it has stemmed from mission and in unity drives toward the renewal and mission of the Church. If oneness is a mark of the very nature of the Church we should be able to observe its outcroppings through the centuries, which is indeed the case. Generally, however, we date its modern expression from the great missionary conference at Edinburgh in 1910. As recently as 1954 the official Roman Catholic position was opposed to the ecumenical movement, and it is only during the decade of the sixties that the Roman Catholic Church may be said to have been a part of it. Some would, of course, place this movement, as movement, at the opposite pole from the institutional expression of the movement.

Actually we can differentiate what some have termed three ecumenical movements. The first one was what might be called "charismatic ecumenism." It was pioneered by gifted individuals — laymen and clergy alike — who discerned that God was doing a new thing; that following centuries of division, he willed that his people express their unity once more. Collaborative Christian efforts began to take place which transcended denominational separations. The Y.M.C.A., Y.W.C.A., W.S.C.F., especially the national Christian Councils, and many others are examples of this trend. Here one recalls the names of John R. Mott, Robert E. Speer and Robert H. Gardiner — all laymen. Mott, Speer and Joseph H. Oldham laid the foundation for the International Missionary Council. Or consider Bishop Charles H. Brent, who pioneered the Faith and Order movement; or Archbishop Nathan Soderblom, father of the Life and Work movement.

These three organizations represent strands now intertwined in the present World Council of Churches. Other names could be added: W. A. Visser t'Hooft, Archbishop William Temple, Bishop George K. A. Bell, or Daniel T. Niles—the list is long. To these must be added the name of Pope John XXIII.

What might be termed a second ecumenical movement might be dated from 1948, when the World Council of Churches was initiated. It is quite clearly a manifestation of "churchly ecumenism." With the establishment of the World Council of Churches notice was given that the denominations had taken over the ecumenical movement. Some observers have been highly critical of this trend which they have seen as a taming or domestication of the ecumenical movement. A strong positive case for the W.C.C. and other councils can be made, but this churchification may tend, some would say, toward a kind of prostitution of the movement. The earlier manifestation accented Christian unity; the latter emphasized unity also but unity among churches. By its very nature it is more institutional than charismatic. It is more dependent on the structures as they are now. The council is a council of separated churches. It proceeds by consensus or by even a kind of least common denominator. Communication is basically by means of normal hierarchical lines. Its life moves from assembly to assembly, with everything pointing to and leading from these assemblies.

As the council grows, consensus is harder and harder to reach. Parliamentary procedures in the World Council of Churches, for instance, are likely to be heavily Anglo-Saxon, with the burden of adaptation falling heavily upon the non-Westerner. Such councils are prone to become merely cooperative movements with little prophetic voice. As a result of such factors, councils at every level are at the present time in trouble. So far our structures have not been devised adequately to convey the full force of a unitive ecumenism. It must be acknowledged, however, that both in executive staffing and in constitution of committees, the W.C.C. has more recently reflected in fuller measure its global nature.

Not surprisingly, therefore, there emerged during the 1960s what could be designated the "third ecumenical movement." It might be called "grass-roots" ecumenism or even "guerilla" ecumenism. It is harder to describe then the other two, but it is also fundamental to our theme. It is widespread, discursive, a folk movement; often one must rely on a kind of folklore to grasp it. It is not entirely restricted to the churches, but is related to the worldwide "revolution of rising expectations," a worldwide linking of arms based on common humanity.

To the extent that the third ecumenical movement is evident within the churches, it is largely lay in orientation. Many laymen, although by no means all, increasingly "sit loose" to traditional denominational loyalties. This form of the movement is less interested in the organizational forms of unity than in the experience of unity. It is a peoples' movement and takes the whole world as its arena. It is not represented by an official dialogue between the churches but exists among peoples. It moves toward the depths of humanness and, with ever increasing seriousness, even celebrates its humanness.

Such Christians have often already left their traditional confessional settings. They see their commitment not so much to the past as to the future. They are not ecclesiastical leaders, but rather the rank and file who wish to participate more fully in whatever shapes their lives. No leader can today "deliver a constituency." They all want to be consulted. Quite clearly one cannot point to specific organizations and say, "There is the third ecumenical movement," for it is not institutional. Nevertheless, this third movement should be understood as a reality recognizable both within and without the Church today — a reality which cannot be ignored.

The third ecumenical movement is evident in a good deal of the disenchantment with regard to organized religion today. It exists in the tension between institution and movement.[6] It is not antireligious in its thrust and may be attractive to those who have broken with their denominations but not their commitment to Christ. Perhaps its chief peril is that it can so easily succumb to negativism. Nor should we oversimplify and conclude that all unrest in the Church comes from a kind of vocal ecclesiastical Left, thus ignoring potent reactions from the right, from those who precisely do not want the church to be involved meaningfully and concretely in the human struggle.

The third ecumenical movement is not by any means restricted in its manifestations to Protestantism. It is clearly present in the unrest so in evidence within the Roman Catholic Church, whether it stems from the celibacy issue, or the more profound one of collegiality, or the challenge to infallibility, or the exodus from the priesthood and women's orders. A kind of massive erosion seems to be taking place there, and it should give no pleasure at all to those within the Protestant fold. Their pain and sorrow and sickness is also our own. What is involved is a wholesale critique and reappraisal of lifestyles which for centuries have been taken for granted. This could, of course, spell disaster or, on the contrary, be the birthpangs of great new possibilities.

Quite clearly these developments are reflected in all manner of experimental ministries throughout the world. Some of them bridge the Protestant-Catholic gap, a kind of ecumenical underground, such as is commonplace nowadays in Holland. Or we find them in guerilla churches or house churches, or in little congregations which relate in celebrations with the larger congregations. Or they are present in ad hoc manifestations of the Church or in issue-centered congregations which "do their thing" in relation to peace, drugs, air pollution and so on. Many Christians everywhere are seeking to live more authentic Christian lives as they gather to celebrate the Gospel and scatter again to do justice among men. My intent is here to affirm the third ecumenical movement in its intent if not in every particular.

THE CRY FOR HUMANITY

Once again, let it be said that the third ecumenical movement is not a humanism in the usual sense; but it is a call for authentic humanity on the part of all humanity. The cry for humanity comes from every quarter: from the new nations of the world; from Viet Nam, North and South; from Czechoslovakia as it yearns for freedom; from Poland as it strives for economic justice. It comes from "Down under" where an Australian poet claims that the dream cannot be realized until "the country is irrigated and the people humanized." The cry for humanity comes from youth. A professor asked a young man why he let his hair grow long. He replied, "Just to annoy my parents." He was pressed to say more. "All right, I mean it to say something: Hold it! Hold it! Hold it right there! Why does it have to be *this* way? Could it not possibly be *that* way?" The cry says that what always has been does not always have to be.

The cry for humanity comes from women in our time. They no longer are willing to fill a role assigned them by men. They are determined to live in their own right. Long ago Ibsen saw this and in his *Doll's House* we find Hjalmar telling his wife: "Before all else you are to be a wife and mother." Nora replied: "That I no longer believe. I believe that before all else I am a human being, just as much as you are — or at least that I should try to become one." That cry is nearly universal today!

The cry for humanity comes from students in their protest against overemphasis on creature comforts; their insistence that man is more than a brain, a fleshly computer; their conviction that a university must not be manipulated to serve just any old social end. It is seen in their desire that higher education be not just the privilege of the elite; that they themselves be taken seriously for what they are; and that when beneficial change can be effected, it must be.

The cry for humanity comes from Africa. There one hears the word *Muntu,* found in all the Bantu languages. It means "man," as the early missionaries knew, but it means also mankind; it means human and humane, and all that relates to true humanness. There is *Muntu* in nature, in song, in dance, in mystery, in letting go, in entering into life, in expressing "soul." This quality is not lost entirely among contemporary black citizens in America who today lift up, as if with one voice, their cry for human dignity. And the rest of mankind must hear.

Particularly, the Church must hear. All that we have been saying is embraced by what may be called the third ecumenical movement. Can it somehow be integrated into the second or churchly movement, or at least strongly affirmed by the churches, and in turn become a fulfillment of the vision of the pioneers of modern ecumenism who sought a comprehensive unity and renewal for mission in behalf of all mankind? If so, then this movement will have proceeded toward that goal to which we initially alluded; namely, that literally ecumenism has to do with "the whole inhabited world." Is it not true that periodically there must be a kind of marriage of the church movements with the established Church? History would seem to say so.

EXPRESSIONS OF INSTITUTIONAL ECUMENISM

In a real sense the Church cannot organize or control this peoples' movement; but an attempt can be made for it to be more effectively represented in churchly forums, for a completely formless ecumenical movement would be impossible or ineffective. The world is too well-organized for that. Let us examine two current expressions of institutional ecumenism with regard to this matter.

First, the World Council of Churches, which is taking this task with great seriousness. Already plans are afoot for the fifth Assembly of the W.C.C. to be a far more broadly representative body than its predecessors. It is hoped that it may not be nearly so heavily laden with ecclesiastical "brass" and by the same token be more inclusive of laity, women, youth, minority groups, smaller churches, and those who possess special equipment to deal with the complex problems confronting the Church in the contemporary world. So far, it appears that the churches will accept a considerable change in the representative principle to enable this goal to be accomplished. At the same time, it is hoped that a more spontaneous presence of ordinary lay Christian people at assemblies may be evident to symbolize and manifest the profound human movement of our day.

Meanwhile, at the Geneva headquarters, a less formidable bureaucratic structure has been sought. It is hoped that it will prove to be smaller, more flexible and more responsive to the needs of people than in the past. The months ahead will tell whether or not this ideal may be realized. For the World Council in January 1971 unanimously adopted a far less rigid structure of its divisions and departments than that approved in 1954 at the second Assembly in Evanston. Replacing all this administrative machinery, three program units have been authorized: Faith and Witness; Justice and Service; and Education and Communication. The first embraces activities formerly subsumed under Faith and Order and under Missions. The second gathers together the areas of inter-church aid and the Commission of the Churches on International Affairs and other social emphases. The third is new, for from Amsterdam to Uppsala there was no specific department for educational matters in the World Council, whereas communication in the past was largely conceived of as having to do with press relations. It is believed that in this structure is a real opportunity for the World Council to become less bureau-laden and more adequately equipped for mission.

A second massive test for relating the third ecumenical movement to churchly structures is seen in the Consultation on Church Union. This exploration for a church truly catholic, reformed, and evangelical was launched in 1962. During March 1970 in St. Louis a draft Plan of Union was given tentative approval and submitted to the nine member-communions for their initial study and response. It offers the churches an exciting possibility, and during the 1970s they must alter, accept, or reject the proposed plan. The scheme is widely known, and no detailed exposition or critique is needed here.

It is maintained, however, that the member churches do not differ much on essentials of faith; only in accent. This is of basic importance, but in our day the whole Church has been given what may well be called an ecumenical faith. The participating churches do not vary widely in matters of worship and sacrament either. On ministry they are further apart — especially in practice and emphasis. The plan speaks of one ministry of Christ given to the whole church which is shared by the whole *laos*. It then acknowledges three offices of ordained ministry: the diaconate, the presbyterate and the episcopate — the latter to be both historically and constitutionally defined. Strangely, the order of these offices in the plan is presbyterate, episcopate and diaconate.

Oddly enough, it is structure that excites the most defensiveness, for apparently no denomination is prepared to move easily into unaccustomed surroundings. This reluctance suggests that nontheological questions may still be decisive for the participants. Real breakthroughs in creative structure are already manifesting themselves in original ways at both the local and regional levels. It is here that the proposed Church of Christ Uniting (COCU) may grapple most effectively with the phenomenon of the third ecumenical movement. The plan provides for a quite familiar four-fold structure of the church: manifestations of the church locally, in districts (conferences or dioceses some would say), regionally, and nationally. No less familiarly, the typical church organization is triangular with the apex pointed upward; the Western world has known this sort of thing since the formation of the first Roman legion, perhaps before. Now, suppose that the triangle were to be inverted and rest upon its apex. That is a somewhat precarious position, so, better still, lay it on its side with the base facing forward. This represents and exalts the local manifestation of the Church. All the other manifestations of the Church — district, regional and national — appear behind it in a supportive, connected relationship. That is the basic model of the Church of Christ Uniting.

The local and regional aspects of the plan are important because at these points new ground is being broken. They are significant not only for what is being specifically proposed in each instance but also for the psychological value of the proposals; for in neither the local or regional instances can any of the participating denominations point with pride and say, "This is the way we do it." In other words, there is sufficient newness about these elements as to put all parties in essentially the same posture with regard to them. The district and national aspects are quite similar to the present arrangements in the member-denominations, and no comment need be made about them here.

The draft plan proposes that the local church be composed of two forms: the task group and the parish. The task group will focus the efforts of action and prayer on specific ministries and projects. It will be made up of persons with special interest or competence in a particular need and a vocation to care for it. A task group may be formed at any level of the church, but will fulfill its ministry locally and usually for only a limited period of time. An example might be a task group devoted to ministering to the problem of drug abuse in a community.

The more basic shape of the local church would be the *parish*. This is a specialized use of the term. It would be made up of one or more than one (usually more than one) congregation, related for common governance of their life, for planning in participation in the total mission of the church and their own specific mission, and for common exercise of ministry. This structure will enable both ethnic and social variety and inclusiveness. In the view of many observers, one of its strong points is that it affords an authentic possibility of breakthrough on the race issue, for it affords the opportunity to be constituted multiracially with respect to its congregations and ordained ministers. Typically, its ministry would be collegial. This plan is not at present precisely characteristic of any of the traditions; nor is it entirely alien to any of them. There seems to be a widespread reaching for such a shape of the local church within many denominations, and there is a great need for exactly this sort of structure. All over the country, some experimentation of this character has been taking place for some time.

With respect to a regional structure for the church, another really new possibility presents itself. If this idea is taken seriously and fully implemented it will be the chief guarantee against the Church of Christ Uniting becoming a superchurch. Indeed, there would seem to be grounds for believing that it could be less topheavy, less bureaucratic, less hierarchical, and more decentralized, than any one of the predecessor bodies are at present. It is proof against a monolithic structure, for leadership would be dispersed and decentralized, with a relatively *lean* bureaucracy at the national level (but enough provision to afford adequate correlation of the whole and the possibility of speaking and acting as one when it is required). The point is that decisions would be brought closer to the people and involve many more of them. The proposed shape of the local church and of the regional expression of the church offer peculiar possibilities of responsiveness to what the third ecumenical movement strives for.

On paper, there is even now regional structure within some, if not all, of the nine participating churches. Who would claim that these are really effective, as constituted at present? In fact this level never has "come off" in any tradition in church history. This is true regardless its designation: archdiocese, province, synod, or jurisdiction. This deficiency has been due to three reasons: (1) failure to decide what a region is; (2) failure to define the task or mission of a region; and (3) failure to grant adequate authority, money, and personnel to fulfill that mission. Each of these failures the plan proposes to overcome. Note, by the way, that we are speaking here of regionalism and not of sectionalism as, for example, in the expression the "solid South."

Now what do we mean by a region? Fortunately, this is not a theological matter, and neither searching the Scriptures nor prayer and fasting will shed much light on the subject. Rather, we must turn to the social scientists for guidance. They can help us, although gradually regions shift. We all experience our lives regionally. State lines are not always the best guides. One could hazard the guess that there are about thirty-five to forty-five natural regions in this country. COCU would propose an ecclesiastical structure to correspond to them. Training, communication, social service, and elements of mission clearly best served in and by the region itself would suggest the tasks of such regions. The church would then provide for authority and resources to the region adequate to such tasks. Control and participation would be closer to the people yet under the correlation and review of the national body.

In both the local and regional arrangements, let it be repeated, a real breakthrough seems possible. This will be most appealing to young people — lay and ministerial — and could be major means of renewing the total life of the Church. At present, many young people feel they are caught within aged and often outmoded structures.

A greater sense of urgency is visited upon the churches all the time. Neither the Church nor the world will stand still. We cannot keep everything as it is or was. There is an eschatological aspect to the situation in our day, and there is no turning back. Church incomes decline in many denominations, secularism grows apace, yet the demands upon the People of God increase. We must decide, and we must decide against the background of the new era in which God has placed us. Many local situations reveal redundancies and over-lap. In many places there is an eagerness to seize the initiative locally in order to solve the ecumenical problem. It is increasingly clear that this may be a disastrous course unless the denominations them-selves move at the same time. Furthermore, there appears to be the possibility of the Church fracturing even more than it already has unless, while it is still open to them, leaders of the churches take steps to reverse the process. We have suggested by way of these somewhat elaborate illustrations that both the restructuring of the World Council of Churches and the taking seriously of COCU may afford the renewed institutional means of furthering the mission of the Church.

UNITY IN MISSION

But what is the mission of the Church in our day? Much confusion exists on traditional mission fields as well as in the minds of mis-sionary strategists. Once the nature of mission seemed clear; but not of late. Recently the writer asked two outstanding missionary leaders what they had to say about the mission of the Church. One was an American white person with experience in Asia; the other a black person from the Caribbean. The first replied that the missionary role is that of midwife—to bring to life faithfulness to the Gospel; it was healer of all the hurts within and between men; it was a catalyst to bring about change in the systems which cruelly oppress men and women. The other said that the mission today was to be found in dialogue with men of every faith and ideology; it was lib-eration for people from every bondage; it was changing the institu-tions and structures of society. They both offered helpful insights, but somehow their replies were not satisfying. Perhaps it is because the mission today must be *concrete* and not merely *conceptual*.

What we suggest is that it is God who raises with his Church the question of its mission. Given the present context in the world and in the Church, suppose the Church is confronted with God's question: "What does the Lord require of you?" An answer to this question should reveal the nature of the Church's task. Would not an answer be that the Church is required to go through the fires of change, the fires of a new and rapidly changing world if it is to be renewed after the image of its Lord whose Body it is? This, it seems to this writer, is exactly what the Church has been undergoing during the years just past.

In the painful situation which is the Church's lot today, again it is asked: "What does the Lord require of you?" Then, perhaps we will see our task if we are to labor in the Lord. What the Lord requires of us is precisely to go through this fiery furnace. This is the glory of the Church! When she most suffers is she not then clearly bearing the cross of her Lord? It was in the midst of the burning, fiery furnace that the enemy of the faithful Hebrew witnesses saw not three men but four! When the Church suffers then is her Lord most clearly present with her.

More than this, it is in the agonizing situation in which she finds herself that the Church once again finds her mission. In the turmoil of the human order and the anguish which sears the souls of men, our essential role as men and women of faith becomes clear once more. From the brewing and brooding depths of men everywhere —the poor, the young, the dispossessed, women, students, those disenchanted because of race or class—from every breast is arising a new call for freedom, the cry for full humanity, for possibility. It is in the hearing of these cries, and responding to them in the name of the triune God, that the Church finds its mission.

Yet it is because our task presents itself in so concrete a guise that many turn away. They long to be merely "spiritual," forgetting that a person as sensitive as Dag Hammarskjold said that nowadays the road to holiness leads through the world of action. Theology today is not the application of a perfect theoretical system to the real world. Rather, it is interplay; it is dialogue between faith and the world. This, after all, is what incarnation is all about: spirit and matter, matter and spirit constantly intermingled.

So, it is clear, religion and politics must be embraced together; but the clergy, in particular, have too often forgotten of late that the two are not identical. We must not remove ourselves so far from the world that we cannot be heard, nor identify ourselves so closely with the world that we have nothing to say. Nor should we forget the testimony of Martin Niemöller about his failure to speak as a Christian in times of turmoil and crisis: "In Germany they first came for the Communists, and I didn't speak up because I wasn't a Communist. Then they came for the Jews, and I didn't speak up because I wasn't a Jew. Then they came for the trade unionist and I didn't speak because I wasn't a member. Then they came for me — but by that time no one was left to speak up." [7]

1. The mission of the Church in our day is still directed to the whole world. In our global situation, in which as never before we have an international consciousness, it cannot be otherwise. For the world is one.

2. The mission of the Church in our day is a setting forth of the whole Gospel in declaration and in deed that cannot fail to be comprehended. The word and the deed go together, for ours is not just a protestation of the love of the Lord but a seeing to it that his sheep are fed. The word must be kept in history. But to declare the living word of God's endless love and forgiveness is never easy.

3. The contemporary mission of the Church is to obey God, to voice his demand and offer wherever people dwell. This will mean that we cannot wait for people to find their way into our increasingly alien sanctuaries. We must push out into the fields and into the streets of crowded cities to address the people on their own terms and in accordance with their own felt needs. This calls for experimental forms of service to be devised and encouraged, for cooperative parishes or clusters from various congregations and from among the different denominations. It goes without saying that at every level the Church will find occasions to make common cause with secular agencies in an effort to fulfill common goals.

4. Today's mission is precisely in response to and in terms of man's universal cry for his full humanity. This is really what the Gospel of the incarnation involves. The Word made flesh is God's permission and power for men to live as men before him — as men. The Church, therefore, must be found being the Church. It will be about its chief business of laboring for the increase among men of love of

God and love of neighbor. This is no mere pious admonition but sets us to the most concrete tasks imaginable. To meet such needs every church has been called to realign its priorities.

The Church will find itself serving radical students, militant crusaders for women's or minorities' rights, long-haired youth, bewildered aging ones, and those best known to us as countless forgotten men and women. We will discover ourselves involved in political activity in a new key; we will uncover utterly new ways to minister to humankind. And we will be fulfilling an essential role of the Church — that is, injecting new hope into individual and collective experience. For the Church is rightly the living, prophetic conscience of the drama of mankind. It alone has the solemn responsibility of bearing witness to the sacred, the eternal and depth dimension of human existence, what Eliade calls the "really real."

Increasingly the responsibility for mission will belong to the local church, which is where the Christian usually experiences the Church. In brief, each congregation or group of congregations must be renewed not for its own sake, but in order to enable each community and all communities to enter into that full experience of humanness which God both intends and empowers. This is not achieved by councils and conferences and hierarchies, but by pastors and people in each place and in all places availing themselves of the resources God supplies as he leads his people.

NOTES

1. It is worth observing that the Church "Establishment" was the *first* to feel the present anti-institutional pressure. This may just suggest that the churches may have been at their proper task at the frontier-posts of society.

2. See, for example, Muelder's work, in collaboration with Nils Ehrenstrom, *Institutionalism and Church Unity* (New York: Association Press, 1963).

3. N. A. Nissiotis, "The Ecclesiological Significance of Inter-Church Diakonia," *The Ecumenical Review* (January 1961): 193, 195.

4. Sam Keen, *Apology for Wonder* (New York: Harper and Row, 1969), p. 39.

5. The uniting of two world confessional groups, namely the Presbyterian and the Congregational, is an illustration of this point.

6. See H. Richard Niebuhr, *The Kingdom of God in America* (New York: Harper and Bros., 1937, Torchbook, 1959), p. xiii. Niebuhr probably first introduced this distinction, drawing on Henri Bergson.

7. "When I have used this statement first (it is long long ago) I do not know, nor can I say if ever I have used it in any publication." Letter from Martin Niemöller to author, 28 October 1971.

12 Public and Private Dimensions of
Ethical Responsibility   *L. Harold DeWolf*

I<small>N</small> his book *Social Salvation*, published in 1935, John C. Bennett devoted most of a chapter to "Three Half-Truths Concerning the Relation Between Individual and Social Salvation." The three ideas against which he was protesting, despite the measure of truth which he recognized in each, were as follows: (1) "that individuals can rise above any combination of social circumstances"; (2) "that since individuals control institutions and systems it is enough to change individuals"; and, on the other hand, (3) "that you can change society without changing individuals."[1] Such tendencies to divide social reform from Christian concern with individuals are still with us, although the forms of expression and the ways in which they are now institutionalized are considerably changed. With these tendencies the man honored by this volume is in striking contrast.

Walter G. Muelder is widely known for his teachings and writings concerning social ethics. He has devoted major attention to the ethics of ecclesiastical, political, and economic life. Moreover, he has worked not as a "loner" but as a member of a team, in fact of many teams. He never showed inclinations to become a prima donna. As a dean he was always an integral part of the faculty and sought faithfully to administer policies developed by a majority of his colleagues. He has worked within and through the Church, from local congregation to major committees and assemblies of the World Council of Churches.

Less well known to the general public are his personal piety and individual self-discipline. He has always been ready to make lonely decisions and to stand by them with courage. His personal life is a model of probity. Moreover, when he preached in chapel or led the devotions of smaller groups, it was evident that he was a man of prayer steeped in the great traditions of Christian devotion. When the new School of Theology on Commonwealth Avenue was planned he selected the great saints of the prayer life and prescribed the themes for the beautiful and richly meaningful windows in the little prayer chapel. By the spontaneous and insistent recommendation of the faculty and student body the prayer chapel was named by the Trustees of Boston University the Walter G. Muelder Chapel. It is therefore especially fitting that a book dedicated to him should include a chapter seeking to place the public and private aspects of ethical responsibility in proper perspective.

This book is being written in a time of such moral confusion as to be unusual even in a world chronically aberrant ethically. The extraordinarily rapid social changes, the population explosion, the vast increase in available knowledge of facts and techniques, and the mingling of diverse cultures have together overwhelmed the traditional conscience and established patterns of moral behavior. The resulting confusion has profoundly affected both personal morals and the recognized social responsibilities. In this situation which is, in many ways, new and confusing, it is needful, as well as fitting, that we make a fresh appraisal of the relations between public and private dimensions of ethical responsibility. As we do this we will first look critically at contemporary onesided views, then try to see ethical responsibility whole.

INDIVIDUALISTIC PIETISM

An article in the July 1970 issue of *Christian Life Magazine* is entitled "How We Can Save The Methodist Church" and is written "by the Honorable Samuel Teague, Former Mayor, Tallahassee, Florida." The writer begins by pleading for the removal of "paper members" and requiring genuine "devotion, sacrifice, and hard work of every member." The article is a winsome pleading for less formal ritual and more spiritual substance in worship, for protecting the minister from empty chores and inordinate requirements of time with a few neurotic members, and for suggested specific rules to secure a genuinely working fellowship. Then Teague comes to the question of a Social Gospel or a "personal gospel": "There is only one Gospel of Jesus Christ and its focus is upon an individual's personal commitment and relationship to God," he says. Elaborating, he continues, "Once we have come to love God with all our hearts, all of our minds, and all of our souls, we will find ways and means to overcome attitude structures that are disadvantageous to any one of our brothers — regardless of his race, color, or creed." It must be noticed, however, that it is "attitude structures" which are to be overcome and not social, political, or economic structures. There is specific condemnation of "mass marches for various causes," any association with councils of churches, and becoming "involved in social issues and worldly affairs." "Christ," we are told, "would never permit Himself to become involved in civic movements or worldly disputes."

Attention has been drawn to this one article because it expresses individualistic pietism at its best, while still maintaining its typical center. The writer does not defend racial discrimination nor attack labor unions. He assumes that "getting right with God" must involve "getting right with all our brothers [else] the experience is not genuine." While he would like to see ministers brought into business boards of directors so that they will understand the laymen, he also wants them to "join in the councils of our labor unions." There is so much that is appealing here and so much of needed truth that I could wish for more laymen who would take the Christian life and church obligations as seriously. The truths of such earnest individualistic pietism are worthy of explicit inventory. In making such inventory we shall not be limited, of course, to Teague's statement, nor attempt to include all the true and useful insights he expresses which are not especially characteristic of such individualism.

There is great need for changed and committed individuals. A minister cannot work long in a pastorate without learning of many lives which are broken by marital disloyalty, alcoholism, lack of love by parents for their children, drab purposelessness, obsession with material gain, or long-harbored hostilities. People who are victims of their own sins or shortcomings of such kinds injure others and are seldom able to give much service to the needs of neighbors or community. They are not only themselves alienated and spiritually lost, but they spread the infection to others whose lives they influence. There is need for ministry to all such persons by pastors and laymen. Part of the care must be concerned with the stirring or renewal of faith and repentance. Indeed, all persons are infected with sin, and all need such ministry from others in the community of faith.

Resources of preaching, worship, and prayer can lead to changed lives. In every church which has long had an effective ministry, there are persons whose lives have been radically changed by the preaching of the Gospel and by participation in worship and prayer. Some of the changes have been sudden and dramatic; others have come slowly and, at the time, almost imperceptibly. But the important truth is that they have occurred.

Evangelism is vitally important and often neglected. By evangelism is here meant, not only the preaching or teaching of the Gospel, but quite specifically the winning of individuals to faith in Christ. There is no one right method of evangelism. Mass revival meetings, for example, were unknown throughout most of Christian history. So far as we know, Augustine, Luther, Calvin, and Wesley never invited people to come to the front of an audience or congregation for commitment to Christ. Such invitations were effective in the nineteenth century and in some places are effective today. But less public and dramatic methods are generally more useful.[2] It is sad, however, that many churches, in giving up mass evangelism, have given up all effort to gain forthright commitment of faith by individuals. Instead, many simply receive children into the church at some stage in instruction and invite adults to join the church with, or even without, some instruction and without so much as asking for a personal decision in either case.

Such neglect of individual commitment is a tragic default on the part of church leadership. As a result there are large numbers of people in the churches who customarily make their practical decisions without reference to Christian life. However, in the denomination of which Teague wrote, a large number of members did, at least in 1959, regard themselves as obligated to choose in accord with Christian teachings and apparently were affected by such teachings in some aspects of practical life.[3]

Changed individuals are needed for changing institutions and operating them responsibly. If institutions which perpetuate racial discrimination, war, poverty, and crime are to be changed, there must be large numbers of persons with strong and reliable purpose to change them. It is not enough to have large numbers, even preponderant majorities, who would like to see all these evils eliminated. There must be effective majorities willing to pay the price for the necessary changes. This will involve yielding old privileges, accepting new risks, and giving up positions of economic advantage. These are precisely the kinds of renunciation and sacrifice which Christ called upon his disciples to make. Genuine, understanding acceptance of Christ as Lord brings into being the kind of will required. The pity is that in churches where evangelistic calls to Christian commitment are most frequent, there is seldom any understanding of such meaning; and where there is understanding there are few evangelistic calls for decision, public or private.

Even where good institutional structures are established, if they are operated by men and women who are mainly concerned with personal advantage, new tyrannies, exploitations, and other evils will quickly displace the old. This is the history of innumerable political reforms in municipalities and nations alike. A new world requires new persons.

Along with its truths, individualistic pietism carries some errors which have always been serious, and in the complex social structures of today they are no less than disastrous.

It is falsely supposed that institutional environment is unimportant to personal development. Whenever some churchmen urge programs to relieve poverty or to provide equal opportunities for all citizens, others are sure to raise vigorous opposition. Often they point to their own humble origins, in contrast to their present affluence. An individual's life is what he makes it, they insist. With hard work and thrift, anyone can succeed. People who have worked hard to gain their present economic security should not now be called upon to subsidize by taxes the people who have been too lazy, wasteful, or immoral to get ahead.

These are precisely the arguments used by Robert C. Byrd — Baptist, Gideon, and United States Senator from West Virginia — as he opposes legislation aiming for some measure of economic justice. He enjoys especially contrasting the allegedly shiftless poor in Washington, D.C. (where most of the poor are black) with his own modest origin and present success. Senator Byrd does not mention, of course, that he was not handicapped by being black. And he could not have been subjected in childhood to the protein-deficient diet which in itself condemns many children of the poor to lives of low energy and early death; for if he had he would now have neither the physical nor the mental energy to carry on his present activities. Neither does he take account of the fact that when the total number of available jobs falls short of total employment by millions, millions will inevitably be left out of work.

Often the glorification of individualism is stated in such a way as to make it appear that personal character and the qualities that are truly important are independent of the economic and political environment. Yet the conservative church people who maintain this view as an argument against making any effort for social change show a remarkable anxiety about any movements which tend, or which they fancy to tend, in the direction of a socialist or communist society. They appear to believe that it is individual character and not social environment that counts, but *only* within one particular social environment, namely the status quo! Of course, a few individuals do come out of wretched surroundings to register remarkable achievements. But a Christian or any humane person should not be satisfied with a society which tolerates conditions from which only a very few can emerge to meaningful and useful lives. Moreover, an economic system which produces such vast disparities of wealth and poverty as are present in ours damages people at the top of the heap, as well as those at the bottom.

In 1924, when I was a theological student, a law student and I happened to see the famous socialist leader Eugene V. Debs on a train, and we had a long and memorable conversation with him. The law student asked him what kept him from bitterness against the wealthy and powerful men who had so often misrepresented him and had put him in prison for his opposition to World War I. Debs replied that he truly cared about the well-being of rich and poor alike. He wanted to change the system because it was "making materialists of people both at the top and at the bottom." The people at the top had so much wealth that it preoccupied their attention; and the ones at the bottom were forced to give most of their attention to material things just to stay alive. Was Debs far from the truth? Does not great wealth pose a powerful temptation to pride and to insensitiveness toward the less fortunate?

It is mistakenly believed that good individuals assure a just society. Frequently the individualistic pietists agree that many aspects of our social order are evil. They say, however, that churchmen ought not to join any efforts to change it, for to do so will only divide the Church while interfering with its real work. The genuine task of the Church is to convert individuals, they insist; and when enough real conversions to Christ have occurred, the good people will inevitably produce a good society with justice for all.

This argument fatally ignores two realities. First is the fact that when people are persuaded to faith in Christ without instruction about the social implications of true Christian faith, they are likely to remain unchanged in their voting, business practices, and assumption or evasion of public responsibilities. Often they become even more damaging than before because they help to spread a cloak of self-righteous pride over the worst kinds of social injustice, exploitation of the environment, and military dominance of national policy. That this is no mere speculation is shown by the many letters of hatred which a minister receives when he becomes conspicuously identified with civil rights or antipoverty programs and which conclude their expressions of hate by such phrases as "Yours in the name of Jesus" of "Yours for Gospel preaching." Similarly, the most viciously racist radio propaganda frequently comes from stations devoting many hours of broadcast time to revivalistic Bible teaching.

The other important truth ignored by the belief in question is the fact that it requires careful attention and special knowledge to make good will effective in a business corporation, in urban renewal, or in international affairs. A few skillful men of power concerned only with their own selfish interests can manipulate policy in all these and many other areas so as to have the most exploitative, cruel, and violent effect on many, while people of good will are relating their Christian ideals *only* to individual virtue in personal relations. Actually, sincere Christian people contribute heavily to systematic cruelty because the victims are screened from their view by housing patterns and lack of trained perceptions.[4]

In fact, if people are simply kind to their friends and neighbors and pay little attention to political and economic structures, in the urban, industrialized society in which most of us now live, grave injustices will arise and be perpetuated simply by default. The physically handicapped, the children of the poor, and the aged will be left to personal charity, and most will be condemned to fatal neglect. There is much viciously selfish and merciless exploitation in our society; but such positive evil is not even required to injure and cruelly destroy the weaker members of our society. For this, *in*action will suffice. Especially in a competitive economic system, the merchant who uses skillful but unscrupulous advertising, packaging, and exploitation of labor has such an influence on the market that the manager who wishes to be fair to workers and customers alike can find little room for maneuver without economic ruin. That is, he cannot unless such structures as labor unions and consumer legislation have limited his irresponsible competitors.

Contrary to fact, it is thought that biblical Christianity is concerned only with personal religion and character. The individualists never tire of urging that the Church return to the Bible and the old-fashioned Christianity of personal salvation. Actually, most of the Old Testament concerns the social implications of the belief that God had made a special covenant with the people Israel which included an elaborate system of law to which they were subject. The law and the prophets dealt with every aspect of political, economic, and international policy, as well as marriage, relations between parents and children, and prescribed religious rites. The New Testament records the origins of the Christian movement, which was a minority in Judea and, in the period covered, a very small and illegal minority in the Roman Empire. In neither political entity could it have much influence on immediate public policy. However, this fact did not prevent Jesus from denouncing the eviction of widows from their houses by men who made a great show of their piety. Neither did it prevent his condemnation of laws which were both religious and political. Boldest of all his incursions into public affairs was his action in the court of the temple in Jerusalem. There, in the center of the political and economic, as well as religious life of Judea, he boldly overturned the tables of the money-changers and drove out the merchants who, he said, were making the place "a robber's cave." It was for teachings and actions like this that Jesus was crucified.[5]

In The Acts and the Letters of Paul, most of the instruction concerns the structure and life of the Church. However, it is also worthy of note that the apostles led in the wholehearted plunge of the Church into economic life and particularly the relief of poverty.[6] From New Testament days to the present, when the Church has been vigorous and healthy it has taken active part in public affairs and often deeply influenced the course of history.

EXCLUSIVE EMPHASIS ON SOCIAL CONCERNS

There are more than a few persons now, mostly young, who insist that only the broad social concerns are worthy of being regarded as raising moral issues. Many of these young people have grown up in the Church and have taken seriously the New Testament ethic of love. Most of them are disillusioned with the Church. They have observed church people expressing moral anger against bad language and even rough clothes, but remaining indifferent to the forcing of black people into rat-infested slums. They have heard expressions of outrage against the violence of fighting with sticks and stones on campus and in the streets from church people who ignore or defend the violence by which the United States sends fifty thousand of her own youth to death in Asian jungles on a mission to kill hundreds of thousands in defense of a military police state. In reaction, these young people find it hard to take seriously the gnats they see being strained by the pietist's moral sieve, while the same pietists are asking them to swallow camels by participating in the most monstrous violence.

In their reaction, many are going on to consider the use of marihuana and then heroin as without ethical significance. Some also accept sex without marriage as only a matter of private taste. They regard themselves as ethically superior to their parents and teachers, who are mainly concerned about personal activities which the young rebels believe to be of consequence only to the people choosing them. To this new way of thinking, immoral violence is the wholesale violence of war, the human destructiveness of racism, or the exploitation of the poor. These are the real denials of Christian love, while personal "morals" are mainly important as evasions of the prodigious evils which threaten to destroy all mankind.

These reactions to wide moral blindness in the social order are useful as correctives of one-sided ethical individualism in the Church, even apart from the protest against condemnation of such petty irrelevancies as beards, long hair, and dungarees. (On the renunciation of moral restraints on personal conduct, more will be said below.) The exclusive social emphasis of this critique does, however, lead to some false beliefs.

It is falsely concluded that society alone is responsible. Under the influence of modern social sciences and especially of psychology, many people come near to agreeing with one of the positions described by Walter Moberly and expressed as follows: "That any individual is what he is, is not a matter of merit or demerit. Ultimately, every one of us, and not only the social failure and outcast, is the product of the psychophysical constitution with which he was born and of the society into which he was born." So viewed, the individual is only a cell in the organism of the whole society. If there be responsibility somewhere it belongs, then, to the whole of which he is a part. Moreover, in the modern world, to quote Moberly again, "the individual's education, his recreations, his way of earning a livelihood, are determined by social institutions which seem to have acquired a momentum and an energy of their own."[7] Hence, only the society is responsible.

Anyone who has worked with convicted persons in a prison can feel the attraction of such a view. Again and again, as I have heard the life stories of prisoners and confirmed them by reading the official case histories, I have found haunting my mind the words of Shakespeare, "More sinned against than sinning." (*King Lear,* act 3, scene 2.)

The extreme belief, nevertheless, far overshoots the mark. The society, however large and complex, is constituted of individual persons. If it is to be purposely changed for good, this must be accomplished by individual persons. The responsibility of society is the responsibility of all the persons who constitute it. This responsibility is not equally distributed, of course, but varies according to the freedom and power possessed by its participants.

It is unfortunately supposed that individual self-discipline is of little relevance to social reform. Many young people who are keenly interested in promoting civil rights, economic justice, and world peace overreact to individualistic pietism by repudiating interest in personal virtue. For them, not only physical cleanliness, but also chastity and marital faithfulness, honesty, and freedom from addictive drugs, are regarded as insignificant, or even as aspects of a hypocritical and enslaving establishment, and therefore evil.

Personal and institutional life are not to be so neatly separated. When an individual loses his own freedom to drug addiction, this much of society has been enslaved. Moreover, the cost to social institutions is heavy. The institutions must pay for care and treatment of the addict. He may commit crimes to secure the drug, meaning more cost to the economic system, the victims, the police, the courts, and the penal system. All that is paid for such costs is unavailable for public housing, expansion of medical care, foreign aid, and other public causes the reformer may espouse.

If illicit sex is his personal interest, this will have the effect of drawing off his attention and energy from the causes he advocates, besides undermining the institution of marriage and family. Along the way he will be using and hurting other people, too, regardless of the principle of "adult consent." Even with such consent, when sexual intercourse is entered into with less than total commitment to faithful marriage, there are bound to be frequent tragic discrepancies in degree of involvement of the two partners and in personal consequences.

If social reforms are sought for any worthy purpose, must it not be for the sake of persons? If one is truly concerned about persons, how can one be careless about personal relations which are bound to affect persons deeply?

Indeed, some youthful rebels against conventional morality intentionally withdraw from the large society into small groups of their own. It is obvious that such self-exiled persons are not giving much assistance to the removal or alleviation of injustice and violence in the larger society. In one way or another they still depend upon the larger economic system, with all its wrongs, while doing nothing to correct it. Like the medieval monasteries, the withdrawn groups might establish small models of justice, brotherhood, and human quality. To do so, however, requires superior levels of self-discipline seldom achieved for more than a few weeks or months. Even if successful they would not give much help to people who are trying to develop a just and peaceful community, not merely for a few like-minded persons, but for radically disparate cultures, races and classes, divided by many conflicting interests and living in massive urban societies.

Finally, the person who does not discipline his personal life with firmness will be unable to contribute anything approaching his maximum capacity. This is true not only because he will be incapable of bringing his full powers to bear when and as he purposes, but also because he will lack the respect, confidence, and cooperation of the many other persons needed to participate with him if his

286

goals are to be achieved. Social reform is not accomplished by lone individualists. It is true that calls to reform have often been made by lonely voices "crying in the wilderness." But before the needed social changes are ever accomplished, especially in complex, mostly urban societies, many must respond to the calls, band together, and cooperate in concerted effort. Self-indulgent individuals are not capable of contributing their full powers to such efforts.

It is erroneously believed that the real concerns of the Bible are all social. Some enthusiasts, building on Old Testament emphasis and on selective New Testament study, maintain that the whole biblical message is properly understood as relating to social institutions, even though it has been traditionally distorted by individualists. From the ancient covenant with Israel to the promise of the coming righteous Kingdom of God, the real interest, it is said, is social. Does not *The Magnificat* of Mary promise the tearing down of imperial powers, and the lifting high of the humble, the taking from the rich and satisfying of the hungry? Does not Jesus attack the whole establishment of religion, politics, and economic life by his condemnation of Pharisees, scribes and chief priests and by his dramatic demonstration in the Temple; and is it not that for which he died? When he described the Last Judgment, did he not make the providing for the poor, the weak and the friendless the sole norm of judgment? If you truly want to care for such needs today, must you not make such care a matter of social policy? Does not the Revelation make an all-out attack on imperial Rome and all the kings and merchants who profit by dealing with her? [8]

In such arguments there is much truth which needs to be heard. What is affirmed by it is, indeed, true. It is only against its denial of stress on the personal that protest must be made. Along with much which concerns public institutions, the Bible has much to say about individuals and their personal relationships to God and their neighbors also. Indeed, quoting from Deuteronomy, Jesus says that the greatest commandment is this: "You shall love the Lord your God with all your heart, and with all your soul, and with all your mind." He then quotes from Leviticus the command which he says was second greatest: "You shall love your neighbor as yourself." [9] These love commandments have far-reaching institutional implications which need attention, emphasis, and action. Yet the commandments are immediately personal. Only persons love. Institutions do not love, although they may be fashioned by the loving purpose of persons and may assist in the development of such persons.

Love for God and man is clearly at the center of New Testament teaching and of genuinely Christian ethics. But there are many teachings in both testaments concerning other personal virtues, attitudes, and relations as well. Pronouns of the first person are frequent in the Psalms. The laws include many concerning marriage, relations of parents and children, and neighbor with neighbor. Although the deeply corporate nature of responsibility is heavily emphasized, in the later prophets, Jeremiah and especially Ezekiel, individual responsibility is given special attention too.[10]

In the New Testament too there is much dealing with individuals. Whoever has faith in Christ is to have eternal life, and faith is a very personal thing, even though it is elicited in the community, creates communal relations among believers, and deeply affects the wider community. Salvation and holiness are communal in nature, according to both testaments. Yet the community of the New Covenant is generally described as entered by individuals, one by one, as they commit their faith.[11] Both in the gospels and in the letters there are many admonitions to personal virtues and warnings against personal self-indulgence and vices of various kinds.

There are, indeed, many biblical teachings about social institutions, and all biblical teachings have implications relevant to institutions. But all have relevance also to the lives of individuals, and many are specifically directed to the inner spirit, the life-style, or the quite personal relations of individuals.

THE RESPONSIBLE PERSON SEEKING THE RESPONSIBLE SOCIETY

Love requires expression by all means available. Christ teaches that we are to love our neighbors as ourselves. By the parable of the Good Samaritan he shows that there are no boundaries limiting the love to which we are called. We are to love and serve all human beings. In his parable of the judgment, he stresses particularly the obligation to feed the hungry, clothe the naked, and minister to the imprisoned.

How are we to obey these commands? If I truly will to feed the hungry, am I free to support public policies which will inevitably leave many to die of hunger or be handicapped by malnutrition? If I obey the command to clothe the naked, can I be indifferent to efforts to provide housing for all and the economic means of life for the handicapped and the aged? If I care enough about the imprisoned to minister to them, will I not support actively efforts to bring hope and training for useful self-support into the penal system? In all these matters, to depend upon private charity is to leave acute needs unmet. Love requires both private and public expression, person-to-person, church-to-individual, special agencies to families. Municipalities, states, and federal governments are called to pursue policies of just opportunity for all. To refuse means by which love can accomplish its will is to fail truly to love. As the Letter of James makes especially emphatic, love is not mere sentiment or words, but effective action to meet need.[12] To be effective, action must use whatever means concerted effort can devise in the service of love.

Respectful care for God's world requires both public and private action. In these days we are increasingly aware that our natural environment is made sacred by God's creation of it and by the incarnation through which Christ put on not only human flesh, but the flesh of all earthly being. Hence, not only for the sake of human generations to come, but also for the good earth itself, with all its beauty and variety of life, a genuine piety requires care of the environment. How is this to be accomplished? The clearing of polluted streams and air, the preservation of the oxygen cycle, the conservation of soil and other natural resources, all require appropriate public policy of massive proportions. But what shall we say of the individual who demonstrates for clean air, yet fouls indoor air with the carcinogens of tobacco smoke? Will not the same reverence for life which supports public conservation policy require the guarding of one's own body from addictive drugs and other abuses? Will not love that is real seek also to protect others by setting an example which will point to life rather than death?

Walter G. Muelder appropriately entitled his most comprehensive development of social ethics, *Foundations of the Responsible Society.* He took the concept from the Amsterdam Assembly of the World Council of Churches, from the report of which he quotes the following definition: *"A responsible society is one where freedom is the freedom of men who acknowledge responsibility to justice and public order, and where those who hold political authority or economic power are responsible for its exercise to God and the people whose welfare is affected by it."* [13] He further cites the assembly report which makes clear that in the responsible society power must be widely "distributed . . . through the whole community," and that "economic justice and provision of equality of opportunity be established for all the members of society."

At the time Muelder wrote *Foundations of the Responsible Society,* little public attention had yet been given to ecology, and basic theological thinking about it had scarcely begun. The basic conception of the responsible society needs enlargement at this point. Muelder has written briefly about responsibility for conservation in agriculture, and he treats this and other problems of agriculture with unusual skill.[14] However, he seems to have viewed our responsible stewardship of the soil as solely related to human values. I believe that we are responsible for the natural order for the sake of its goodness in God's creation and plan of redemption, in addition to its instrumental usefulness to man.[15] Moreover, responsible stewardship must go far beyond stewardship of soil and water for agricultural use, if even the human species is to be preserved much longer.

It is especially to Muelder's credit that he has held the ideals of the responsible society and the responsible person in such close unity. The two cannot, in a coherent ideal, be separated. One cannot be a responsible person without concern for a responsible society, and a responsible society cannot be conceived apart from many responsible persons participating in the responsible direction of its power. The integral character of this relationship is emphasized even more by the truth in the doctrine of original sin. Sin has a deeply corporate character. It is not transmitted genetically — and no biblical writer said it was — but it is socially infectious, transmitted by example and emotional injury from parent to child, friend to friend, individuals to institutional structures (like those of war and exploitative industry), and by these structures to other structures and to individuals.

If we would evangelize and educate for the development of responsible persons, we must be incorporated into the redemptive body in which righteous love is incorporated. Through that body of persons who are learning responsible love, we must penetrate and redeem the community structures (as well as the individuals) which perpetuate evil. What then are the responsibilities of the individual Christian in a society behaving irresponsibly?

He sets an example of responsibility. All present associations and communities are to a greater or less extent behaving irresponsibly. All societies, including the actual, empirical churches, fall short of full responsibility. Some are predominantly evil. The irresponsibility of a society is seen in its concentration of power in the hands of a few, in the high premiums it places on material values, in its exclusion of many from its benefits, in its limited horizons, in its hostilities toward other societies, and in the limited concerns of its policies and members for the needier members.

A person who is seeking to participate in development of a responsible society must first of all set a personal example of responsibility. Such responsibility implies self-discipline, generous assumption of obligations toward others, and loyal work for the higher goals which he envisages, if possible in cooperation with others — including non-Christians when their specific goals and methods are compatible with those to which his Christian practices impel him. The person who simply refuses to participate in community responsibilities because the community is evil, makes himself part of the problem, not of its solution. He also gives an example of self-righteous pride which is the very opposite of Christian responsibility. The truly responsible person feels too deeply the pain and guilt of others to permit the luxury of self-righteousness. When Jesus said, "Do not think that I have come to bring peace on earth; I have not come to bring peace, but a sword," he was not encouraging warfare.[16] The context of the passage and of the whole of his teaching and life disprove such a notion. He is speaking, however, of the division which he brings between people, a division which takes many forms.

A person who makes a fully earnest commitment of faith in Jesus Christ does by that commitment separate himself in some ways from others. He is bound, for example, to order his life and make decisions from presuppositions which differ in some respects from those of neighbors or even members of his family who lack this serious commitment.

And even among people of committed faith Christ brings division. Because they have become Christ's people they cannot lightly gloss over serious problems of public policy or personal conduct. They are bound to express their beliefs with care for accurate representation of facts and of opposing views, but they are not free to make the easygoing compromises of people who do not really care very much for God, man, or the earth.

On many serious affairs of the day—from foreign policy to the use of beverage alcohol—there are differences of opinion among earnest Christians. We need to accept this as normal among people of limited knowledge and also imperfect wills. Earnest discussion, study, and debate about controversial matters in the light of Christ must be accepted within the Church if the Church and its members are to take their proper roles as responsible though imperfect participants in a highly imperfect society. Not to study and debate controversial issues in the Church is to leave them for discussion and decision apart from the light which Christ throws upon them when they are opened to his spirit.[17] Such failure also condemns the Church to increasing superficiality and pettiness.

In the debate about remilitarization in West Germany during the chancellorship of Konrad Adenauer, Karl Barth took a vigorous part—in opposition to the government and the Church. After some discussion of the concrete issues, he trumpeted forth that remilitarization in that situation would be contrary to the Gospel. He was accused of causing dissension and threatening to "tear the church to pieces." Barth replied that if the defenders of remilitarization were acting in earnest, under God, then they should speak, not just as politicians, but rather joining the debate on the ground of "the Word of God." Such a debate should not be shunned, he insisted. He continued: "In a church that is alive, and not dead, it must be not only possible but necessary for its insights to be questioned, only to be rediscovered on a higher level, in a later hour of our history." [18]

Division is accepted for the sake of a higher reconciliation in Christ. When we are divided by controversy, if we are responsibly Christian, we accept the division and engage in the controversy in such spirit as to keep the way open for return into full unity. In fact, even while we differ, we continue to worship together and acknowledge the unity which embraces us as one body under the Lordship of Christ.

Indeed, when we must divide, it is for the sake of love for God and his creatures. This love is responding to God's love which we have seen in Christ and which is the ground of our hope for universal responsible community. Any unity which would require us to be unfaithful to that love as we understand its working in the world today would be the denial of true brotherhood. At the time, such denials might make possible that easy kind of silence or evasive utterance which smooths things over and leads to an appearance of peace. But this would be the saying " 'Peace, peace,' where there is no peace." [19] Christian responsibility requires that we not evade division, but that we accept it as the price of the deeper unity in which is our true and lasting peace.

NOTES

1. John C. Bennett, *Social Salvation* (New York: Charles Scribner's Sons, 1935), esp. p. xii.

2. On February 10, 1965, in conversation, Billy Graham was asked what method he thought was most promising for renewing the life of the Church and evangelizing the nation. He replied that it was not mass meetings — although, he said, that was one method he himself seemed able to use effectively. Rather, it was the use of small groups in Bible study, prayer, and Christian action.

3. See the results of a careful statistical study (1959) of The Methodist Church reported by S. Paul Schilling in *Methodism and Society in Theological Perspective* (New York: Abingdon Press, 1960), chap. 5. It is true that The United Methodist Church of today includes the

Evangelical United Brethren Church as well as The Methodist Church. However, the membership of the United Methodist Church in Teague's home city of Tallahassee is little changed from that of the Methodist Church.

4. For examples and elaboration of this and related themes, see J. Edward Carothers, *The Churches and Cruelty Systems* (New York: Friendship Press, 1970).

5. Mark 12:40; Luke 20:47; Mark 11:15–17; and Matt. 21:12–13 (New English Bible).

6. E. g., see Acts 2:44–46; 1 Cor. 16:1–4; 2 Cor. 9:1–4.

7. Walter Moberly, *Responsibility* (Greenwich, Conn.: Seabury Press, 1956), p. 15.

8. Luke 1:53–53; Matt. 21:12–13; 23:15,23,39 and 25:31–46; and Rev. 18:1–24.

9. Matt. 22:36–39; Mark 12:28–31; cf. Luke 10:25–28.

10. See particularly Ezek. 18:1–9,20.

11. Apparent exceptions are the narratives of the whole households being baptized after declaration of faith by the head of the house. Acts 16:14–15, 31–34.

12. James 2:15–16.

13. *The Church and the Disorder of Society,* p. 192, quoted in Walter G. Muelder, *Foundations of the Responsible Society* (New York: Abingdon Press, 1959), p. 19 (italics Muelder's); see also his *Religion and Economic Responsibility* (New York: Charles Scribner's Sons, 1953); and *Moral Law in Christian Social Ethics* (Richmond, Va.: John Knox Press, 1966), pp. 152–72.

14. Muelder, *Foundations of the Responsible Society,* pp. 162–83, especially p. 165. Subsequently he has written further about ecology. See "The Ecological Era," three lectures delivered March 3–4, 1970, at Gammon Theological Seminary, printed in *The Foundation* LXVII, 1 (Summer, 1970).

15. I have developed this view further, with biblical and other argument, elsewhere, especially in my book *Responsible Freedom: Guidelines to Christian Action* (New York: Harper and Row, 1971).

16. Matt. 10:34.

17. I have discussed the norms and methods of authentic Christian decision in *Responsible Freedom.*

18. Karl Barth, *Against the Stream* (New York: Philosophical Library, 1954), p. 155.

19. Jer. 6:14.

Communitarian Christian Ethics:

A Personal Statement and a Response

Walter G. Muelder

A *Festschrift* is a deeply personal honor and I am profoundly moved by the recognition given to me by Boston University, my colleagues, former students, and scholars in my field. The excellence of the essays bespeaks a serious devotion to Christian social ethics and constitutes at several points an important development in both method and substance. I am grateful to the editor, Paul Deats, Jr., who has been at once a stimulating student, a brilliant colleague, and a loyal friend. If my retirement has occasioned the convergence of essays by younger and creative minds on important themes, the effort may not be entirely "in praise of folly." I appreciate the contributions of both theoretical and practical aspects of social ethics.

Mindful that some readers of essays in this volume may not have been students of mine and that many fewer have read widely in my essays and books, I shall respond with personal or autobiographical notes as well as with comments on the essays.

I am deeply rooted in the personalistic heritage of Boston University, although I have outgrown, I believe, the individualistic limitations of Bowne's ethics. He hardly had what would today be called a social ethic. Person is always person-in-community, and community is lockstitched into the institutional structures and procedures of society. I still appreciate Bowne's attack on the fallacy of abstract universals and his insistence that if the individual person is zero then society is zero. Moreover, man ought not to be viewed as mere fuel at the fireside of society. Bowne's work has always been a reminder of the method of empirical concreteness in terms of personal consciousness and a protest against all schemes that reduce personal experience to impersonal terms. Edgar S. Brightman, to whom I owe more than to any other philosopher, had not yet become a social philosopher when I was the Bowne Fellow in the Department of Philosophy. He encouraged me, however, to develop Personalism in a social-ethics direction. I soon discovered that such a lifework required cross-disciplinary and interdisciplinary research and adventure. Brightman himself subsequently developed social philosophy significantly.

My predisposition for Christian social ethics grew out of the circumstance that my father was a graduate of both the School of Theology and the Graduate School. He was a devotee of Bowne and also of Walter Rauschenbusch. Since I was reared in a Methodist parsonage home that was liberal, warmly evangelical, and socially committed, it was almost natural for me to walk in the way of personalistic philosophical theology and of social Christianity. There were other elements that pushed me along the road also. At Knox College I was a history major. About 1926 I joined an ad hoc group that tried to eliminate the R.O.T.C. there. Having been selected to give a short oration at the commencement exercises in 1927, I chose to speak on the Chinese Revolution. By the time I entered the Boston University School of Theology that fall I was a convinced socialist as represented by Eugene V. Debs. Inter-racial solidarity and the need for developing institutions for world order were for me moral commonplaces. Company unionism was capitalistic paternalism. The Sacco-Vanzetti case aroused me deeply. I recall searching out in Boston the celebration of the tenth anniversary of the Russian Revolution only to find that the "comrades" there were utterly uninterested in the presence of a theological student. Although only a junior in the School of Theology I was already at a point where radicalism in social questions had no need to be tied to sophomoric materialism or atheism. I was free to be open to new ideas and movements while seeking graduate education for the ministry. Boston excited me. It excites me now. That excitement is part of the image I have of Boston University as well as of Boston.

Some of the essays above have referred to my piety and my interest in the great mystics of the Western Christian tradition. This interest has indeed been important to me. I can only wish that my experience were even more deeply disciplined by the various devotional criteria of practices followed by the greatest mystics both East and West. They have helped me in self-examination, in sorting out motives, in ecumenical understanding, in handling personal attacks, in radical dissent from established institutions, in awareness of the spiritual continuity in the Christian tradition, in distinguishing genuine from superficial piety, and in developing the trust which lies at the heart of faith. I shall refer again to this below, for the life of devotion is both serenity and struggle.

As I was reared, there was no warfare between piety and philosophy or science, or between piety and moral responsibility. Pietism as followed in German Methodism had already been chastened, deepened intellectually, and broadened by my father's education under the influence of Bowne, the other Boston University faculty, and the Social Gospel of Walter Rauschenbusch. Moreover, I had no serious authority problem and basically trusted my elders both at home and in school situations. Evolution, relativity theory, and social-science reforms were ideas that fit in well with history and a religious devotion to Jesus Christ and the God who was ultimate reality.

My devotional convictions were deepened by a course on mysticism which I took under Professor E. S. Brightman, under whom the class read many classics of East and West. He helped me ask four questions of every mystical writing or experience: (1) What was the preparation for the experience? (2) What was the experience as described? (3) How did the mystic interpret his experience philosophically or theologically? (4) What were the practical fruits of the experience? Devotional piety and reading great mystics has helped keep alive the first hand religious experience of the "amateur"; it has constantly corrected tendencies toward second-hand "professionalism." I often have a mild mystical experience in the midst of corporate worship. At the same time, I have been aware of the danger of short-circuiting worship experiences as criticized by William James and William E. Hocking.

I must say a little more about my intellectual development as a graduate student and my early teaching career in Berea College and the University of Southern California. As I continued an interest in history and biblical studies, I found that my central concerns were philosophical and ethical, particularly the concern to change the "system" radically. My technical equipment in philosophy in college was limited to a course in history of philosophy. Before I completed my six years as a School of Theology student and a doctoral candidate I had done the grand historical sweep from the pre-Socratics to Schopenhauer and Nietzsche five times, from as many different teachers at Knox, Boston University, and Frankfurt, Germany. I built up my background in doctoral prerequisites in the College of Liberal Arts while taking the regular theological curriculum. As my competence in history, philosophy, and theology developed I became very impatient with intellectual history taught as the algebraic chain of concepts. My social-science concerns and independent reading in Marx gave me additional tools with which to criticize the capitalist system and made me ready to appreciate thinkers like Troeltsch and Tillich. At the University of Frankfurt I studied principally under Tillich, along with Karl Mannheim and Max Horkheimer.

Knudson first introduced me to Troeltsch, but not the Troeltsch of the *Social Teaching of the Christian Churches*. Knudson was very Kantian, like Bowne his teacher, and appealed to the "religious a priori" which Rudolf Otto and Ernst Troeltsch expounded. This idea seemed to protect religious experience from reductionism as practiced by the illusionists like Comte, Marx, Freud and many others. Knudson liked a self-validating principle in his epistemology of religious criticism. In this he differed from E. S. Brightman, whose Personalism was more Hegelian and whose appreciation for wholes, for dialectical method, and for coherence as the criterion of truth permanently influenced me. Knudson and Brightman both encouraged me to do my dissertation on Ernst Troeltsch. My year in Frankfurt confirmed this interest. I felt that by working on the problem of historical wholes in Troeltsch's philosophy of history I could make progress on my deepest intellectual and existential needs of relating ideal religious values to radical social change. Troeltsch helped me to place men and ideas in the dynamic context of sociological, economic, and historical forces without surrendering the uniqueness of personal genius to antimetaphysical positivism. "The levels of moral discourse," to use the phrase of Henry David Aiken, could be coherently conserved. Personalism and Marxism could both be synoptically confronted in the dialectic of history.

During the thirties I struggled with the Depression as a graduate student, as a pastor for a year in northern Wisconsin, and then for six years at Berea College in the foothills of Appalachia — where in the mountain counties the average annual income was about $200. I had a good education in elemental poverty and a first-hand experience of the correlation of the social problem as "regionalism" became a new perspective in sociology. In this setting President William J. Hutchins gave me, as chairman of the Department of Philosophy and Bible, the charge "to build a golden bridge between the impossible mountain theology and the modern world." This was, of course, only one facet of the college's total commitment "to lift the mountains from the bottom." I was secretary of the Socialist Party local and also active in the Fellowship of Reconciliation.

World War II found me at the Graduate School of Theology of the University of Southern California. Whereas in Berea my duties had been primarily in philosophy, at the University of Southern California my responsibilities were more in Christian theology and ethics. On the theoretical side, my theological position was becoming more crystallized in opposition to the neo-Augustinian anthropology of Reinhold Niebuhr and Emil Brunner, particularly Niebuhr's pessimism and his attack on reason. He seemed not to grasp fully a personalistic and communitarian view of reason and the interpenetration of theory and practice. In the area of social philosophy, I came greatly to appreciate the work of Robert M. MacIver. I also discovered the profundity of John Elof Boodin's *The Social Mind*. While he differed substantially from Troeltsch, he had a grasp of the reality of social wholes, the role of will, and the primacy of the category of purpose in social wholes which made a permanent contribution to my thought. On the social-science side, the greatest influence was the great work by Gunnar Myrdal, *An American Dilemma*. I studied it thoroughly, particularly its handling of cumulative causation, the ranking of prejudices, the possibilities of a benign social spiral, and the handling of valuation in social science. Myrdal's method is more dynamic than MacIver's, but I found the social philosophy inherent in *The Web of Government* coherent with Myrdal's approach to the social dilemmas. Racial problems were acute in Los Angeles as persons of Japanese origin were forcibly relocated and as Negroes poured into the city to turn "Little Tokyo" into "Bronzeville" — and later, Watts. For several years I was chairman of the Race Relations Committee of the Los Angeles Church Federation and was active on the Council for Civic Unity. Boodin and Myrdal strengthened my conceptual framework for practical tasks, which included in addition to the above, participation in the Civil Liberties Union, the Fellowship of Reconciliation, and concern for labor's rights in the burgeoning war industries. Throughout the War I strove continually on the ecumenical front and in social action through the Methodist Church. In 1945 I came to my present position.

Having shared a bit of my inner pilgrimage I should now like to respond more specifically with thoughts stimulated by the various essays of this book.

As Paul Deats' insightful and penetrating essay shows, the interior cross-disciplinary character of social ethics does have several focal points. How these distinguish a particular writer depends in part on the state of the art at the time and in part also on the ethicist's driving concerns. Paul Deats' own concern for understanding the nature and method of strategic response inclines him toward the focus of social policy where he has made outstanding contributions.

His critical quest for a social ethic exhibits a thorough knowledge of the ethicists whose conflicting views he analyzes. He expresses an appropriate surprise that a reviewer like Father Blanchette questions whether I have faced up to the implications of the interdisciplinary approach, and whether I have left social philosophy and sociological theories "in a sort of extrinsic juxtaposition." Christian social ethics has an inherent eclectic character about it, and so the quality of extrinsic juxtaposition may be a permanent limitation of the method to some extent at least. But there is another consideration easily lost sight of. *Moral Law in Christian Social Ethics* was originally planned as an integral whole with *Foundations of the Responsible Society* and would, if published together, have given more the impression of L. Harold DeWolf's *Responsible Freedom* which belongs on the whole to the same heritage and tradition as my work.

Ralph Barton Perry remarked at the Seventh International Congress of Philosophy at Oxford that he would recommend a greater effort on the part of philosophers to read each other's books. I generally favor that idea for intellectuals. Some reviewers are limited too closely to their impressions of the single work they have been invited to read. My several writings do not tend to repeat my total standpoint and so a single one may mislead the reviewer; a number have apparently been so misled judging by their comments.

The spirit of the interdisciplinary approach is not entirely new, at least not as a cross-disciplinary effort. Francis Greenwood Peabody concluded his famous book *Jesus Christ and the Social Question* with a chapter entitled, "The Correlation of the Social Question." By the nature of social problems and their involvements, one is led into many dimensions. Unless one is responsive to these dimensions and synoptic in method, one is likely to be simplistic or reductionist. Much as I have sought to be consistent with the method which I have announced, I am aware that the work in my generation has been more programmatic than complete. All critical writing is to a degree more corrective than autonomously systematic. Certainly my responses show a corrective posture toward Reinhold Niebuhr. When Martin Luther King, Jr. decided to do his doctoral studies at Boston University, he was wrestling with the basic theological differences between Reinhold Niebuhr and myself. As he states in *Stride Toward Freedom,* he took a major step of his pilgrimage into non-violence as a consequence of his reflection on these differences.

In the 1930s the ecumenical movement rediscovered the doctrine of the Church, both with respect to "Life and Work" and with respect to "Faith and Order." The much quoted imperative "Let the Church be the Church!" referred not only to Church-state relations but to the whole range of church life within community. The Oxford and Edinburgh conferences, followed in 1938 by the Tambaram conference of the International Missionary Council, decisively influenced worldwide theological and ethical discussions, raising in a strongly self-conscious way the distinctive meanings of terms such as *Christian, Church, community,* and *state.* These conferences also exposed afresh the ways in which social factors affected institutional realities and threatened the autonomy of Christian witness. Over all hung the threats of totalitarian revolutions and regimes and imperialist colonialism.

Among the efforts helping the Church be the Church, the Christocratic influence of Brunner and Barth must be noted. Barth's dialectical theology, however solitary in stressing the transcendence of the word of God, tended to discourage, on the one hand, study of philosophy of religion and philosophical ethics and, on the other, empirical social-science analyses in many Protestant circles. The present renewed interest in the interdisciplinary method of social ethics has had to overcome the negative consequences of the neo-Reformation methodology. In European circles the once popular Ernst Troeltsch was a victim of the church struggle in Germany. Fortunately, the Anglo-Saxon countries maintained at least a modest interest in his historical and sociological achievements.

Troeltsch's *The Social Teaching of the Christian Churches* is better known than his *Der Historismus und seiner Ueberwindung.* James M. Gustafson's essay should encourage those who have been fascinated by the typology of the first of these books to pursue the mode and problematic of the latter as well. I can only endorse the emphasis of his argumentation. Troeltsch's significance lies not in his conclusions but in the irrepressible significance of the issues he raises. When sketched on a canvas that is truly universal, Troeltsch's wrestling with relativism is even more relevant today than in the first two decades of this century. The real dialogue of world cultures and world religions is now upon us. What is the lordship of Jesus Christ in an age of universal history? Is there a doctrine of man, of humanism, that speaks to every section of the globe? In dealing with questions of historical analogies, Gustafson asks whether they presuppose some continuities in human nature: "Does it suppose that man has a nature as well as a history? Or at least that there are universals in human experience, which, while not denying the uniqueness and precise unrepeatability of events, nonetheless are a ground for continuities?"

Troeltsch's historicism foundered on his reliance on the neo-Kantian idea of a religious a priori, an a priori in man more inclusive than the cognitive, the ethical, or the esthetic a priori. He tried to find a formal principle which would be universally validating. In the end he dissolved this idea into a religious intuition or *Evidenz-gefühl.* When he tried to use the idea of personality as such a principle, he found that in some cultures the principle of personality was not as self-evidently primary as in the Christian West. This fact shattered his confidence that a universal principle could be found. One of the difficulties is that he followed an analytic Kantian method instead of pursuing person as person-in-community and community-in-history. Anthropologists have shown that there are cross-cultural norms and that the themes of culture are paradigms that are variously conjugated in differing social systems. The anthropological evidence since the death of Troeltsch indicates that relativity with respect to person-in-culture (community) holds, but that relativity does not predetermine a universal valuational relativism. In a sense, Troeltsch did not tackle the question sufficiently within the arena of history, for history has a nature as truly as personality does. In Troeltsch's era, the case for the *Geistewissenschaften* had to be made in radical contrast to the *Naturwissenschaften* which seemed to require a necessitarian or deterministic principle of causation. This contrast led him to view the person as transcending not only nature but history as well, through the principle of the religious a priori. Therefore the person was regarded as outside history. But this solution failed when his historical method disclosed that the very category of personality was lacking in certain non-European cultures. Today a temporalist view of nature is quite compatible with both physical science and metaphysics. Indeed, there is even some experimental evidence of the nonreversible character of time at the infra-atomic level.

Troeltsch's concern for a doctrine of development compatible with the conception of historical wholes as unities of meaning and value, unique and unrepeatable, is being reasserted in new forms. In the current debate stirred up by Kung and Rahner one reads as follows in the *Ecumenist* for March–April, 1971: "If the truth is historical, then the truth of a doctrine cannot be preserved simply by repeating it; to protect and promote the truth, the doctrine must again and again be re-interpreted in the church's ongoing history." Here we need to employ the doctrine of the Holy Spirit in theology, but in a critical way so that the ontological and the historical variables are kept in a dynamic tension. Troeltsch's doctrine of development needs itself to be developed, making more use of the category of purpose, as in Boodin above. Purpose canalizes social energy, the purposes which are disclosed in the Universal Declaration of Human Rights adopted by the General Assembly of the United Nations disclose goals of development which are roughly analogous the world over — even where they are repressed.

The sharpest challenge to my conception of Christian social ethics in these essays is made by Ralph B. Potter, Jr., who would restrict the ethicist primarily to the " 'mode of ethical reasoning' concerned with the procedures for defining relevant considerations and alloting them appropriate weight." I am glad to have this challenge so that ethicists may seriously consider whether the broad view which is attributed to me can be brought into sharper focus and into manageable units of work. Potter's essay criticizes both the ideal list of competencies which I have mentioned and the development of middle axioms. However, I miss any focused attention to my discussion of the moral laws. They are central to the task. I do not find in Potter's method any relief from mastery of the empirical disciplines that are specifically relevant to complex moral decisions; any relief from wrestling with theological issues; any relief from mastery of the principles of philosophical ethics. I would also point out that middle axioms are time-bound, although perhaps neither as cramping as he suggests nor as guilty of easing off onto others the demanding work leading to concrete decision. As one who is following Potter's work with a great deal of interest, I am impressed by the fact that he, like myself, leaves the door of decision-making open to the agent and does not conclude the moral reasoning for him. His style of doing ethics can be encompassed within the program I have embraced. Since the range of social ethics problems is today so wide and complex, I see no way of avoiding the most comprehensive perspective, even though one tries to enter the universe of moral discourse each time by way of a concrete issue requiring a decision, as Potter proposes. One wonders whether Potter's model for doing ethics raises issues as radically as they should be, or whether the framework of moral discourse is limited by the universe of moral discourse of those who seek his expert advice?

In response to the wholistic evangelical thrust of DeWolf's essay I should acknowledge those points in which he corrects or supplements my published positions. Our views are very close together, although his work has continued to be more systematically theological while mine has been more historical, philosophical, and social-theory oriented. If Paul Deats' interdisciplinary work, as noted above, tends to the social science–social policy end of the spectrum, L. Harold DeWolf's tends toward the theology–social policy end of the spectrum. DeWolf is thoroughly immersed in the social data, but not as thoroughly at home in the hermeneutic of social theory as Deats. I have appropriated DeWolf's communitarian moral laws into my system.

DeWolf notes, appropriately, that in my main period of work there was little attention given specifically to ecology and that basic theological thinking about it has scarcely begun. Certainly the basic conception of the "responsible society" needs enlargement here. This enlargement requires a deeper working relationship with both the physical and biological sciences. Ecology is a much deeper problem than reform of wasteful and polluting practices and of social policy. Social ethics needs profounder knowledge of biology, including genetics, and also of the total planetary balances of life. Ecology and demography interpenetrate. Yet, the tendency toward equilibrium theory in ecology must be held in tension with a doctrine of development capable of radical changes in behalf of person-in-community and in behalf of cultural quality. Ethically, ecology becomes a method of responsibility in relation to immediate and ultimate environment. It is not a program to turn the world into a wild-life preserve.

There are other areas besides ecology for which the idea of the responsible society is incompletely formulated as a middle axiom. It is an awkward model for family studies, although not an erroneous middle axiom. It is also not fully apt as a guideline for global political and economic institutional growth in an era of multinational corporations. In short, as a middle axiom, it is historically conditioned and needs to be constantly reexamined. Some find it inept in a situation of revolution, but the revolutionary needs it as a corrective to excessive zeal or utopian visions of power following a successful revolution.

François Houtart warns of the fundamental issue raised by southern Africa and the Portuguese colonies, there being real danger for serious international conflict. Here, once again, the so-called Christian nations have not learned or practiced social ethics. "The countries designated Christian find themselves on the side of the economic exploiters, while the countries labelled materialistic are the only ones to support the struggle for liberation, which is a part of the collective effort of mankind to break free from underdevelopment, of which the principal characteristic is the absence of responsibility for one's own lot." Development and self-determination within the interdependent community of nations is a theme which has played an increasingly large role in ecumenical bodies — Protestant, Orthodox and Roman Catholic. François Houtart has been a congenial colleague in this field and is helping to arouse Christians to the true urgency of the situation. I rejoice that a number of my students and colleagues have given so much leadership to the fundamental theory that should inform a responsible philosophy of development. I should express indebtedness to Richard Dickinson whose work has been exemplary. Dean Freudenberger has applied the "moral laws" method and the model of "strategic response" to agricultural aspects of development.

In this Second Development Decade, international bodies must play an increasingly greater role in guiding the power of multinational economic institutions and encouraging the developing countries to respond to the new situation with farsighted discipline and initiative. Christian social ethics should take particular note of the humanistic philosophy that animates African countries, which do not wish to embrace either full-blown capitalistic or socialistic ideologies. K. D. Kaunda of Zambia comments on humanism in Zambia as follows: "This high valuation of man and respect for human dignity which is a legacy of our tradition should not be lost in the new Africa. However 'modern' and 'advanced' in a Western sense this young nation of Zambia may become, we are fiercely determined that this humanism will not be obscured."

I am impressed by the insight given to political aspects of social ethics in these essays. This fact deserves some specific attention, for it signifies that the economic aspects have, relatively speaking, receded into the background, although they are not disregarded. This situation is almost a reversal of the earlier situation when industrial relations and labor issues, along with corporation power and the evils of the capitalist profit system, aroused so much attention. In the development of the Social Gospel movement, the "labor question" was the red thread that ran through the period from 1865 to 1915. From the strikes of the post–Civil War period to the New Freedom of Woodrow Wilson, Christian reformers were concerned with the new industrial situation, the plight of immigrant workers, child labor, women's exploitation, and the unequal bargaining power of organized labor and corporation management. The Social Creed of 1908 was almost exclusively focused on the rights of human beings as workers. There was minor attention paid to Christian Socialism and Marxism. The Reverend George D. Herron nominated Eugene V. Debs for president when the Socialist Party of America was organized in 1900. Walter Rauschenbusch envisaged a broad range of issues, to be sure, in *Christianizing the Social Order* but most prominent were the factors of economic power and predatory profit interests. All of this economic concern was quite understandable in an era extending into the twenties when the President of the United States could say that "the business of America is business."

The essay by Preston N. Williams notes that "the Social Gospel not only spoke weakly to the question of race but that it helped to create a method of analysis that makes more difficult, even today, a solution of the racial problem." He explicitly attacks Rauschenbusch, stating that in part his (and Gladden's) failure was due to the fact that racism was endemic to American life, a ruling idea. I am not yet convinced of the historical thesis here. There is considerable literature to support the idea that many northern Christian leaders believed that the suppression of slavery had fundamentally solved the race question. They supported many enterprises and educational ventures to improve the Negro's lot. They saw the frontier issues of their time in the growing industrial and urban centers. The Civil War raised the question of the place of violence in social reform. In his early work, *The Righteousness of the Kingdom,* Rauschenbusch discusses slavery in this context. Slavery had been overcome by force, yet the terrible cost in life on both sides and the ubiquitous anger persistent in North and South and the continuing sad condition of the Negroes (about 1890) made the young social gospeler wonder whether there was no other way.

Williams' essay raises a basic question not only about the Social Gospel, which I must emphasize was more a movement than a formal set of ideas, but also about black theology as a cultural phenomenon. If racism is an independent variable, how is it to be eradicated? If racism is dependent on a cluster of interdependent variables, why should Social Gospel advocates be criticized for not treating it as if it were an independent variable? Social gospelers, like all Christians, deserve criticism for complacency, but the sweeping charge of racism only confirms the suspicion that it lacks historical and scientific precision. The fact that social Christianity has been revitalized by the life and work of Martin L. King, Jr. points to the multifaceted character of the movement and its pragmatic cause-oriented tendencies. It is yet to be proved that the problem of racism "is the white man's fear of black skin and kinky hair." Skin color and hair form may become the badges for many structures and processes of marginalization, but are hardly basic independent variables. They do not provide the key to the forces that make for marginalization in technological development, economic institutions, and political process. Fortunately, the law can deal with objective elements in social systems, and the Church has as its vocation to convert and redeem persons in the full range of their existence.

Preston Williams is correct in pointing out the tension between the historical Social Gospel and the Church as an institution. The former rediscovered the idea of the Kingdom of God and stressed its realization. In the present time, many who are most militant for social causes are very critical of the Church or even reject it entirely. However, as noted above, the Oxford and Edinburgh Conferences of 1937 saw the rediscovery of the Church and thereafter ecclesiology developed rapidly. The social teachings of the World Council of Churches have greatly emphasized the nature and role of the Church. In the case of the black church, there has been a significant renewal of awareness of its nature and potential power. It has been late in developing self-consciousness, although the actual role of churches and clergy in the civil rights movement is a conspicuous one. This was particularly true of King's activities, even though he was not an organizer of black churchmen. The revival of the black church owes much to the spiritual appeal and methods of the civil rights movement. In any case, every defensible program to overcome racism must include the principles of cumulative causation and of autonomous choice of persons-in-community.

For those who were heirs of the Social Gospel movement, victims of the Great Depression, and citizens pressured to think in black and white terms about Communism and capitalism, the political seemed to be secondary to the economic. They had to learn the ubiquity of government and to reappraise the nature, role, and meaning of the state. It became quite clear that in the Soviet Union the state was not withering away, that in fascism and nazism, state and community had significantly close relationships, and that in the

U.S.A. drastic leadership in the federal government was required if there was to be an economic recovery. These phenomena called for a basic reconsideration of social causation, historical causation, and especially of economic theories which assumed the priority of the economic powers and relations in society.

But, just as Christian thinkers in many denominations were facing up to the need to enlarge the social creed by dealing, not only with individual reforms in behalf of labor and trade unions, but also with the profit system as a whole, the thought of more state action was partly quenched by the various powerful repressive states of Europe. The contradictions and anachronisms of the colonial-imperialist state were veiled by the extremism of its alternatives until the whole colonial system collapsed. At the Oxford Conference in 1937 the state as well as the economic order received major attention. New church-state issues were identified.

It is an interesting phenomenon that American social ethicists became seriously aware of Weber and Troeltsch almost as early as they were aware of Marx. For many of them, Rauschenbusch, Troeltsch, Weber and R. Niebuhr were as significant as Harry F. Ward and others who thought seriously in Marxist as well as in biblical categories. Although Max Weber became increasingly popular because of the typology of *The Protestant Ethic and the Spirit of Capitalism* — many liberals using it and R. H. Tawney's *Religion and the Rise of Capitalism* to debunk middle-class culture Protestantism — the essential conflict between Weber and Marx has generally been overlooked. Weber was in basic sociological disagreement with Marx on the role of religion in culture and in Western history. His friend Ernst Troeltsch had a profounder appreciation than Weber of the significance of the materialistic interpretation of history. Both Weber and Troeltsch have made less than their full impact on social ethics because the works translated into English and read by theologians have been principally in sociology of religion and in history. The full range of their methods deserves more attention.

My own teaching has stressed the importance of all the social sciences, but my relatively greater competence in economic theory and in sociology has overweighed political science, except that in teaching the history of Western ethics I have always included the classical political philosophers. I suppose that I have been one of few theologians who has taught in a regular cycle a course on Religion and the Labor Movement. Twenty-five years ago the course was much more popular than it has been recently. I was one of those who opposed certain provisions in the Taft-Hartley legislation, and I later entered publicly into the struggle against the passage of right-to-work laws. They were and are a moral and national disgrace. My standard course on Christian Ethics and Social Reconstruction has been heavily weighted on the applied side of economic institutions and issues. For a number of years Dr. Glen Trimble and I (later Paul Deats and I) offered a year's program of study on reform movements which concentrated heavily on nineteenth- and twentieth-century socialist ideologies, parties, and revolutions along with a Christian dialogue with and critique of them. Paul Deats now has the teaching of these courses.

I was not surprised when Alan Geyer as a graduate student was dissatisfied with the relative lack of political science and current political theory in the social ethics offerings. He made an imaginative and comprehensive proposal at the time to balance the situation. Except for budgetary considerations I would have liked to rectify the emphases. Graduate students were encouraged to do dissertations in areas which were of political concern, even though regular courses had to be supplemented by a great deal of independent work in directed study. A number of them will recall that they were encouraged to spend a year at the London School of Economics — and some did — a year which greatly added to both their political and economic sophistication as well as their critical perspectives on the American scene.

The above paragraphs serve to highlight the emphasis which several of the essays have given to social ethics in the arena of political theory and practice. In the future, as international questions of development grow even more prominent in the Second Development Decade, the troika of sociology, economics, and political science should be kept in an inter-disciplinary balance, not losing sight of philosophical ethics and theology as well.

The three essays by Geyer, Sample, and Stamey redress a lack and indicate contributions to the present state of the art. Geyer's essay shows that the struggle for political consciousness has not yet been entirely won. In the churches, affluence has aided and abetted the backlash against civil rights and made white racism more bitter in the suburbs. If Christianity could only be separated from political consciousness in general, the white racist and the anti-welfare reactionary would have a more secure hold on the status quo of the local parish! Geyer is therefore correct in going back to elementary principles: "a positive valuation of the political is the beginning of proper ethical analysis." It almost echoes Aristotle's dictum that ethics is a branch of politics. His stress on empowerment integrates well with Stamey's discussion. As another contemporary says, there is little alienation that some genuine empowerment will not cure.

The ubiquity of the political rightly structured is one of the best defenses against exaggerated and abusive state power. On the American campus, the problem has been twofold: to provide continuing motivation for participation by students and faculty in university governance and to maintain continuing political concern for national and international issues in spite of youth's penchant for only episodic involvement. On both these problems, there is a lack of both good theory and good process. The pragmatic and even expedient posture of students and faculty — and their moral immaturity in not being willing to discipline their peers — fall short of true political consciousness. When Geyer argues that the denial of politics in the Church becomes the denial of humanization of the Church, his remarks can be extended to include the university. For, while no formal repudiation of politics is made in the university, it cannot become fully humanized until its patterned irresponsibility with respect to governance has been rectified. Geyer is quite correct in citing the emergence of black caucuses as a real gain in the life of the Church, even though on numerous occasions the tactics seem indefensible and the demands unrealistic. Sound political awareness gives hope and aids empowerment. Here we may also cite the concern which Dr. John Gardner has implemented in Common Cause — the renewal of the nation through responsive and widespread political participation. This wider scope of participation now includes youth from age eighteen years on. An idealistic, vigorous youth movement can serve on college campuses, in churches, and in other community groups to update political processes and policies. Yet, there is no more guarantee that youth will provide wise political participation than that giving women the vote fifty years ago has assured the purity (as was claimed) of the nation's morals.

The significance of the political in social ethics today is reflected in the growing differentiation of its vocabulary. In this development of vocabulary, particularly with respect to the spectrum and dimensions of power, political values follow a cultural law. The greater the role of a cultural function or institution, the more precisely defined are its various terms and the more differentiated its meanings. At the present time, writers are groping for a more precise language for such terms as *violence, nonviolence, force, coercion, noncoercion, resistance, nonresistance, power, powerlessness, passive resistance, nonviolent resistance* and many other operational and rhetorical varieties of meaning. The distinction between power-order and power-structure is useful. This differential development of political vocabulary overlaps many other disciplines, particularly as psychology, sociology, economics and political science deal with the goals, methods, and means of social change. Theories of conflict, conflict resolution, revolution, and reconciliation intersect with efforts to clarify the rhetoric and the practice of radical reform.

We must anticipate that the quest for an updated political vocabulary will be complicated by the varieties of method employed to effect social change in all parts of the world. The essays have the merit of keeping the discussion close to the more generic issues and of relating the meaning of terms to ethical analysis as well as to operational and descriptive meanings in various sciences. There is always the danger in social science of either concealing normative values under apparently descriptive concepts or of lifting the descriptive terms to the functional level of the normative. Also, in the sphere of theology and ethics there is the danger of blurring the morally dysfunctional aspects of a judgment in the interest of being relevant. There is a great temptation to condone physical violence in behalf of much-needed radical change and to blur the evils of physically violent revolution by pointing to the violence within established laws, institutions, procedures, and practices that are not overtly physically violent. Some condone physical violence against property so long as persons are not killed. In such areas of discourse a much more precise vocabulary must be developed and would be welcome.

Where such redefinition is attempted, it is important to trace the functional consequences of the meanings of terms throughout a whole social system and to study the evolution of the terms and values involved longitudinally in history. Impatience with history and the criticism of history is costly in terms of real progress in clarifying and maturing political consciousness. In developing the nomenclature of the social ethics of politics, it will be increasingly important to study the experiences of different developing countries in Africa, Latin America, and Asia. The perplexities of Western civilization can be finally seen as quite parochial. G. Myrdal, in *Asian Drama,* found it necessary to challenge many Western values and assumptions before proceeding basically into the causes of poverty in South Asia. We must beware of devising a new nomenclature of political power that is insufficiently generic or universal.

Tex Sample's critique of Reinhold Niebuhr's approach to power is very relevant. A further point or two may be added. Niebuhr has been deservedly very influential as a theologian, but on both theoretical and practical ground some difficulties in his view should be noted. His realistic ethics separated too sharply justice and love, a point frequently made by his critics. The two qualities became virtually two different principles. Joseph Fletcher has argued persuasively that they should not be thus divided, for justice is love distributed. Martin Luther King, Jr. rejected the Niebuhrian view of human nature in favor of one which made the love ethic, as expressed in the personalistic heritage, primary. In *Stride Toward Freedom,* when discussing his pilgrimage into nonviolence, Dr. King stated that he responded positively at Boston University to "a passion for social justice that stemmed, not from a superficial optimism, but from a deep faith in the possibilities of human beings when they allowed themselves to become co-workers with God." He added: "It was at Boston University that I came to see that Niebuhr had overemphasized the corruption of human nature. His pessimism concerning human nature was not balanced by an optimism concerning divine nature. He was so involved in diagnosing man's sickness of sin that he overlooked the cure of grace." I may add that any Christian social strategy requires, as Sample and Wogaman also note, the factor of reconciliation.

Although the personalistic heritage at Boston University School of Theology cannot be simply or exclusively identified with Dr. King's interpretation and practical methods for effecting social change, his positive use of *agape* in his nonviolent civil rights struggle was undoubtedly an instance of the concrete unity of theory and practice. Interpreters of King have rightly pointed to his intensive study of the methods, strategy, and tactics of Mahatma Gandhi; but it is only fair to record his continual awareness of the personalistic view of reality, his Christian faith, and his commitment to *agape* love. As a practical historical embodiment of the ethic of peace and love which emerges from the Christian social ethics which I have represented, Dr. King's work expressed it preeminently in the civil rights field. *Agape* ethics as nonviolent action must be viewed not simply as a method but as a way of life. Those who measure King by the criteria of proximate success often miss this point entirely.

I am not convinced that Sample has fully made his case in holding that "a sequential relationship exists between power order, responsible society, and reconciliation." Taken strictly, this might mean that the Church should hold off in its work of reconciliation until the first two stages have been fulfilled. The first two are parts of the work of reconciliation, as with empowerment and responsibility alienation is to a degree broken down. But reconciliation as the work of Christ often performs direct miracles of grace and is not necessarily sequentially phased. Here the essay by Wogaman makes a good point on theory and strategy.

Sample is correct in noting that I do not hold simply to an implicit functional consensus model of society. Certainly I do not hold finally to an equilibrium model. I have affirmed this in acknowledging my appreciation for Myrdal's model of cumulative causation. My adherence to MacIver's dictum that society is held together by its myth-structure is not so much a consensual response to Niebuhr as to certain classical theories of the relation of the state to community and of law to ethos. It is instructive to realize that in the ideologies of developing countries there is almost universally an appeal both to the traditional roots of culture as well as to modernizing nationalism. For example, Kaunda of Zambia calls for the consolidation of humanism in his country, affirming both the traditional community values and the achievement of African democratic socialism.

I have learned a great deal not only from the essays by Geyer and Sample but also from the analysis by Stamey. He has thoroughly grasped my problematic with respect to authority. There is an important tension between the *legitimation* that comes from the covenantal roots of society and the *justification* of social change that comes from a vision that goes beyond the consensual ethos that created government. The doctrine of the new covenant in Jeremiah 31:31–34 expresses this tension. The declaration by Jesus in Luke 4 that he is the fulfillment of the law and the prophets also expresses it.

I must acknowledge particularly Stamey's identification of my vision of the world as "religious actualism." His relating my pacificism to this actualism and to a strain of religious mysticism is quite sensitive and perceptive. It belongs in a book like this precisely at this point. Methodologically, it is part of the theological component that makes its decisive contribution to social ethics as cross-disciplinary work, a theological component that is not immanentist alone but also an awareness of the transcendent ultimate.

As in the case of politics in general so also in the matter of social strategy, others in the Department of Sociology of Religion and Social Ethics have contributed much more than I. The discussion by Philip Wogaman carries the theory of strategy forward and tests it by concrete illustrations and recent critical analyses by others. I can only express admiration for it, urging that its treatment of power be read dialectically with the other essays. One implication of his essay is that the development of political institutions at the world level is a matter of critical urgency. With multinational and transnational conglomerates and other economic institutions growing rapidly, only an adequate world political power structure can control the whole with a goal to effect responsible society. If developing countries are to develop humanistically and with appropriate freedom, the United Nations must itself develop rapidly so that, as Wogaman says, political power can effect "the maximum point of strategic leverage upon everything else."

As Francis Greenwood Peabody stressed the correlation of the social problem in the early days of the Social Gospel movement, so these essays contribute to what Wogaman calls the "systematic consolidation of strategy." Nothing is more rewarding to me as a social ethicist than to see the emergence of a group of scholars who contribute so much to the systematic growth of a discipline. The emergence of strategic theoretical coherence in a field like Christian social ethics makes a major contribution to the systematic consolidation of strategy.

When one moves from theory to political participation, it is good to have the testimony of one, such as Senator George McGovern, who interprets his role from a Christian perspective. He was one of the delegates from the United Methodist Church to the Fourth Assembly of the World Council of Churches in Uppsala in 1968. His emphasis on the pervasiveness of the political picks up a theme that illuminates the relationship of the state to the community, the ubiquity of government. McGovern's further emphases on political participation as process and the dangers confronting pluralism give a sense of urgency to the social ethics of policy formation and decision-making. Like Niebuhr he gives a solemn warning against self-righteousness in the midst of the ambiguities of power.

I feel especially honored that Bishop James K. Mathews has contributed an essay on ecumenism. His leadership in behalf of Boston University and his range of church leadership give his essay a special note of authority.

The relationship between Christian social ethics and the ecumenical movement has been very close and has been recounted many times. I have emphasized it in many writings and have elaborated its significance in more than one book. The goal of Christian social ethics must be to fulfill its task within the total evangelical and missional vocation of the Church and of the wider ecumenical movement. Inherently moral law is universal. So too, the public verifiability of scientific hypotheses. Universality is also one of the marks of the Church. Universality belongs to the doctrine of man and to the doctrine of God. Along with universality belong the concrete embodiment and expression of moral decision, scientific hypothesis, the Church's fellowship, the particularity of man, and the creative, preserving, and redeeming activity of God. Given such reference points the Christian social ethicist must be in a global dialogue within the "household of God" and the whole family of man. It is a challenging curiosity that the phrase "family of man" has a wider extension than the household of God. The dilemmas and contrasts of these two phrases set the terms of reference for the ecumenical movement. One unitive theme in church and in secular social action is race. The race is, absolutely, one. Many moral judgments have to be qualified by conflicting values, but within Christian social ethics we may say there is absolutely no place for willful racism. The struggle for the complete elimination of the remnants of past racism must be vigorously and tirelessly pressed. It must be pressed not simply by the victims of past and present racism but by all persons. The vocation of the Church and the university requires it.

I am grateful to have had the privilege of living and working in the era of the ecumenical movement. The year I was born marked the birth of the Social Creed of the churches and the publication of Walter Rauschenbusch's *Christianity and the Social Crisis*. In the decade of my college experience, many liberals were contrasting Christianity and churchianity. The fundamental issue was not very different from Bonhoeffer's religionless Christianity. My middle year in the School of Theology was the first in which theological students were invited as participants in assemblies of the Federal Council of Churches. The student movement was impatient with denominations and tended to go nondenominational, as did docetically some theological seminaries. The preparations for the Oxford Conference and the Edinburgh Conference excited me a great deal. I thrilled at the thought that everywhere in the world Christians would bear a common witness to all states and economic orders and would participate in freeing nations from colonialism. It was not only pacifism and democratic socialism that made me oppose entrance into World War II. Ecumenical ethics required that the "Church be the Church" and to me this meant a degree of autonomy and self-understanding by the Church that refused to be dragged in — nation after nation — in the wake of the foreign policy of the several nation-states. I still envision an ecumenical movement — Protestant, Orthodox, Roman Catholic — that will give transnationally a unified moral witness. One aspect of this I tried to express during World War II in an essay in *Christendom* on "The Ecumenical Significance of the International Labor Organization."

In the symbiotic relationship of ecumenics and ethics, the themes of the responsible society and development must remain central. The decade of the sixties brought, as Bishop Mathews notes, the Roman Catholic Church into the ecumenical movement. There now exists the basis for cooperative and joint action in the area of development at the very time when the United Nations is making a fresh effort to give productive effectiveness in development leadership. Development played a major role in the Uppsala Assembly of the World Council of Churches and marks a new era in ecumenical relations. Responsible development may well be a theme for which new middle axioms should be drafted. Responsible development could provide an overarching criterion against which one measures many impulses and programs of revolution and of international action.

Finally, I must relate my sense of stewardship as a teacher and administrator particularly at Boston University School of Theology. Others must judge the performance, but I must confess that I have taken my duties seriously under the personalistic rubric of the concrete unity of theory and practice. A position in a School of Theology faculty or in the administrative staff of the university is not primarily a platform from which one launches on occasion into militant action in the world. The university is itself a vital part of the world's social order and therefore it is the time and place for the embodiment of the responsible society. Here conflict, conflict resolution, and reconciliation should be the expected order of the day. The university is chartered for dissent — for responsible dissent. No institution in society is in a better position to recognize that all previous foundations of truth and art, of virtue and piety are historically conditioned and that its present efforts are also under judgment. No community has a better opportunity to prepare leaders through living in to-morrow's world by anticipation. No anticipation of the future carries with it a greater obligation to be responsive and responsible than the day-by-day experiences of the academic community.

Since embodiment is required for the responsible exercise of freedom in relation to the continuous practice of virtue, I am grateful particularly for my participation in the Ecumenical Institute of the World Council of Churches, the establishment of the Boston Theological Institute, the ecumenical developments in the United Methodist Church, and above all the Boston University School of Theology. For the confidence that has been placed in me I wish to give thanks to Presidents Daniel L. Marsh, Harold C. Case, Arland F. Christ-Janer, Calvin Lee, and John Silber who have tolerated the adventure.

A Bibliography of the
Writings of Walter G. Muelder

BOOKS

Historical Outline of the Bible. With Edgar S. Brightman. Berea, Ky.: Berea College Press, 1936.

The Development of American Philosophy: A Book of Readings. Edited, with Lawrence Sears. Boston: Houghton Mifflin Co., 1940.

Religion and Economic Responsibility. New York: Charles Scribner's Sons, 1953.

The Idea of the Responsible Society. Boston: Boston University Press, 1955.

In Every Place a Voice. Cincinnati, Ohio: Woman's Division of Christian Service, Board of Missions, The Methodist Church, 1957.

The Development of American Philosophy: A Book of Readings. 2nd ed. Edited, with Lawrence Sears and Anne V. Schlabach. Boston: Houghton Mifflin Co., 1960.

Foundations of the Responsible Society. New York: Abingdon Press, 1960. (Later translated into Korean by B. I. Chang for the Christian Literature Society, 1966.)

Methodism and Society in the Twentieth Century. Methodist Social Thought and Action, vol. 2. New York: Abingdon Press, 1961.

Institutionalism and Church Unity: A Symposium. Edited, with Nils Ehrenstrom. New York: Association Press, 1963.

Moral Law in Christian Social Ethics. Richmond, Va.: John Knox Press, 1966.

CHAPTERS IN BOOKS AND SYMPOSIA

"Personality and Christian Ethics." In *Personalism in Theology: A Symposium in Honor of Albert Cornelius Knudson,* edited by Edgar S. Brightman. Boston: Boston University Press, 1943.

"Cumulative Power Tendencies in Western Culture." In *Conflicts of Power in Modern*

Culture, edited by L. Bryson, L. Finkelstein, and R. MacIver. New York: Harper and Bros., 1946.

"Methodism's Contribution to Social Reform." In *Methodism,* edited by William K. Anderson. Nashville: Methodist Publishing House, 1947.

"The Function of Social Ethics in a Theological Seminary." In *Education for Professional Responsibility,* by E. D. Smith and others. Pittsburgh: Carnegie Press, 1948.

Introduction to *Hindu View of Christ,* by Swami Akhilananda. New York: Philosophical Library, 1949.

"Power, *Anomie* and Personality." In *Perspectives on a Troubled Decade, 1939–1949,* edited by L. Bryson, L. Finkelstein, and R. MacIver. New York: Harper and Bros., 1950.

"Norms and Valuations in Social Science." In *Liberal Learning and Religion,* edited by Amos N. Wilder. New York: Harper and Bros., 1951.

"Religion and Human Destiny." In *Human Destiny,* edited by William D. Nietmann. Stockton, California: College of the Pacific, 1951.

"Methodism." In *The Quest for Christian Unity,* edited by R. S. Bilheimer, New York: Association Press, 1952.

"The Organization of Economic Life." In *The Church and Social Responsibility,* edited by J. R. Spann. New York: Abingdon-Cokesbury Press, 1953.

"Ethical Aspects of Income Distribution and Consumption." In *American Income and Its Use,* by Elizabeth Hoyt and others. New York: Harper and Bros., 1954.

"Report of the Preparatory Commission on Church-State Relations in Social Welfare." In *Reports of the Preparatory Commissions,* National Conference on the Churches and Social Welfare. Mimeographed. Cleveland, Ohio, 1955.

"The College Community." In *The Responsible Student,* by Peter A. Bertocci, Paul K. Deats, Jr., and others. Nashville, Tenn.: National Methodist Student Movement, 1957.

"Social Changes in the Lives of Theological Students." In *Report of Fifth Biennial Meeting,* Association of Seminary Professors in the Practical Fields. Boston: Boston University School of Theology, 1958.

"Ethical Frontiers." In *Patterns of Ethics in America Today,* edited by F. E. Johnson. New York: Collier Books, 1962; reprinted in *The Range of Ethics,* edited by H. H. Titus and M. T. Keeton. New York: American Book Co., 1966.

"Christian Responsibility with Respect to Revolution." In *Papers on the Theology of Mission,* New York: Division of World Missions of the Board of Missions of the Methodist Church, 1962.

"Uniting Churches as Social Institutions." In *The Challenge to Reunion.* Edited by Robert McAfee Brown and David H. Stitt. New York: McGraw-Hill, 1963.

"Theology and Social Science." In *Christian Social Ethics in a Changing World,* edited by John C. Bennett. New York: Association Press, 1966; also translated into German as "Theologie und Socialwissenschaft." In *Die Kirche als Faktor einer Kommenden Welt-gemeinschaft.* Berlin. Kreuz-Verlag, 1966.

"The Right and Wrong Use of Religion in Politics." In *Political Studies: Essays in Honor of Eddy Asirvatham,* edited by S. C. Tiwari and S. R. Sharma. Agra, India: Shiva Lal Agarwala and Co., 1966.

"To the Secularist." In *Sermons to Men of Other Faiths and Traditions,* edited by Gerald Anderson. New York: Abingdon Press, 1966.

"Christian Responsibility with Respect to Revolution." In *Christian Mission in Theological Perspective,* edited by Gerald Anderson. New York: Abingdon Press, 1967.

"Religious Frontiers in Political and Economic Responsibility." In *Religion in Philosophical and Cultural Perspective,* edited by J. C. Feaver and W. Horosz. Princeton: D. van Nostrand Co., 1967.
"Diakonia: Der Christ in der Gesellschaft." In *Die Kirchen der Welt,* Der Methodismus, vol. 6. Edited by C. Ernst Sommer. Stuttgart: Evangelisches Verlag, 1968.
"Methodism and Ecumenism in the United States." In *Methodism's Destiny in an Ecumenical Age,* edited by Paul M. Minus, Jr. New York: Abingdon Press, 1969.
"La Risposta Metodista All 'incredulita' e All 'ateismo.'" In *L'Ateismo Contemporaneo,* vol. 4. Rome: Societa Editrice Internazionale, 1971.
Introduction to *Ethical Issues in Biology and Medicine,* edited by P. N. Williams, W. G. Muelder, and G. Fulton. Cambridge, Mass.: Schenkman Publishing Co., 1972.

ARTICLES IN PERIODICALS AND JOURNALS

"Naturalism Faces Prophetic Religion." *Crozer Quarterly,* October 1939, pp. 241–50.
"Principles of Constructive Peace." *Prophetic Religion,* June-July 1941, pp. 5–8.
"The Ecumenical Values of the International Labor Organization." *Christendom,* Spring 1942, pp. 177–88.
"William James and the Problems of Religious Empiricism." *The Personalist,* April 1942, pp. 159–71.
"Religion and Postwar Reconstruction." *World Affairs Interpreter,* Autumn 1942, pp. 275–85.
"The Church Takes Courage." *Intercollegian,* May 1943, pp. 149–50.
"Labor after the War." *Fellowship,* September 1943, pp. 160–63.
"A Philosophy for Post-War Pacifism." *Fellowship,* December 1944, pp. 200–01.
"Dumbarton Oaks." *Now,* March 1945, p. 3.
"What the Resurrection Means to Me." *Christian Advocate,* 22 March 1945, p. 345.
"Limitations to Social Effectiveness of the Church." *Social Questions Bulletin,* April 1945, pp. 1–2.
"Reinhold Niebuhr's Conception of Man." *The Personalist,* Summer 1945, pp. 282–93.
"From Sect to Church." *Christendom,* Autumn 1945, pp. 450–62; reprinted in J. Milton Yinger, ed. *Religion, Society and the Individual.* New York: Macmillan, 1957, pp. 480–88.
"The Peace We Preach." *Zions Herald,* 20 February 1946, pp. 184–85.
"Our Twofold Insecurity." *Christian Advocate,* 28 February 1946, p. 271.
"National Unity and National Ethics." *Annals of the American Academy of Political and Social Science,* March 1946, pp. 10–18.
"The Pittsburgh Conference." *Christianity and Crisis,* 17 March 1947, pp. 3–6.
"The School of Theology of the Future." *Bostonia,* May 1947, pp. 5–6.
"Concerning Power in the State." *Philosophical Forum,* Spring 1947, pp. 3–14.
"Pacifism and Politics: A Reply to Felix Greene." *Fellowship,* June 1947, pp. 93–94.
"Basic Strategy of Religion in Public Education." *Christendom,* Summer 1947, pp. 370–80.
"The Church and the Labor Movement." *Religion in Life,* Autumn 1947, pp. 483–93.
"Brawn on the Inside." *motive,* December 1947, pp. 11–12.
"What about the Methodist Federation?" *Zions Herald,* April 1948, pp. 315–17.

"Essential Human Rights." *The Adult Teacher,* August 1948, pp. 8–17; and September 1948, pp. 10–12.

"Why Are Things As They Are?" *Vision,* 22 August 1948, pp. 12–13.

"Organization of Power for Spiritual Ends." *motive,* January 1950, pp. 12–14.

"Mr. Stanley High's Fringe of Conscience." *Zions Herald,* 15 February 1950, pp. 147–48.

"Basic Principles of the Methodist Federation for Social Action." *Zions Herald,* 12 April 1950, pp. 339ff.

"Communism, Secularism, and Christianity." *Zions Herald,* 19 April 1950, pp. 370–71.

"The Future of the Federation." *Zions Herald,* 14 June 1950, pp. 563ff.

"The Social Philosophy of Edgar Sheffield Brightman." *Philosophical Forum,* Spring 1950, pp. 9–14.

"Christianity and Communism Bibliography." *Bulletin of the General Theological Library* (Boston), October 1950, pp. 4–6.

"Graduate Ecumenical Administration." *Zions Herald,* 21 February 1951, p. 183.

"Truth and the Social Zealot: Mr. McMichael and the U.N. Commission on Korea." *Zions Herald,* 14 March 1951, pp. 243–45.

"Hope for a Sick Church." *Zions Herald,* 7 November 1951, pp. 1065–66; 14 November 1951, pp. 1090–91.

"Dangers of Total Conscription." *NUEA* Handbook, 1951–1952, pp. 207–10.

"Social Action in The Methodist Church." *Zions Herald,* 6 February 1952, pp. 128–31.

"Shall We Have an Official Organization on Social Action? Yes, to Make our Christian Witness more Effective." *Christian Advocate,* 3 April 1952, p. 9.

"The Future Belongs to Non-Violence." *Zions Herald,* 28 May 1952, pp. 507–08.

"Minorities Can Be Integrated." *Intercollegian,* February 1953, pp. 16–17.

"The Efficacy of Prayer." *Pastoral Psychology,* September 1953, pp. 11–16.

"Some Implications of World Conditions for Christian Education." *Religious Education,* January–February 1954, pp. 13–18.

"Impressions of the Evanston Assembly." *The Ecumenical Review,* October 1954, pp. 1–8.

"Methodist Emphases in the Light of Current Theological Discussions." *World Parish,* October 1954, pp. 3–16.

"Assumptions for Economic Life." *Christianity and Society,* Winter 1954–1955, pp. 16–17.

"Right to Work Laws." *The Machinist,* 13 January 1955, pp. 1–3.

"Right to Work Laws Victimize the Worker." *American Federationist,* February 1955, pp. 22–24.

"The Role of the Church in the Responsible Society." *Chicago Theological Seminary Register,* March 1955, pp. 13–18.

"The Nature of the Ecumenical Conversation." *United Theological Seminary Bulletin,* second quarter 1955, pp. 3–5.

"The Attack on the Social Gospel." *The Socialist Call,* June 1955, pp. 9–11.

"The Second Coming of Jesus." *Christian Advocate,* 25 August 1955, pp. 1009ff.

"Institutional Factors Affecting Unity and Disunity." *The Ecumenical Review,* January 1956, pp. 113–26.

"The Labor Merger." *The City Church,* January–February 1956, pp. 7–8.

"Appeal to a Right-to-Work." *Congressional Digest,* February 1956, p. 61.

"Personalism, Theology, and the Natural Law." *Philosophical Forum,* 1956, pp. 3–20.

"Walter Rauschenbusch and the Contemporary Scene." *The City Church,* March–April 1957, pp. 10–12.

"The Idea of a Theological School." *Nexus,* no. 1 (1957), pp. 12–14.

"Institutionalism in Relation to Unity and Disunity." *motive,* November 1957, pp. 12–13.

"Memorial Address for Charles M. McConnell." *Methodist Rural Fellowship Bulletin,* Winter 1957, pp. 11–22.

"Ethics and the Interior Life." *The New Christian Advocate,* June 1957, pp. 18–22.

"The Nature of the Unity We Seek." *Zions Herald,* June 1957, pp. 5–6.

"The Unity We Seek." *The Christian Evangelist,* 10 June 1957, pp. 4–5.

"The Nature of the Unity We Seek." *World Outlook,* July 1957, pp. 27–28.

"Organized Labor Comes of Age." *National Council Observer,* September 1957, pp. 25–26.

"Institutionalism is Relation to Unity and Disunity." *The Chaplain,* December 1957, pp. 23–36.

"Philosophy of the Curriculum: An Analysis." With L. Harold DeWolf. *Nexus,* no. 2 (1957), pp. 53–76.

"The Ethics of Outer Space." *Zions Herald,* February 1958, p. 13; reprinted in *The Churchman,* August 1958, and *The Chaplain,* October 1958.

"The Message Beyond the Crisis." *The Methodist Woman,* July–August 1958, pp. 36–39.

"Relations of Men and Women." *The Presbyterian Outlook,* 17 November 1958, pp. 7–8.

"New Theology and Old Social Gospel." *The New Christian Advocate,* October 1958, pp. 26–28.

"The Albert V. Danielsen Chair of Psychology and Pastoral Counselling." *Nexus,* no. 4 (1958), pp. 15–16.

"Middle Age: Its Problems and Challenge." *Pastoral Psychology,* November 1958, pp. 9–13.

"What Is the Place of Religion in the Satellite Era?" *Zions Herald,* November 1958, p. 8.

"Prologue to Involvement." *motive,* December 1958, pp. 29–30.

"Values in Graduate Education." *Boston University Graduate Journal,* December 1958, pp. 41–50. Excerpts in *Nexus,* no. 7 (1959), pp. 31–34.

"The Place of Religion in a Satellite Era." *motive,* January 1959, pp. 4–5.

"A Rejoinder: 'Theology and the Ethics of Outer Space.' " *The Chaplain,* February 1959, pp. 1–3.

"Social Change and Christian Freedom." *The Church Woman,* March 1959, pp. 3–7; and April 1959, pp. 12–16.

"Bibliography on Social Issues." *Bulletin of the General Theological Library* (Boston), May 1959.

"Some Issues Facing the Future of Theological Education." *Zions Herald,* June 1959, p. 3.

"From a Social Creed to World Consciousness." *Nexus,* no. 8 (1960), pp. 11–16.

"Methodism and Segregation: A Case Study." *Christianity and Crisis,* 4 April 1960, pp. 39–42.

"Some Historical Notes on the Theme of Religious Education." *Nexus,* no. 9 (1960), pp. 33–36.

"Operating in Anticipation." *Bostonia,* Spring 1960, pp. 2–3.

"Reaching the Unchurched." *Methodist Story,* June 1960, pp. 3–8; reprinted in *The Church School,* September 1960, pp. 6–10; and in *Workers with Youth,* October 1960, pp. 6–8.

"Vocational Responsibility." *Christian Education Bulletin,* July 1960, pp. 2–4.

"The Church's Dialogue with the World." *School of Theology at Claremont Perspective,* October 1960, pp. 5–6.

"A Sudden Awakening." *motive,* October 1960, pp. 29–31.

"The New Dialogue between Science and Religion." *Nexus,* no. 10 (1960), pp. 9–14.

"Renaissance of Bowne." Symposium in *Bostonia,* Fall 1960, pp. 23–27.

"Theological Aspects of Vocation." *Pastoral Psychology,* September 1961, pp. 9–13.

"Berlin Notes." *Nexus,* no. 13 (1961), pp. 19–21.

"The Significance of the Third Assembly of the World Council of Churches." *Nexus,* no. 14 (1962), pp. 2–6.

"Theological Education and the Neglect of the Gospel." *Bulletin of the American Association of Theological Schools,* June 1962, pp. 200–15.

"Power Structure, Ethical Concern, and the Church in the World." *World Outlook,* September 1962, pp. 27–29; and in *Laity,* November 1962, pp. 29–38.

"Person and Community." *Philosophical Forum,* 1962–1963, pp. 35–59.

"Aspects of Ministerial Recruitment." *Nexus,* no. 17, (1963), pp. 1–4.

"How Does the Ministry Attract Recruits?" *Nexus,* no. 17 (1963), p. 27.

"Institutionalism and Church Unity." *motive,* April 1963, pp. 5–8.

"Christian Social Ethics Bookshelf." *Christian Century,* 30 October 1963, pp. 1336–37.

"Persons and Traditions: Address in Honor of Edwin P. Booth and Paul E. Johnson." *Nexus,* no. 20 (1964), pp. 16–22.

"Frontiers that Challenge Mission." *World Outlook,* February 1964, pp. 7–10.

"Christian Social Ethics Looks Forward." *Nexus,* no. 21 (1964), pp. 3–10, 42–45.

"Tribute to Albert and Jessie Danielson." *Nexus,* no. 22 (1964), pp. 7–8.

"The Heritage of Devotion: An Address in Honor of Retiring Professors Jannette E. Newhall, Richard M. Cameron, James R. Houghton, and Harold Ehrensperger." *Nexus,* no. 22 (1964), pp. 25–30.

"Recruitment of Negroes for Theological Studies." *Review of Religious Research,* Spring 1964, pp. 152–56.

"An Observer at Vatican Council II." *Bostonia,* December 1964.

"Recruiting Negro Ministers." *Christian Advocate,* 28 January 1965, pp. 12–13.

"How Ecumenical is the Vatican Decree on Ecumenicism?" *Nexus,* no. 23 (1965), pp. 23–26.

"The Church in the Modern World: A Critique of Schema XIII." *The Ecumenical Review,* April 1965, pp. 113–26.

"The Second Vatican Council: An Observer Reports." *Nexus,* no. 24 (1965), pp. 23–29.

"Just Emerging — A New Dimension to the Ecumenical Dialogue." *Christian Advocate,* 3 June 1965, pp. 14–15.

"Decision Time Arrives in Ecumenical Affairs." *Christian Advocate,* 1 July 1965, pp. 7–9.

"Apostles of Growth: Howard Thurman, Donald M. Maynard, L. Harold DeWolf." *Nexus,* no. 25 (1965), pp. 29–34.

"The Philosophy of the New Curriculum." *Nexus,* no. 26, (1966), pp. 1–6.

"Role of Women in Church and Society." *The Methodist Woman,* January 1967, pp. 4–7.

"Amiya Chakravarty: Poet and Peacemaker." *Nexus*, no. 29 (1967), pp. 37–42.
"What Has Theology to Do with Social Action?" *Nexus*, no. 30 (1967), pp. 3–8.
"Frontier Issues at Uppsala." *Nexus*, no. 34 (1968), pp. 5–12.
"The Role of the School of Theology in Boston University." *Nexus*, no. 35 (1969), pp. 3–12.
"Lively Theology." *Bostonia*, Fall 1969.
"Scholars of Stature: Ehrenstrom and Schilling." *Nexus*, no. 37 (1969), pp. 34–39.
"New Hopes Involve Many Risks." Report on Conference on *The Identity and Dignity of Man* from the Perspective of a Theologian and Ethicist, *Boston University Currents*, 14 January 1970.
"The Identity and Dignity of Man." *Nexus*, no. 39 (1970), pp. 1–8, 26–29.
"Martin Luther King, Jr. at Boston University." *Boston University Currents*, 1 April 1970.
"The Ecological Era." Three addresses delivered at Gammon Theological Seminary as the Thirkield-Jones Lectures, *The Foundation* of Gammon Theological Seminary, Summer 1970, pp. 3–25.
"A Sermon on History and Being Radical." *Nexus*, no. 41 (1971), pp. 13–14.
"The Muelder Chapel Windows." *Nexus*, no. 43 (1972).

SELECTED UNPUBLISHED MANUSCRIPTS

"Individual Totalities in Ernst Troeltsch's Philosophy of History." Ph.D. Dissertation, Boston University, 1933.
"Essential Elements in the Christian Conception of Man." Presented at Garrett Biblical Institute Conference on Christian Education, November 1947.
"Secularism." Presented at Institute of Religious and Social Studies, Harvard Divinity School, 25 November 1947.
"Why I Believe in Pacifism." Presented at Conference on Church and War, Detroit, Spring 1950.
"Home Missions and Basic Human Rights." Presented at Annual Assembly, Division of Home Missions, National Council of Churches, Buck Hill Falls, Pa., 9 December 1951.
"Edgar Sheffield Brightman: In Memoriam." 25 February 1953.
"Distinctive Characteristics of Christianity." Presented at American Theological Society, Union Theological Seminary, 11 April 1953.
"The Heresy of Irrelevance." Commencement Address at Holy Cross Greek Orthodox Theological School, 6 June 1965.
"William Ernest Hocking: Religious Meaning in Human Existence." Presented at Memorial Meeting, Department of Philosophy, Harvard University, February 1967.
"The Family in the Revolutions of Today." Four lectures at Wisconsin Area Family Life Conference, October 1967.
"The Renewal of the Church." Three Willson Lectures, Board of Education of The Methodist Church, Scarritt College, Vanderbilt University Divinity School, and Board of Evangelism of The Methodist Church, 28–29 February 1968.
"The Social Witness of the United Methodist Church." Presented at Commission on Social Principles of the United Methodist Church, February 1969.
"Christian Bases of Morality and Ethics." Presented to the Council of Bishops of the United Methodist Church, 9 April 1969.

"Basic Issues in Seminary Student Protest." Presented at Convocation of Theological Faculties of United Methodist Theological Schools, 20 June 1969.

"Methodism in the United States." Presented at Commission on Structure of Methodism Overseas of the United Methodist Church, Atlantic City, April 1970.